PUBLISHED FOR THE PRINCETON CENTER
OF INTERNATIONAL STUDIES

*A list of other Center publications appears
at the back of the book*

DIVISION
AND COHESION
IN DEMOCRACY

A Study of Norway

BY HARRY ECKSTEIN

PRINCETON, NEW JERSEY
PRINCETON UNIVERSITY PRESS
1966

Printed in the United States of America
by Princeton University Press, Princeton, New Jersey

Second Printing, 1971

Preface

IF THIS STUDY were intended to be a detailed, comprehensive account of Norwegian politics, of the sort that country specialists generally write, it would not only be much longer but an impertinence. It is based on only four and a half months' stay in Norway, a limited number of interviews with Norwegian academics and political figures, and considerable, but far from comprehensive, reading of Norwegian historical, political, and sociological studies. Such a background hardly suffices for a sure and comprehensive treatment of the manifold details of any political system.

The essay, however, is differently conceived. My overriding interest as a political scientist is not in any particular polity but in the comparative study of political systems and in problems that can be dealt with only through such study. This interest does not originate in a belief that configurative studies of particular countries are without value. Those who produce such studies have done much distinguished and necessary work—necessary most of all to the generalizer, who can hardly learn everything for himself, but must draw on configurative studies, with confidence in the powers of those who produce them to get things right. My interest in comparative study, however, does arise from the view that the materials produced by configurative case studies must be used, among other things, for more general purposes, such as the construction of typologies of political systems, the formulation of general propositions about such systems, and the solution of special problems in regard to which data from a single case, or from a very limited number of cases, cannot be conclusive. It is also premised on the conviction that the theoretical fruits of broader studies can sharpen one's understanding of particular cases, much as psychoanalytic theory, laboriously derived from many case studies, sharpens inquiry into further cases to which it is applied. The end of political inquiry, as I see it, is a close joining of broad and deep studies; but doing both on the scale ideally required is beyond any single work or any single scholar. What is needed is a long, deliberate, and mutually sympathetic dialogue by those whose tastes run to the general and those who prefer to deal with special cases.

Either mode of study entails shortcomings. The generalizer sacrifices sure mastery of detail, the narrower scholar relevance to theory and the excitement of imagination that comes from broad horizons. For that reason alone the work of using specific studies to inform general ones, and of the latter to inform the former, can never be fully and finally done. Especially in the early stages of inquiry, the special studies available for pursuing any broad concern are likely to be very incomplete and to a large extent irrelevant. That problem can be progressively reduced only by a serious interest in general theory on the part of those preferring to work on special cases, but is unlikely ever to be removed completely. Then too, when special studies are used for general purposes, it is only too possible that the generalist (who, like any human being, is limited in time, energy, and background) will misunderstand or be merely superficial, or be misled by mistakes or biases of specialists that he cannot detect himself. Only constant criticism by specialists will help reduce this problem, provided that they understand the generalist's concerns and that the latter is willing to take well-informed criticism into account. Hence the interplay of general and special work in political study must be unrestrained, sympathetic, and above all continuous. But to continue, it must begin. And to begin one must be prepared to write on a level of great tentativity and very insufficient knowledge, hoping that others will not misunderstand one's intentions.

The present essay is conceived in that manner—as a tenative "theoretical case study." It grows out of an interest in discovering the conditions that produce stable or unstable rule, especially in democracies. I have long been impressed by the shortcomings of interpretations bearing on that problem that have been arrived at by specialists on particular countries; none of these survive for long when taken as generalizations. I have also been dissatisfied by the fact that the problem of the conditions of stable democracy has been closely studied in very few instances, and by the superficialities of generalists attempting to deal with large numbers of relevant cases. This study represents a first attempt toward a more satisfactory treatment of the problem through a combination of the genres of specialists and generalists. It tries to use detailed studies (and my own observations) of Norway, a country unfamiliar to practically all students of democracy, for the purpose of applying, testing, and revising theories developed in studies of other cases or in comparative studies. But it is only a beginning, using as yet insufficient, and not always directly relevant, materials to examine tentative theories. It should not be regarded as an attempt at anything more ambitious.

Perhaps this discussion will generate interest in, and provide some knowledge of, a country about which most of us know little, but which, I feel, holds many lessons for democratic and general political theory. Perhaps it will even illuminate matters previously dark to specialists on Norway or raise for them new questions and perspectives. If it has these results, so much the better. But these would be happy by-products, not essential to my purpose. I neither can nor will claim to be an "expert" on Norway, but claim only to have taken here a small step toward a remote destination: the union of comparative generalizations and configurative data in well-formulated theories resting on a sound empirical base.

I fully intend to take further steps in that direction, if possible along with others who see the point of my approach. Many other unfamiliar cases must be examined as Norway is examined here. Many familiar cases need reexamination as the work of developing empirically solid theory unfolds. More hypotheses than those treated here need consideration. Theories of stable democracy need to be made congruent with larger theories of political structure and society and to be subjected to special testing. Not least, a great deal of empirical work, informed by theoretical concerns like those expounded in these pages, still needs to be done in Norway itself, among many other countries.

In the last of these tasks, I myself hope to participate in some manner, not least because I liked the country and was stimulated by its political scientists. In this connection I particularly ask indulgence of my Norwegian friends, many of whose studies are represented here—I hope without much distortion. I trust that they will bear in mind that in this essay I grope through territory that they intimately know, but which to me is new, insufficiently charted, and crowded with as many obstacles to progress as their rugged and beautiful land. No doubt there are errors and misinterpretations in the study, despite precautions. But I trust that they are minor, and that they will not impugn, or divert attention from, my major arguments.

ONE fundamental misimpression to which any case study may give rise should particularly be avoided by readers: namely, that I consider Norway's political system or society to be, in any substantial sense, unique. This misimpression may arise because of the very fact that this is not a systematic comparative study, and because, for reasons stated in the last chapter, the passing references to other democracies generally point out differences between them and Norway, not similarities. No doubt, Norwegian politics and social life do have distinctive characteristics, as do all concrete phenomena, be they persons, relationships, objects, or events; it is after all the distinctiveness of concrete phenomena that permits one to recognize them as such in the first place. The ways in which and extent to which Norway is peculiar can, of course, be established only by thorough comparisons that are not, and could not, be made here. But the fact that this is a "theoretical case study" necessarily implies a strong assumption on my part that Norway is *not* unique, in one or both of two senses: first, that what is the case in Norway may also be substantially the case elsewhere, however exotic some aspects of Norwegian life may seem; second, that there are general principles which can account for

any distinctive characteristics of Norway and for the undoubtedly distinctive general configuration of the whole society.
It is the search for just such principles that animates this study.

Although I do not systematically compare Norway with any
other democracy here, I have, of course, tried throughout to
juxtapose Norwegian experience on one hand and empirical
generalizations on the other; in that sense the study is certainly
comparative: it compares a case with a body of theory pertinent to it. More often than not, alas, the theories fail to fit. And
in so far as those that run counter to Norwegian reality seem
plausible generalizations and are deeply entrenched in the re-
ceived opinion of social theory and common sense, the impression that Norway is very singular, hence mysterious, will be
especially enhanced—above all, perhaps, in Chapter III, which
deals with Norway's political divisions. It may be, however,
that Norway raises puzzles—as it certainly did for me—only
because our current theories are so widely at variance with
reality. And it may be that aspects of Norway which at first
sight seem uncommon will, on further consideration, turn out
to be quite usual. If so, all the better, for my object here is not
to generate mysteries but to dispel them. This despite the fact
that the organization of this study represents my own history
of puzzlement, as well as what I take to be gradually growing
comprehension, as I searched through Norwegian realities with
the all too feeble interpretative guides provided by contemporary comparative politics.[1]

---

[1] After this preface was written, an article appeared that comes extraordinarily close to arguing for just such a research approach as I
follow in this study: Barney G. Glazer and Anselm L. Strauss, "Discovery of Substantive Theory: A Basic Strategy Underlying Qualitative
Research," *American Behavioral Scientist*, VIII, 6 (February 1965),
5-12. To make sense of the conception of this study, that article should
by all means be consulted, despite the fact that the authors' ideas differ
from mine in some minor respects. A book similar to mine in conception is Lucian Pye's case study of Burma, *Politics, Personality and Nation Building* (New Haven, 1962). Both Pye's work and mine are designed to cope with a dilemma that Max F. Millikan discusses in a fore-
word to Pye's book: that between case studies which emphasize the

To AVOID likely misunderstandings of my arguments, readers should also note some other points.

Throughout the study—especially in Chapter V, which deals with Norway as a "community"—I speak of large social aggregates without distinguishing special units or segments comprised in the aggregates. In some cases the aggregate is the whole of Norway. In others it may be a geographic region of the country, or a demographic group, or a social class or occupational group. Wherever such large aggregates are treated here in general terms, there is no implication that the attitudes or behavior of their members are absolutely uniform, only that they exhibit "typical" (frequent, modal, predominant) patterns. In many cases we have evidence, systematically gathered and incontrovertible, that establish the patterns; in some the generalizations have a more tenuous basis in my own impressions and require much further study. In no case, however, do I mean to argue that the Norwegians have a "national character," or even certain distinct subnational characters, in the simplistic sense of that term: that Norwegians are all alike, in ways that are somehow permanently fixed. I imply only that Norwegians, at various levels of inclusiveness, exhibit characteristic (but not uniform) and relatively stable (but not unchanging) attitudes and behavior patterns.

In many parts of the study the characteristic patterns sketched involve attitudes and "orientations" rather than behavior. This might be taken to imply that the subjective components of Norwegian life seem to me more important than objective aspects of Norwegian social structure, or that they appear to me highly autonomous of the latter. They do not. At-

---

unique features of particular cultures and comparative studies that gloss over the distinctive features of particular contexts. This, in my view, is not really a "dilemma," if general theories can be useful in interpreting correctly special cases and the study of special cases helpful in the construction of general theories. A case study that illustrates these possibilities, and was especially influential in my choice of genre, is Lipset, Trow, and Coleman, *Union Democracy* (New York, 1956).

titudes, after all, are not formed in a vacuum. We know pretty well by now that they may have three immediate sources, the relative significance of which varies under varying circumstances. First and foremost, they are implanted by socialization processes—learning processes in early life—that link generation to generation; to the extent that they originate in such processes they may be quite autonomous of present experience, hence of the direct impact of objective social structure. Second, they are usually related in some degree to adult experiences, hence likely to reflect, to an extent, such matters as occupation, status, and social mobility. Third, they may result from efforts to integrate one's attitudes, or one's attitudes and position in life, in order to reduce strain and dissonance in the personality. Attitudes, therefore, are never mere reflections of objective conditions, nor ever fully independent of them either. They shape, and are shaped by, the external environment and the internal needs of the personality. And even where they are implanted by socialization processes one can usually demonstrate a close connection between attitudes and social structure at some point, near or distant, in the past. I suspect, therefore, that one could, if one wanted, find good "structural" explanations of all the attitudes sketched in this study. Where such explanations are not presented, the reason is quite simply that searching them out did not seem germane to my objectives.

Finally, in many cases my characterization of Norwegian atitudes is premised on implicit comparisons with other societies rather than the close correspondence of Norway to ideal models. Take, for example, the assertion that Norwegians are "egalitarian." In terms of some abstract ideal of social equality one might well dispute this statement; in terms of political values—a commitment to still greater equality—one might dislike it; and individual Norwegians, in light of their personal position, might feel unrepresented by it. But in terms of a comparative ranking of societies on a realistic equality-inequality scale, Norway certainly is highly egalitarian; at any rate, that is all the statement alleges.

SEVERAL organizations helped to make this study possible, and I wish here to express my gratitude to them. A summer grant from Princeton's Center of International Studies, a faculty fellowship from the Social Science Research Council, and a McCosh Faculty Fellowship from Princeton University combined to provide a year's leave from teaching duties, during which the research and writing that went into the study were done, along with some other work. The Center of International Studies also provided secretarial services and, through its faculty and research associates, a forum on which to try out my ideas, some of which were formulated not in connection with this study but in earlier work supported by the Center. After completion of the first draft, Princeton University also provided funds for a second trip to Norway that enabled me to get the draft criticized directly by Norwegian social scientists. The criticisms I obtained were kind, thorough, and very helpful, although I must confess that in revising the manuscript not all of them were, or could be, taken into account. As usually happens in these cases, some suggestions made to me were contradictory one with another, some involved references to research not yet published or completed, and a few involved personal impressions different from my own but not necessarily more solidly grounded. In regard to such criticisms I chose to follow my own inclinations, recognizing, however, that careful research may prove me to be mistaken.

My debt to certain Norwegian social scientists will be evident in the text and footnotes and need not be underlined here; but I want particularly to thank the Institute for Social Research in Oslo for providing me with space, secretarial help, and much general kindness during my stays in Norway. Numerous American colleagues, in Princeton and elsewhere, also helped with criticisms and encouragement. Mohammed Guessous, Manfred Halpern, Gregory Massell, and Lawrence Stone, all of Princeton University, raised my morale with kindly comments and a generous forbearance from criticism. Klaus Knorr, the director of the Center of International Studies, and two Princeton graduate students, Eric Nordlinger and Michael East, all provided useful comments. Among members of other universities, I want particularly to acknowledge the help and encouragement of my former mentor at Harvard, Samuel H. Beer (with whom I spent two delightful days discussing the problem of "operationalizing" the concept of community as used in this study), of R. A. Dahl of Yale University, William C. Mitchell of the University of Oregon, and Sidney Verba of Stanford University. My wife, Joan Campbell Eckstein, helped me to form my impressions of Norway with hers, curbed (not, I fear, altogether successfully) my penchant for premature generalization, and patiently endured large oral doses of my nondeclamatory prose. My thanks also to Mrs. June Traube, who patiently typed, again and again, the manuscript, and to Mrs. Patricia Rosenblad, who prepared the index.

HARRY ECKSTEIN

Princeton, New Jersey
December 1965

Contents

Tables

DIVISION AND COHESION IN DEMOCRACY

Introduction:
The Relevance of Norway

WHY should anyone want to study Norwegian politics? Among the questions I was asked after a research trip to Norway, that was much the most frequent. Usually it was not asked to elicit information about the pertinence of Norwegian data to general problems in political study, but, unmistakably, to question the relevance of such a small country to any large academic concern.

Indeed the smaller European countries are strangely overlooked by American political scientists, who seem to know more about Uganda or the Ivory Coast than about Denmark or Holland. Comparative politics has, after all, always had something of a great-power fixation, particularly in regard to Europe. Unlike many small countries elsewhere, those in Europe have not recently raised prominent international problems, and comparative politics still takes its intellectual cues largely from currently perceived difficulties in international affairs. For some years the foundations have done much to encourage research in neglected foreign parts, but they have not until recently recognized Europe as a foreign area or seemed to realize that parts of it are at least as shadowy to American social scientists as more remote countries. Academics who might have seen some intrinsic value in studying the Scandinavian or Benelux countries have been diverted not only by grant-getting strategies, but also by language barriers. Who, for example, learns Dutch in school? Who would invest his time in acquiring Norwegian when he might be learning multipurpose languages like Spanish, Arabic, or French?

1. Let us immediately indicate, then, why a country like Norway does have strong claims on our attention. A full cata-

logue of reasons would be enormous, but listing a few of the more basic ones will make others readily apparent. That the points I shall make are obvious when stated makes them all the more weighty.

First and foremost, we are concerned in political study with discovering broad generalizations about political systems and broad strategies for making sense of them, and Norway is a political system. Like any other, its experiences may suggest new hypotheses and serve to invalidate or support old ones. The grand strategies that have been used in and proposed for the study of political systems—formal-legal study, the elite approach, group theory, the political culture approach, communications theories, input-output schema, functionalism—can be put to work in Norway as well as anywhere, and revised, filled out, or impugned by the materials it provides.

This point comes first, because it ought alone to suffice. But equally obvious and important is the fact that Norway is highly relevant to a host of special topics and problems in comparative politics. It has a bureaucracy, local government, a legislative process, parties, voluntary organizations and pressure groups, news media, political socialization processes, a constitution, foreign policies, welfare policies, legitimacy notions, elections. Anyone who generalizes about such aspects of politics and government is talking about Norway, whether he realizes it or not. As well, to touch on a highly contemporary concern, Norway is one of the newer nations of the world, having been for all practical purposes a Danish colony until 1814 and, more loosely, an adjunct of Sweden until 1905;[1] in other senses too

---

[1] Technically there was a Danish-Norwegian "union" until 1814, but to say that Denmark was the "predominant" partner in the union is to put it mildly. The events of 1814 were certainly treated by the Norwegians themselves as amounting to liberation. The Norwegian-Swedish union involved less, but still considerable, inequality, and 1905 also figures in Norwegian attitudes as a year of liberation. Good introductions to Norwegian history are Karen Larsen, *A History of Norway* (Princeton, 1948), and T. K. Derry, *A Short History of Norway* (London, 1957). For a special account of the events of 1905, see Yngvar Nielsen, *Norge i 1905* (Horten, 1906) and for a comprehensive history

it has been rapidly "modernizing" (industrializing, urbanizing, rationalizing, etc.); so that anyone who speaks of new nations or rapid modernization speaks of Norway, willy-nilly. The same applies to anyone who speaks of the effects that the lack of a feudal tradition has on democratic politics, of the effects on such systems of one-party dominance, of the social bases of stable democracy, and a host of other issues.

Political scientists have often shed bitter methodological tears over the scarcity of cases relevant to such topics and problems. Some have gloomily inferred from that alleged scarcity a need to descend to the lowest regions of probability, others a need for redefining the subject matter of politics so as to take politics, conventionally understood, out of it. It is hard to see a necessity for such desperate conclusions while plenty of cases lie fallow, waiting to be cultivated.

A case for studying Norway can also be made from the opposite of this perspective. In certain ways Norway, like any other country, has distinct features as well as shared characteristics —distinct either in that they are peculiar to Norway or at least highly uncommon. Such peculiarities serve a vital function in inquiry: that of allowing one to learn from contrasts and of illuminating the normal by means of the rare. One example may suffice to illustrate this point. Political scientists are much concerned with "problem cases"—that is, cases that pose conspicuous policy problems—and rightly so. But why not a similar concern with what one might call "solution cases": societies that have managed to deal well with problems that preoccupy us? Why always original panaceas? The Scandinavian countries are among the, sadly, few that have dealt remarkably well with certain vexing practical problems. Social welfare, land use, industrial relations, conservation, the promotion of the arts and aesthetics of life, and controlled economic growth come readily

---

Edvard Bull *et al.*, *Det norske folks liv og historie gjennom tidene*, 11 vols. (Oslo, 1935); for the period 1814-1844, Sverre Steen, *Det frie Norge* (Oslo, 1951-62); and for a summary in Norwegian, Magnus Jensen, *Norges historie*, 3rd ed., 2 vols. (Oslo, 1963).

to mind: we can profit from studying their policies in these and other fields. This is no plea for imitation, which rarely works, but for considering instructive experience where it is available.

Often the relevance of the policies of a country like Norway, as well as the pertinence of data it presents in areas of theory, are impugned precisely because Norway is such a "small" political system. Perhaps it is (although one could make quite a case to the contrary). But smallness may be an asset, not a liability. There are, after all, many small countries in which many people, for various reasons, are in fact interested; if scale makes much difference in political systems we are handicapped in studying such countries with notions derived from cases of quite different dimension. Anyway, who can say what the significance of scale is in political systems unless he studies systems of assorted sizes? And the smaller the country, the more likely it is that one can get a decent grip on it in a reasonable amount of time—read the literature, interview important actors, explore its various regions and social segments—in other words, achieve economies in inquiry. Considering the great complexity of political study, that is no small advantage.

2. In view of this, it is pleasant to be able to say that a broadly useful and penetrating literature on Norway is at last beginning to appear, the product of both Norwegian scholars and Americans. Of course, Norwegians, and a few others, have long written about their country's government, but until recently they have done so within very narrow limitations. Treatments by foreigners have been invariably brief, superficial, and ultraimpressionistic.[2] Those by Norwegians can best be characterized as "solid" within the limits of continental historical-constitutionalist scholarship—not variegated or relevant to the majority of concerns of contemporary political studies, however

[2] For examples, see the treatment of Norway in Royal Institute of International Affairs, *The Scandinavian States and Finland* (London, 1951), pp. 151-231; the section on politics in David Rodnick, *The Norwegians* (Washington, D.C., 1955), pp. 122-144; and the section on the political labor movement in Walter Galenson, *Labor in Norway* (Cambridge, Mass., 1949), pp. 55-77.

admirable in themselves.[3] Impressionistic essays, special and general histories, and constitutional commentaries continue, fortunately, to be written, but a new literature is adding to such studies previously neglected and at least equally valuable dimensions. Two recently published books illustrate in what sense this is so: James Storing's *Norwegian Democracy* (Oslo, 1963) and Henry Valen and Daniel Katz's *Political Parties in Norway* (Oslo, 1964).

Storing's *Norwegian Democracy* tries to present a full picture of the Norwegian political system in all its aspects; it is a broad survey based on wide, although far from exhaustive, reading and considerable personal acquaintance with the country. As the author himself says, the book is "reasonably traditional," which means that its foundations are largely in the historical-constitutionalist school, to some of the chief Norwegian exponents of which (Castberg, Wyller, Steinnes) the author acknowledges special obligations, while omitting from his menu of acknowledgments (as well as from his bibliography and reading) such names as Rokkan, Valen, and Torgersen, who have explored quite different approaches to the Norwegian polity. This makes some of his chapters and sections rather thin, and one of them particularly so: that on parties, which happens to be the special subject of Valen and Katz's work. But this was bound to be the case in so broad a study. Storing at least provides a book that can serve as a broad foundation from which English-speaking political scientists can proceed to deeper and narrower studies, as well as a basis for taking Norway into account in their broad theoretical speculations.

Valen and Katz's *Political Parties in Norway* is a more intensive study and written in a different mode. Its concerns and style can be inferred from its authors' credentials. Katz, a pro-

[3] Outstanding examples for both their quality and limitations are Frede Castberg, *Norges statsforfatning*, 2 vols. (Oslo, 2nd ed., 1947), Johan Andenaes, *Statsforfatningen i Norge* (Oslo, 1945), Edvard Bull, *Arbeiderklassen i Norsk historie* (Oslo, 1947); the massive official history of parliament, *Det norske Storting gjennom 150 år*, 4 vols. (Oslo, 1964); and Jens Arup Seip, *Et regime foran undergangen* (Oslo, 1945).

fessor of psychology at the University of Michigan, is one of America's more illustrious "behavioralists," whose work has been concerned with such matters as rigorous research methods in social science (especially survey research and measurement techniques), industrial psychology and sociology, and, as here, political sociology. Valen, the Norwegian partner, studied political science at Oslo University shortly after the field was established there in the postwar period and is now head of political studies at Oslo's Institute for Social Research, which since its founding in 1950 has produced much admirable empirical work in occupational and industrial sociology, theoretical and experimental psychology, family sociology, and political science. The Institute has been much visited and, apparently, influenced by American sociologists and psychologists (e.g., Lazarsfeld, Hyman, Katz, Frenkel-Brunswick, Campbell, Coser, Tumin), while Valen himself has spent two years at Michigan's Survey Research Center.

Valen and Katz's book, not surprisingly then, stems directly from the pioneering work of the Survey Research Center in election and related studies. Its data come largely from the Norwegian election of 1957 and a particularly intensive survey of the Stavanger area in Southwestern Norway, selected because, being a small area, it permitted rigorous research, while having characteristics sufficiently varied to make it particularly suitable to the authors' purposes. These purposes were "(1) to measure the effect of party activity on the attitudes, perceptions and voting behavior of the electorate, (2) to evaluate the correlates and determinants of voting preference and the stability of that preference and (3) to compare the various political parties in terms of attitudes of leaders and voters on such matters as party units, party goals, party identification and motivation and character of party leadership" (p. 3). Within this program, the study is particularly concerned with the political effects of rapid social and economic changes and of different levels of economic development. To place its findings in a larger context, it provides succinct analyses of the general

Norwegian political and party systems, with particular emphasis on the actual decision-making structures of the parties, the relation of parties to other social organizations, and the bases of political cleavage in Norway.

Valen and Katz's book thus is at once narrower and broader than Storing's. It is narrower in that the bulk of its data comes from a small segment of Norwegian political life (which necessitates many caveats in regard to statements about its parameter, the whole of Norwegian politics); narrower also in that it does not deal with everything at once but explores only certain specified problems and hypotheses. It is a broader study in that it taps sources of data and uses methods of analysis not touched on by Storing (while not eschewing "qualitative" materials, including historical and constitutional ones), and in that its findings are tied into certain central general concerns of contemporary political science: problems of the determinants of political division and cohesion, of the social bases of politics, of the nature of oligarchy in political organization, of the consequences for politics of rapid socioeconomic change, and of the significance of what parties do for how the electorate acts. The study, in short, combines narrow detail, closely processed, with a treatment of problems that far transcend the Stavanger, or even Norwegian, boundaries. It thus provides just what is needed to make Norway "relevant" to us.[4]

[4] It is important to point out that Valen and Katz were able to proceed from solid foundations which many others were involved in laying. Their kind of political sociology and psychology has a short but rich history in Norway, where Tingsten's precocious work on election statistics, *Political Behavior* (London, 1937), has been carried forward rather more than in Tingsten's own Sweden. The name of Stein Rokkan, Valen's predecessor and collaborator in Oslo and now director of political studies at the Christian Michelsen Institute in Bergen, looms particularly large in this work. For a long list of his uniformly excellent papers, spanning the period 1952-1960, see Stein Rokkan and Henry Valen, "Parties, Elections and Political Behaviour in the Northern Countries: A Review of Recent Research," in O. Stammer, ed., *Politische Forschung* (Cologne, 1960), pp. 245-246. This paper presents (on pp. 103-136 and 237-249) an excellent textual and bibliographic summary of Scandinavian political research, including works by others in Norwegian

3. It is not my purpose here to discuss in detail Storing's book or that by Valen and Katz. Rather, I intend to use them, along with other works,[5] in the discussion of one specific problem to which the Norwegian experience is particularly germane. This is the problem of the conditions under which democratic systems will or will not tend to be stable and effective. Our voluminous speculations on this question have been very much tied to comprehensive knowledge of a small number of overstudied countries (especially Britain, France, and Germany) or very superficial knowledge of a large number of understudied ones (such as broad indices of their economic development), whereas the ideal surely is comprehensive and penetrating analysis of many cases. Going in depth into a case usually represented in our work only by a few indices, with ideas derived from careful studies of a mere handful of other cases, can be, as I hope to show, an instructive experience.

---

political sociology, such as Valen himself, Tertit Aasland, Vilhelm Aubert, Erik Grønseth, Svennik Høyer, Knut Dahl Jacobsen, Jorolf Moren, Sten Sparre Nilson, and Ulf Torgersen. Later lists can be found in Institute for Social Research, *Twelve Years of Social Research: 1950-1962* (Oslo, 1962), pp. 59-76, and The Chr. Michelsen Institute, *The Department of Humanities and Social Sciences: Activities and Programmes* (Bergen, 1962), pp. 23-24.

[5] Among materials not listed in the sources cited in note 4, the following were particularly useful: Stein Rokkan, "Geography, Religion and Social Class: Cross-Cutting Cleavages in Norwegian Politics" (mimeographed; to be published in S. M. Lipset and S. Rokkan, eds., *Party Systems and Voter Alignments*, New York: Free Press) and "Numerical Democracy and Corporate Pluralism: Problems of Protracted Opposition in Norway" (mimeographed; to be published in R. A. Dahl, ed., *Opposition*, New Haven: Yale Univ. Press); Rokkan and Henry Valen, "Regional Contrasts in Norwegian Politics," in E. Allardt and Y. Littunen, eds., *Cleavages, Ideologies and Party Systems* (Helsinki, 1964); Valen, "Nominasjonene" (mimeographed; to be published in Rokkan and Valen, *Valg i Norge*); and Ulf Torgersen, *Norske politiske institusjoner* (Institute for Social Research, 1964).

Norway as a Stable Democracy

A. THE STABILITY OF NORWEGIAN DEMOCRACY

NORWAY, together with some other "small" states, is a country particularly crucial for studies of the conditions of stable or unstable democracy. The reason is that its democratic system has been, by any standards, remarkably stable and effective. This is important because there are so few unmistakable cases of stable democracy with which the more abundant unsuccessful and ambiguous cases can be contrasted and that can serve as "controls" for statements about the latter. In what senses, then, has Norway been a "stable" democracy?[1]

1. First, Norwegian democracy has been remarkably durable. Factors selected to account for its stability must apply not just to contemporary Norway but, to an extent, as far back as the early nineteenth century, for Norwegian democracy has existed and functioned well since the separation from Denmark in 1814. In that year the newly (and very briefly) independent Norwegians adopted what was at the time undoubtedly the most democratic constitution in Europe, modeled in large part on the French revolutionary constitution of 1791 and fashioned, in the plain upstairs assembly room of a merchant's house at Eidsvoll, by an unusually representative assembly. Under this document, domestic government was carried on during the union with Sweden and is still carried on, in amended form, today. The intervening century and a half witnessed only temporary deviations from the pattern of stable and effective representative rule, which was at no time seriously disrupted. Norwegian national independence and stable democratic govern-

---

[1] Throughout the paper I shall use the terms "stable," "effective," and "successful" as virtually interchangeable. They refer simply to the principal characteristics listed in this section, although their equation may portray some biases of mine in favor of certain kinds of democracies.

ment may thus truly be said to have been "indissolubly inter-linked."[2]

To be sure, Norway's democracy throughout most of the nineteenth century was a qualified democracy. The system belonged to the world of representative oligarchies, as did the British and American governments of the time. Suffrage was limited and government dominated, until 1884 (when a true parliamentary regime emerged from executive domination), by the higher officials, who derived their formal authority from the monarchy and were to a considerable extent free from parliamentary control. But among representative oligarchies, Norway, from 1814 to 1884, comes unusually close to the point where oligarchy and popular democracy become hard to distinguish. Nearly half its adult male population was enfranchised in 1815—about 12 per cent of the whole population,[3] compared to infinitesimal percentages in England even after 1832 (about 2 per cent of the whole population), post-unification Italy and Restoration France (a fraction of 1 per cent).[4] This included many farmers who were guaranteed two thirds of the Storting's representatives, thus assuring (because of a relatively egalitarian system of landholding) the presence, if not the dominance, in parliament of nonoligarchical elements.[5] Start-

[2] William Warby, *et al.*, *Modern Norway: A Study in Social Democracy* (London, 1950), 9.

[3] The figure generally given in Norwegian history books is 7.5 per cent. The percentage given here reflects recent recalculations by Norwegian political sociologists. Differences in such figures result partly from the nature of one's data and partly from such other matters as the definition of adulthood. But whatever the bases of calculation, the overall result has the same implication: that Norway early in the nineteenth century had achieved an unusually high degree of democratization.

[4] Valen and Katz, 13.

[5] Rokkan estimates the proportion of those enfranchised in 1815 at 13 per cent of the entire city population (including women and children) and at 10 per cent in the country. These percentages do not differ markedly from Valen and Katz's for adult males only. Rokkan adds: "By the standards of 1815 Norway was a remarkably democratic country. . . . No other Western European country seems to have reached this level so

ing from this unusually broad base of participation, eligibility for the vote and, even more, its exercise, actually declined somewhat until 1880, but only due to population shifts and, as in other early democracies, a low level of registration. As for the *régime censitaire* of high officials, the *embedsmannsstat* (officials' state) as Jens Arup Seip (among others) has recently called it, that was as much a reality as, and little more significant than, the *ettpartistat* (one-party state) that Seip alleges to exist today.[6] As the latter was always qualified by an influential opposition (now, 1965, in fact, in power) so the former operated together with strong representative local government and an active, broad-based national parliament, if not yet with organized parties and the rules of parliamentarism. As the Labour Party's long dominance reflected a widespread unwillingness to experiment in a working system and thus conservatism of a sort, so the *régime censitaire* rested, like the hegemony of Britain's squirearchs and America's post-colonial and bourgeois aristocracies, on a kind of political deference, as well as a great deal of political "parochialism." Norway, during most of the nineteenth century, thus had all the familiar features of emerging democracy, and indeed among European nations to an unrivaled degree.

Among these features is the gradual and peaceful growth of still more democratic forms from an already broadly representative base. The political history of Norway until the achievement of full suffrage in 1913 (when Norway became the first country to establish formal political equality of the sexes, universal adult male suffrage having been achieved in 1898 and partial female suffrage in 1907 and 1912) reads much like that of other stable democracies. It involves, in Rokkan's words, a process of "gradual civic incorporation." Franchise criteria were relaxed and "parochials" mobilized, especially through the

---

early and been able to stay there." (Rokkan, "Geography, Religion, and Social Class," p. 19).

[6] Seip, *Fra embedsmannsstat til ettpartistat og andre essays* (Oslo, 1964).

organization of a modern party system, very much in the British manner and at virtually the same time. The special position of the executive was broken in 1884, when parliamentary government in the strict sense (selection of the executive from, and its full dependence on, the Storting) was established —again a remarkable similarity to Britain. Throughout this process, demands for political reform, also in the British manner, were always relatively limited, making possible easy concessions by those in power and, through these concessions, drawing the teeth of potentially extremist protest movements.[7]

Norwegian democracy thus at least satisfies the criterion of durability that Dahl uses in his famous study of New Haven. Changes in the system occurred, as they must in any living structure. And some of the changes in Norway, as in New Haven, were anything but marginal. In both cases "organized, overt political competition" gained increasing legitimacy and the number of political participants "shot up"; in Norway, moreover, the formal pattern of power underwent one important reconstitution. But, in Dahl's words, "because of, or in spite of, these changes . . . the essential characteristics of the political system . . . have remained substantially intact for the past century. With appropriate techniques, probably one could detect and describe significant fluctuations in the 'intensity,' 'degree,' or 'magnitude' of the various characteristics, but this line of inquiry would not help much. . . ."[8]

---

[7] Torgersen, *Norske politiske institusjoner*, section 14.1.

[8] Robert A. Dahl, *Who Governs?* (New Haven, 1961), pp. 313-314. Samuel P. Huntington assesses the durability of regimes in much the same way. He argues that institutions exposed to changes in their immediate and remote environments gain durability from adaptation to change without essential loss of form, and relates institutional rigidity to institutional "decay." ("Political Development and Decay," *World Politics*, XVII [1963], 386-430.) This viewpoint is also developed, more abstractly, in David Easton, *A Systems Analysis of Political Life* (New York, 1965). Easton depicts the "maintenance" of a system as a process of constant adaptation to more or less disturbing or "stressful" environmental stimuli, stating that "as long as a system does keep its essential variables operating within . . . a critical range, the system can be said

2. The Norwegian system's "adaptability"—its maintenance of essential form, but lack of rigidity—helps account for the fact that its legitimacy has been virtually undisputed by Left or Right since its inception—a hallmark of stable democracy that is especially stressed by Lipset.[9] Norwegian democracy has maintained legitimacy (or "support," in Easton's terminology) on a very high level despite events that in other countries have generally produced deep crises of legitimacy: throughout the process of establishing national independence, the struggle for full democratization, the political mobilization of new social segments, rapid industrialization and urbanization, and constitutional struggles over the detailed form of the state. Political conflicts there were, but no seriously competing ideas of legitimacy, not even during the three high-water marks of conflict: the fight for parliamentarism from 1880 to 1884, the radicalization of the workers that followed the Russian revolution, and the doubts and tensions of the thirties. All the Norwegian radical movements have played themselves out in about five years; the very possibility of a *coup* was only once entertained (in 1884); labor's radicalization after the war of 1914-1918 had no results beyond the stagnation of the Labour Party through disruption for seven or eight years, and was in any case less marked than elsewhere; authoritarian movements of the Right (e.g., parts of *Bondepartiet* and of *Fedrelandslaget*, and Quisling's *Nasjonal Samling*) were invariably puny.[10] Quisling's movement got only 2 per cent of the vote before the war, and while a few opportunists joined it during the occupation, only

---

to persist" (p. 25). The maintenance of a biological organism or personality is usually treated in the same manner, and the idea of system maintenance as variation within "critical points" or short of a "strategic point" of change also occurs in Parsons' sociology. (See, e.g., Talcott Parsons *et al.*, *Toward a General Theory of Action*, Cambridge, Mass., 1951, pp. 228-231). Unfortunately, critical points or ranges are never concretely specified in these works. Hence, in following their approach, it is necessary, at present, to play the matter largely by ear.

[9] S. M. Lipset, *Political Man* (New York, 1960), ch. 3.

[10] Torgersen, *Norske politiske institusjoner*, sections 14.1-14.6.

one small social segment (higher police officials, not surprisingly) gave it any considerable support (and, more surprisingly, less than half even of them). On one or two occasions the system may have smacked of potential violence, but nothing irrevocable ever happened, and extreme opposition was always quickly tamed, especially by timely concessions, first to the Liberals (*Venstre*), then to Labour.

The point is not that there have been no fluctuations in the legitimacy of Norwegian democracy, but that these fluctuations have had characteristics typical of stable polities. Like any other political system, Norway has experienced periods relatively calm and relatively stormy, times of greater commitment and greater doubt. The stormier, more doubtful periods in part reflected purely internal stresses, and to some extent also the impact on Norwegians of international currents in opinion. Especially after World War I and in the thirties a good many Norwegians raised questions about democracy (its efficiency, its ability to cope with economic crises) similar to those raised in virtually all other countries, as a result both of domestic problems and an ecumenical decline in democratic optimism and commitment. But the crisis of parliamentarism in Norway at this time (if crisis is the word) was but a pale reflection of what transpired elsewhere. It was short-lived and involved doubt and debate rather than alienation and sharp conflict. Indeed, the very ability of a political system to limit and overcome stress provides greater assurance of its soundness than if it were never tested. Healthy individuals do get ill, but exhibit symptoms less acute, and revive more quickly and more intact, than the sickly. And even during the worst times of stress, one aspect of Norwegian political life, local government, always functioned as an unquestioned stronghold of democracy and the principal incubator of the country's political elite, as it had even while the national democracy was still qualified by the power of its officialdom.

The absence of significant radical movements and of intransigent movements of the Right is not the only index of democracy's legitimacy in Norway. It only indicates lack of strong dissent. Equally important is the evidence of strong commitment to democratic forms, rather than the mere passive "acceptance" of these forms that Dahl found in New Haven.[11] In Norway's political mythology, the year of the constitution has a kind of mystical significance, as does the not-so-fanciful picture of primitive democracy among the Norwegians of remote times. The idea of democracy is imbibed through the earliest socialization processes, not more tenuously based on rational persuasion, and is central to the Norwegians' conception of their national essence, for through the Danish and Swedish domination Norwegians were spared having to incorporate an indigenous authoritarianism into their self-conception. As a result, to paraphrase what Ferraton has said about the Norwegian workers movement (but could as well have said about nearly all segments of Norwegian life), fidelity to democracy is a principle that simply is not subject to dispute. "To disavow political democracy seems as immoral as to disavow honesty, as absurd as to want to build a house after destroying its foundations." And elsewhere: "[Democracy] is not considered as an ideology, an abstract construction, to be realized in a future society: it is held as a natural element, a way of living, a moral virtue."[12]

3. Stable democracies are not only durable and legitimate, but marked as well by what might be called intrasystem stability, especially the stability of governments and, closely related, their effectiveness in making decisions.[13] In regard to these matters, Norway's record could hardly be much better. The broad history of its governments is much like that of Britain's in modern times: there have been three periods of continuous domination by a

[11] Dahl, *Who Governs?* 314.

[12] H. Ferraton, *Syndicalisme ouvrier et social-democratie en Norvège* (Paris, 1960), 9, 106.

[13] In Easton's terminology, which may be better, I am speaking here of the ability of the system to process "demands" into "outputs," and the tendency to "support" not only the democratic "regime" and its constituent "roles" but also specific "authorities" (i.e., occupants of the roles).

single coherent political force—a different one in each period
(the conservatives and officialdom from 1814 to 1884, the Liberals from 1884 to 1920, and Labour from 1935 to the present)
—and one more turbulent transitional period (1920-1935).
Only the period 1920-1928, when the nonsocialist parties were
deeply at odds over language and temperance questions, and the
socialists split by the impact of the Russian revolution, was beset
by governmental crises, one cabinet, the first Labour government,
actually being forced to resign, after a mere fortnight in office, as
a result of a positive vote of lack of confidence. But even in the
transitional interwar period, the average cabinet lasted nearly one
and a half years (excellent compared to the Third and Weimar
republics), and this in a period of constant minority government, more extremism than usual, and a prolonged economic
crisis that hit Norway with especially vicious force.[14] More impressive still, Norway, from 1935 to the outbreak of war, produced legislation combining many features of the American
New Deal and the postwar British welfare state (based on a
considerable earlier development of welfare legislation), and
did it without a presidential or parliamentary landslide, but
with a *minority* government at the helm.[15] Since 1945 there has
been but one cabinet crisis—although "crisis" seems too strong
a word for what occurred, for Labour's brief lapse from power
in 1963 resulted as much from a statistical accident as from the
King's Bay incident that apparently precipitated it.[16]

Such continuity of leadership and decisional efficiency have,
incidentally, been achieved without any sacrifice of parliamentarism—without default of parliamentary functions to the
bureaucracy or, through enabling legislation, to temporary

[14] In 1932, 42 per cent of Norwegian trade unionists were unemployed!
See T. K. Derry, *A Short History of Norway* (London, 1957), 230.

[15] *Ibid.*, 231 sq.

[16] The accident was a Storting membership of 74 Labour representatives and 74 representatives of the bourgeois opposition, plus 2 extreme
leftist dissidents from Labour who, on this single occasion, used their
unlikely position to make mischief. Gerhardsens government, however,
soon was back in office.

strongmen. Even in the darkest days of economic crisis Norway, in contrast to most continental countries, never ceased to be an "authentic" parliamentary democracy.[17]

4. Finally, Norway displays also some of those features that have been found characteristic of stable democracies but do not themselves denote stability or directly account for it—characteristics that simply tend somehow to be associated with democratic stability. Thus, Norwegian parties are internally highly cohesive, observing about as much parliamentary discipline as do the British. And as far as one can tell short of survey research, Norway has also some of those curiously mixed characteristics that Almond and Verba found in "civic cultures."[18] For instance, political discussion is normal and politics salient in many social relations, but it is kept in place, low-keyed, a dimension of life that is neither all-absorbing nor widely disregarded.[19] The volume of Norwegian party membership indicates, relative to other countries, neither very great nor very little political activism.[20] As for "system affect," Norwegians appear to have a healthy regard for their government and rulers (their competence, honesty, responsiveness), but certainly not without being capable of criticism, irreverence or sarcasm. The present (1964) prime minister, Gerhardsen (popularly known as Uncle Einar), is a much admired but far from august figure, respected more for his common than uncommon qualities, a butt of jokes as well as serious discussion. The odd combination of self-regard and strong self-criticism that many have found

[17] For a definition of "authenticity" in democracies, see Appendix B, pp. 227-230, *infra*.

[18] G. A. Almond and S. Verba, *The Civic Culture* (Princeton, 1963), esp. pp. 473-505.

[19] See, for example, PRIO, "Public Opinion and the Consequences of Disarmament," Three-Nation Study, Program 16, mimeographed, November, 1964, items 9-11.

[20] Storing, 125. See also Maurice Duverger, *Political Parties* (London, 1954), p. 95, comparing the proportion of members to voters in socialist parties.

characteristic of Norwegian life in general[21] certainly characterizes the Norwegians' stance toward their political system. One
gets the impression that they would not have it otherwise, but
seem astonished when it is praised by a foreigner.

Norway and Theories of Stable Democracy

1. One point should be made immediately about the
conditions that make Norway so stable a democracy: it is not
apparently the formal institutional arrangements of her government that make the system successful. The attractive view,
coming to us from the Enlightenment, that governments are
mechanisms which properly work if properly constructed, is dis-
credited in virtually all its theoretical forms by inconvenient
Norwegian facts.

In formal-legal structure, Norway resembles the familiar unstable democracies of continental Europe more than a stable
parliamentary system like Britain's. Much has been made, for
example, of the strong power of dissolution in Britain as a
weapon that leaders wield to enforce party discipline and squeeze
majorities out of parliament; but in Norway there is no power to
dissolve the Storting at all. Nor are there any carefully devised
formal provisions for executive emergency powers. The electoral
system is a variant of proportional representation, not the
simple majority, single-member constituency system; and while
the Norwegian electoral system may be associated with a fair
amount of party fragmentation, nothing else that is supposed to
follow from proportional representation according to the somber
doctrines of Hermens, Duverger, and others has followed in fact.
There is, compared to Britain, little ministerial control over the
parliamentary timetable; interpolations, supposedly the bane of
French regimes, are permitted; and parliament has powerful
specialized standing committees that much resemble in form the
committees which supposedly emasculated French authority in
the Third and Fourth republics. The Norwegian Storting, in

---

[21] E.g., Rodnick, ch. I, and Frede Castberg, *The Norwegian Way of
Life* (London, 1954), pp. 10-11.

short, is much more a true legislature than the House of Commons. And one should reiterate that the whole constitutional structure is, of all things, more an imitation of a French than British model.[22]

2. To the Enlightenment and its inheritors can also be traced another view about the conditions that impinge on politics: that governments are images of their material environment—of such matters as the geographic and economic characteristics of nations. Here we have fewer firm generalizations to weigh against Norwegian experience. Especially in regard to geographic characteristics, the majority of arguments are patent rationalizations, leading to obvious inconsistencies. (For example, poor soil, geographic barriers and a hard climate have been said to promote in Norway a drive for individual self-sufficiency and isolation—and intensive cooperativeness as well.) However, two well-grounded hypotheses relating politics and its environment may be assessed against Norwegian experience. Both only deepen the mystery of Norway's stable democracy.

The first hypothesis relates stable democracy to wealth and a high level, but slow rate, of economic development. It is an old hypothesis, at present most associated with the work of Lipset.[23] True, Norway today, while in no way ostentatiously affluent, is not much poorer than any other European country (although considerably more stable a democracy than most).[24]

---

[22] Details of constitutional structure may be found in Valen and Katz, pp. 12-22, and, in more detail, in Storing, chs. 3-5 and pp. 225-239.

[23] Lipset, *Political Man*, ch. 2.

[24] For what such figures are worth, Norway's per capita G.N.P. in 1957 was $1,130, which put it eleventh in the world and after only Switzerland, Luxembourg, Sweden, Belgium, and the United Kingdom in Europe—although in view of Norwegian prices, especially food prices, this must not be taken too literally. In daily newspaper circulation Norway ranked fourth (out of 14) in Western Europe; in radio sets ninth; in television sets thirteenth (only barely ahead of Ireland). See B. M. Russett *et al.*, *World Handbook of Political and Social Indicators* (New Haven, 1964). The high per capita G.N.P. does not imply that there is much private wealth. It reflects in part a remarkably even distribution

But there is a catchword here: Norway "today." The crucial fact is that Norway's prosperity is recently acquired while her stable democracy is very old. For much of its history as a successful representative system Norway was desperately poor, one of Europe's economic backwaters. Its emigration rate around the turn of the century was surpassed only by those of Ireland and Italy, both much larger in population.[25] Indeed, much of what one reads about nineteenth century Norway has a smack of Ireland about it; and in view of its resources, topography, and long political dependency, this is hardly surprising. The present prosperity of the country thus reflects rapid and rather recent development, with industrialization dating at the earliest to the turn of the century and being particularly accelerated after World War II, when democracy was already firmly established.[26]

But rapid development itself, according to a hypothesis to which Lipset also subscribes, along with many others, including the present writer,[27] should have led to a particularly serious malfunctioning of the political system. In fact, a Norwegian, Edvard Bull, can claim to have been one of the earliest proponents of the hypothesis, since much repeated, that the rate of industrialization correlates positively with the tendency of workers to take an aggressively destructive attitude toward management and the political system. The hypothesis was formulated in 1922, particularly to account for differences in the Scandinavian workers' movements. It fit Norway in the immediate wake of the Russian revolution, but did not fit for long. Torgersen remarks perspicaciously that the hypothesis fails in

---

of wealth, in part a high priority for public things. Norway is on the whole a country of private scarcity and public affluence, reversing the more usual condition of affluent societies.

[25] Derry, *A Short History of Norway*, p. 213.

[26] See Galenson, *Labor in Norway*, pp. 10, 18, and sources there cited; Valen and Katz, p. 4; and Rokkan, "Geography, Religion, and Social Class," p. 66. From 1950 to 1959 Norway ranked fifth in the world and first in Western Europe in regard to gross domestic capital formation as a percentage of G.N.P. See B. M. Russett *et al.*, *World Handbook of Political and Social Indicators*, p. 168.

[27] Eckstein, *A Theory of Stable Democracy*.

Norway because it rests on a crucial *ceteris paribus* clause, namely that the orientations of management and political leaders toward the workers are a constant. But this, he argues, is not so: certain aspects of the Norwegian social and political structures (in my view, not only elite attitudes) prevented the tendency that Bull predicated.[28]

A second hypothesis about politics and its environment on which Norway casts some doubt involves the scale of society. This is the view that "small" societies are more likely to have stable democracies than large. In what sense does Norway impugn it? Is Norway not a "small" society? Here we must repeat my earlier suggestion that a strong case can be made to the effect that our preconceptions on the matter are wrong, or only partly right. Of course, Norway is not a "great power," but there is hardly a one to one relationship between large societies and great powers (think of India or Brazil). Nor has Norway a large population. But there are other measures of the scale of societies, some of which are manifestly more important for the problem of stable democracy, that yield different results when applied to Norway. If the model "small society" envisaged by the hypotheses is something as intimate, neighborly, and internally accessible as Rousseau's Geneva or an Aristotelian city-state, then clearly international power and numbers of people signify less than geographic area, communications, contiguity, and constant intercourse among citizens. From all these standpoints, Norway comes closer to being immense than small. (A British writer, Mikes, has called her "the largest little country in the world.") Her territory is 30 per cent larger than the United Kingdom's; communications among many places even today are difficult and earlier in the century were virtually impossible much of the year; the population is the most scattered in Europe, except for Iceland's; and there is in consequence much regional diversity and further diversity, even isolation, within the regions. England, which has some three quarters of its elite (those listed in *Who's Who*) living in the London

[28] Torgersen, *Norske politiske institusjoner*, section 14.4.

region, is, from this standpoint, much more akin to the tight little city-state with its accessible hinterlands; so too is France. If, on the other hand, the model society envisaged is simply one of few distinct social segments (regardless of other characteristics) so that there are few diversities for politics to reconcile, Norway also fails to fill the bill. She has about as complex a social structure (diverse regions, dialects, occupations, economic interests, cultural stances, voluntary organizations, and political organizations) as much less stable societies.

3. The context, or setting, of a political system includes, of course, nonphysical and nonmaterial conditions too. One of these is a society's history—a factor that looms as large in the theories of modern conservatives as do constitutional mechanisms in the theories of liberals.

In this area too puzzles arise when one applies established generalizations to Norwegian facts. For example, the general notion central to conservative thought that all rapid change has deleterious social consequences clearly does not hold in Norway, where, as we know already, self-government, popular democracy, industrialization, and its concomitants (considerable urbanization, bureaucratization, mobility) all came rapidly into being. Some, to be sure, hold that such major social changes can rapidly occur without poisoning political life, provided that they do not happen simultaneously, but are safely spaced (as in Britain, where the revolution of national identity was firmly settled before the religious "revolution," the religious before the constitutional, the constitutional before the industrial, the industrial before the social, and the social before the recent transformation of Britain's international role). But Norway's major social and political changes virtually coincided. The process of full democratization,[29] industrialization, full national independence, and the intense development of a social service state

---

[29] Especially if one takes into account not formal eligibility for the franchise but actual political mobilization. See Rokkan, "Numerical Democracy and Corporate Pluralism," p. 10.

all fall within the life of a single generation, and while their joint impact has certainly been reflected in a complicated set of party identifications, nothing more serious has ensued.

4. Constitutional forms, environment, and history are life-less forces that affect action only through their impact on human values, feelings, and cognitions, that is, on "culture." Hence, in attempting to account for the performance of any political system, much can be said for considering culture directly, even if one treats it only as an intermediary between human life and its mute setting (perhaps to help one find the noncultural forces that really matter), not, as is also reasonable, as an autonomous force. But in this area too, Norway compounds the mystery of stable democracy. Consider in this connection three hypotheses, all derived from comparisons of a few much-studied cases and concerned with different aspects of orientations and the human psyche.

The first is the hypothesis that a "legalistic" political style is inimical to successful democracy—a hypothesis based largely on a contrast between Britain and Germany (and to a lesser extent France and Italy).[30] A political style is legalistic where there exist a plethora of explicit legal rules, a high regard for such rules as ends rather than means among other means, much emphasis on strict observance of the rules, and a tendency to use litigation for political purposes. Legalism, in this sense, turns all politics into cognition—of the relevant legal rules, of course —removing from its realm affect as well as moral and practical evaluation. In another perspective, legalism involves only the "ego" in politics, and that only in a limited way.

A case, both logical and empirical, can be made to show that legalism "interferes with [the] success" of democracy chiefly by

[30] This hypothesis is mainly associated with Herbert J. Spiro. See his *Government by Constitution* (New York, 1959), esp. pp. 181-182, 187, and 211-236. In what follows I state what I take him to be saying in a somewhat diffuse and unrigorous discussion, using as my cue his remark that political styles are not exclusive, so that one can speak of legalism even where other styles coexist with it, provided only that the behavior specified for it is pronounced.

restricting its adaptability.[31] Clearly, legalism may characterize societies unwilling or unable to deal with their problems on a moral, practical, or emotional level—societies threatened by politics in the normal sense. But legalism in such cases may be more a symptom than a cause of unstable democracy.[32] Norway, at any rate, suggests that a high degree of it may be found in the most stable and effective of representative systems.

Norwegians are not merely law-abiding people, but in a sense addicted to defining formal-legal rules and to their strict observance; and they seem to value legal experts particularly highly. Their constitutional commentaries are large and meticulous to a Germanic extent.[33] Their political struggles on major issues have had a juridical flavor.[34] Their political "science" until very recently was largely legal study. Their political parties are organized according to extremely detailed constitutions, closely observed. Their voluntary associations, even the smallest, invariably have complex and detailed organizational statutes, lovingly printed and lovingly acted out. The educational requirements for public service applicants emphasize law, with economics a very poor second;[35] the chief secretary

[31] *Ibid.*, 187.

[32] A case in point is provided by Pye's study of Burma, *Politics, Personality and Nation Building* (New Haven, 1962), pp. 105-107. Burma does not contradict Spiro's point that legalism may be related to certain difficulties of rule in representative, and perhaps other, polities. Pye, however, does not blame legalism for these difficulties. Rather, he relates it to a more fundamental lack of trust, love of power, and ever-present threat of violence in Burmese society, from which various consequences deleterious to the political system follow; and he represents law as an element of firmness and predictability in an environment remarkable for uncertainty in human relationships. In effect, Pye considers legalism to be a kind of anchor in the flux of Burmese political life, a "functional" response to social patterns that reduce predictability to a minimum.

[33] See, for example, Castberg, *Norges statsforfatning*, prev. cit.

[34] See especially Castberg, *The Norwegian Way of Life*, p. 50, where the role of legal quibbling in Norway's struggle for independence is discussed and the nineteenth century is characterized as the "great era of the lawyer."

[35] Storing, 115.

of the prime minister's office is required to be a lawyer; and the higher civil service is in fact virtually monopolized by legally trained men.[36] Political litigiousness may be a missing ingredient, but everything else that characterizes legalism is unmistakably there—without any of the deleterious consequences that ought to follow.[37] And emphasis on formal law has a very long history in the country, going back to Viking times; "with law shall we build our land," reads the introduction to the country's ancient legal code, compiled in the thirteenth century, but based on still more ancient practices.[38]

A second "cultural" hypothesis to consider is more familiar. It holds that parliamentary systems work well only in deferential societies, where democracy's potential for anarchy is checked by diffuse respect for authority, based on a larger social deference, a certain aristocratic tenor of life. This hypothesis has been in vogue singe Bagehot wrote *The English Constitution*, and is based mainly on a contrast between the deferential British and the independent French. It stresses the normative rather than cognitive element of orientations, the superego, not the ego: the definition of conduct by internalized norms externally defined.

Diffuse deference may tell us much about British political behavior but is far from a general condition of stable democracy. A more undeferential, unaristocratic society than Norway would be hard to find, and this is not surprising since her indigenous nobility was ravaged by the Black Death of 1348-1350 and

[36] In 1960, 37 of 48 *ekspedisjonssjefer* (the highest public service level) were lawyers (77 per cent) and two-thirds of *byråsjefer* were trained in law. (See Torgersen, *Norske politiske institusjoner*, secs. 9.4-9.6.) What is more, these figures reflect a rather recent recognition that other skills are relevant to public service.

[37] The absence of political litigiousness in Norway does not mean, however, that legal processes do not play a large role in resolving social conflicts. The principal student of Norway's legal profession, Vilhelm Aubert, has pointed out that lawyers, even if not the courts, have long played the central role in Norwegian conflict resolution, chiefly by informal mediatory processes. Aubert, "Norske jurister: En yrkesgruppe gjennom 150år," *Tidsskrift for rettsvitenskap*, LXXVII (1964), 310.

[38] Halvdan Koht and Sigmund Skard, *The Voice of Norway* (New York, 1944), pp. 1, 11-12.

never restored. In the nineteenth century her officialdom, like the British squires, had a sort of quasiaristocratic (i.e., gentlemanly) status, and the term "bureaucratic aristocracy" actually occurs in Norwegian writings;[39] indeed, even today families associated with a history of officialdom often claim special respect. A functional elite, however, can hardly be a full equivalent of Britain's awesome aristocracy, and the respect officials often claim in Norway is in fact, to their chagrin, not often granted. Nor does Norway exhibit any of the concomitants of deference to aristocracy that we associate with Britain. Social relations on any level are much more egalitarian. Parliamentarians are accorded nothing like the aura of sacrosanctity they have in Britain; thus there is a considerable interpenetration of parliamentary party and external party both on the national and local levels[40] (for instance, the parliamentary leader of a party is usually its external chairman as well), whereas in Britain party on one hand and Her Majesty's Government and Opposition are distinguished in all sorts of obvious and subtle ways. As for attitudes to executive authority, one finds in Norway at most a distrustful tolerance, quite unlike British deference to ministers as concrete emanations of majesty. Parliament, in fact, keeps itself nominally distinct from its executive, leading some purists to argue that Norway really has a kind of separation-of-powers system. For example, ministers sit and speak in parliament but may not vote or act officially as representatives, much as in the Fifth Republic, except that in Norway the procedure symbolizes parliamentary rather than ministerial autonomy. In other ways, too, such as the careful examination of bills by parliamentary committees,[41] the Storting manifests its sense of autonomy and power.

Finally, consider the hypothesis, also derived from Bagehot, that stable and effective democracy is promoted by a considerable element of ceremonialism and theatricality, by "dignified"

[39] See Torgersen, secs. 10.3.
[40] Valen and Katz, pp. 65-7, 81, 83, 86, 88.
[41] Storing, p. 87.

arrangements that produce affect and feed the libido. The fact is that Norway's political system is drab and untheatrical in the extreme. It lacks pageantry, aesthetic formalism, and titles, except for one inconsequential knightly order. It cultivates self-effacing, matter-of-fact speaking in which Gradgrindish facts, preferably statistical, are at a premium. And it is headed by a monarchy without a court, chosen in 1905 because it seemed "more respectable" than a pure republic, not out of real monarchical convictions; nor is there yet any deep emotional involvement in it; nor does the monarchy itself try to cultivate such an involvement.

> Apart from the most formal state occasions [Crown Prince— now King—Olav] does not allow anyone to call him "Your Royal Highness" and usually addresses men in the Norwegian equivalent of *du* or *tu*. . . . The Crown Prince and Princess go to the cinema and buy their own tickets; their children go to ordinary schools. . . . One American journalist had two appointments with the Crown Prince and let him down on both occasions, without even excusing himself on the telephone. Finally, he turned up at the Prince's yachting cottage at Hankö without an appointment. He was received, but during the interview the Crown Prince was doing the washing up.[42]

This from a much-bewildered British writer. When the present writer was in Norway, a report was spread that Crown Prince Harald was to marry the daughter of a rather rich commoner. Much heated discussion ensued in the press and in private, involving a variety of revealing positions: for example, that the marriage might be a step toward the creation of an informal bourgeois nobility in Norway and, not unrelated, that certain men might, through connections with the palace, obtain undue political influence.

5. These doubts about various constitutional, environmental, historical, and cultural theories of stable democracy do

[42] George Mikes, "The Largest Little Country in the World," *Encounter*, April 1954, pp. 41-42.

not imply that Norway's political system is a fact without an explanation. They only illustrate the relevance of Norway as a test case for hypotheses developed with other countries in mind and narrow the range of possibilities. But not all possibilities have been considered. One hypothesis above all, a "cultural" one, remains: that democracy requires a large political consensus, or (in a more recent, better, but not very dissimilar formulation) a "balance" of division and cohesion.[43]

This hypothesis has not been mentioned so far because, for several reasons, it deserves a separate and more thorough treatment. Of all generalizations about stable democracy that have wide currency, it is at once the most plausible and the most puzzling. Of all such theories, it is the one on which the emerging literature on Norway has most to say, yet the most difficult to deal with on the basis of that literature. Most important, it provides, in my view, the best basis for understanding the Norwegian experience and using it *constructively* to build a theory of stable democracy. All that follows, consequently, is in one way or another concerned with the division-cohesion hypothesis.

To begin with, one should state that a strong case, both empirical and logical, can be made for the hypothesis. Empirically, it seems to fit the "civic cultures" that characterize stable democracies. Logically, one can see why it fits: Democracy, it is readily apparent, implies both elements of division and cohesion. It is a form of polity that liberates conflict in both the system and its subsystems (e.g., in parties), for its legitimacy is acquired by processes that do so. Democracy even presupposes the fact of political competition, for otherwise what sense would it make? Even the most cynical theorists (such as Schum-

---

[43] See, for example, Almond and Verba, *The Civic Culture*, pp. 489-493, and sources there cited. Almond and Verba use the terms consensus and cleavage, not division and cohesion. I prefer the latter because what is really being talked about is the forces that divide and bind polities, because cleavage is a particularly apt term for one *kind* of politically decisive force, and because consensus, i.e., like-mindedness, is not the only cement of political systems. These points should become more apparent in the course of the paper.

peter) have never managed to develop a conception of democracy that does not involve competition in the very definition. At a minimum, that competition must be about incumbency itself, about power; but it can be shown that such very restricted competition tends itself to undermine democratic polities by discrediting politicians, depriving authority of any element of sanctity, making politics irrelevant to most of society, and inducing attitudes in leaders themselves that lead them to act undemocratically, for an empty concern with power is the essence of the crudest of dictatorships.[44] But competition within a nation is only one face of democracy. The other is national authority. Democracies, like any other polities, must resolve diverse aspirations into accepted and enforced decisions. That requires in them cohesive forces, and, since they liberate conflict and cannot rely primarily on coercive power or exclusivist ideas, particularly strong ones, growing from society itself.[45] Ergo, working democracy equals a balance of division and cohesion in political life.

Norway, as we shall see, bears out this general argument; it could hardly be otherwise. But Norway bears it out only in a very special way, and only after the hypothesis has been considerably elaborated, revised, and made more exact. This is precisely what can make an examination of Norwegian experience in light of the division-cohesion hypothesis particularly instructive. For as far as we have gone with it, this hypothesis solves no problems; it only raises them. What is a proper balance of division and cohesion? How much of one, and how much of the other, is required? What kind of division, what kind of cohesion? What specific effects flow from different general balances of the two, from different balances of the various kinds? And how must

---

[44] These points are amply supported by the sad history of *trasformismo* in post-unification Italy and that of boss rule in segments of the American system.

[45] This point is strongly argued in Henry Valen, "Factional Activities and Nominations in Political Parties," *Acta Sociologica*, Vol. III, No. 4, p. 187.

emotional dispositions in politics. For example, between Soviet and American men there intrudes something larger than (anyway different from) specific disagreement: divergent modes of relating experience to action. Or think of medieval and modern men; among these, cultural divergences might be so great that specific disagreements might not even arise. They might have nothing at all to say to one another (although all too often culturally diverse men have no trouble talking—at cross-purposes). A third kind of division is *segmental cleavage*. This exists where political divisions follow very closely, and especially concern, lines of objective social differentiation, especially those particularly salient in a society—such as tribal differences in still rather primitive societies, racial differences in antagonistic multiracial societies, or regional differences in newly unified states. Other sorts of segmental cleavages might be based on rural-urban conflicts, on sex, generation, religion, language, or occupation. In the more extreme cleavage systems one often gets the impression that politics is struggle between distinct, only nominally unified subsocieties, each pursuing not only policy and procedural preferences, but above all autonomy from, or domination over, others, and sometimes these ends alone. The present world of emerging nations teems with examples not only of trival cleavages, but of territorial, generational, religious, linguistic, racial, and sexual ones as well.[3]

[3] To avoid a misunderstanding that arose repeatedly in discussions of the first draft of this study it should perhaps be separately emphasized that, for the present purpose, cultural divergences and segmental cleavages are deemed to exist *only in so far as they are actually manifested in political competition and conflict.* Thus the terms involve more than social differentiation or cultural diversity; they denote politically manifested differentiation and diversity. Note also that segmental cleavage refers to political conflicts that not only pit distinct segments against one another but *especially concern* segmental conflicts. To illustrate, males and females constitute in every society roughly a fifty-fifty segmentation; but to constitute segmental "cleavage" in the present sense, the male-female segmentation has to have two additional features: males and females must be engaged in political conflict, and the conflict between them must involve the society's sex roles in some manner. It follows that segmental cleavages need not exist (even if they are likely to exist)

Kinds of division constitute only one variable dimension of national patterns of political division. Another is the *extensiveness* of division—in a sense, not what kind of but how much political division exists in a polity. This involves a continuum on which societies may be placed according to three criteria. Extent of division may be gauged, first, on the basis of how many "kinds" of political division exist; thus a society that combines disagreements with divergences is more divided, *ceteris paribus*, than one that has only disagreements. Second, the amount of division must be gauged within each kind of division. One wants to know in each case the variety of specific issues at stake and the number of divergent cultural maps and segmental cleavages relevant to politics. Further, in the case of issues, one also wants to know how extensive are their ramifications—in other words, whether they are "fundamental" in the sense of having a large number of implications and consequences. For example, a specific disagreement on constitutional structure usually is far more ramified, hence extensive, than one, say, on the level of state pensions.

A third dimension of political division is its *intensity*. This too involves a continuum, location on which is determined by a combination of measures. One is the amount of "affect" involved in division, since, obviously, where men are tepid over their disagreements, divergences, or cleavages, divisions among them are less significant than where considerable animus is stirred up—regardless of the extent of division. A second criterion of intensity, scarcely separable from affect, is the "distance" among political opponents—how widely apart their political positions are from one another. For example, men who differ over the definitions of powers of a legislative committee are less distant from one another, hence less divided, than men

---

wherever differences in political behavior are correlated with aspects of social differentiation. Women, for example, generally are more "conservative" than men and much more likely to be attracted to confessional parties; but this does not necessarily imply a sexual segmental cleavage.

divided over the general question of legislative power, although both are divided by a specific disagreement; again, two culturally divergent groups of "modernized" men are probably less distant, hence less divided, than either is from unmodernized segments of society. A third criterion of intensity is the extent to which political divisions have become "manifest" in society (for example, the extent to which they are actually organized) rather than being merely latent tendencies in society. Clearly, when a political segment acquires an organized structure— when it becomes an organized party or revolutionary organization, for example—that adds an increment to the weight of political conflict. Political divisions, then, are most intense when organized structures clash over deeply felt differences among highly distant adversaries.[4]

In the existing literature on political division and cohesion numerous hypotheses are intimated that can be stated succinctly through these concepts. Some concern relations among the various dimensions and varieties of political division, others the ways in which patterns of political division affect the stability of democracies. They include the following:

(1) While specific disagreements can exist among men not otherwise significantly divided, cultural divergences are unlikely to exist without concomitant specific disagreements, and segmental cleavages are unlikely to exist without concomitant cultural divergences.

(2) The more extensive are cleavages, the more extensive will be divergences; and the more extensive are divergences, the more extensive will be disagreements (although extensive disagreements *need* not imply extensive divergences, or the latter extensive cleavages).

(3) The more extensive is political division, the more in-

---

[4] These aspects of the intensity and extensiveness of political divisions can, of course, be treated as quite separate dimensions, and for some purposes it may even be desirable to do so, or to take into account one or more without the others. Any one of them, however, seems to me less informative than the combinations.

tensive it will tend to be (although intensity *need* not imply extensive political divisions).

(4) Stable democracy requires:

    (a) political divisions highly restricted in extent; or

    (b) political divisions highly restricted in intensity; or

    (c) little division over general social identifications or broad cultural norms; or

    (d) some combination of (a), (b), and (c).

(5) Whether stable democracy requires (a), (b), (c), or (d), cleavages are most inimical, disagreements as such least inimical, to stable democracy. This is deducible from (1), (2), and (3) above.[5]

These hypotheses, as well as having empirical foundations, appear sensible. It is surely common sense to say that men are more likely to find acceptable common ground if they simply disagree than if the general organizations of their cognitions, values, evaluations, and feelings differ profoundly, and that they are least likely to be reconciled if divergent cultural-political maps coincide to a large extent with antagonistic segmental identifications. Disagreements are at least capable of resolution by compromise; but how does one compromise sets of orientations or profound segmental loyalties? Men argue over their disagreements, differ in orientation, and are separated by cleavage. It seems equally sensible to say that, *ceteris paribus*, the larger the number of matters to be reconciled, the more difficult is the work of reconciliation, or that the more intense men are about their divisive differences (the more emotional and mani-

[5] Almond and Verba stress "higher overarching attitudes of solidarity" (i.e., a relative lack of segmental cleavage or cultural divergence) as basic conditions of working democracy, precisely because democracy also implies conflict over policy (*The Civic Culture*, p. 492). The intensity hypothesis has been most categorically stated in C. J. Friedrich, *Constitutional Government and Democracy*, rev. ed. (Boston, 1946), 585-589. The extensiveness hypothesis is implied mainly in a large literature on the role of consensus in democracy, a typical example of which is H. Finer, *Governments of Greater European Powers* (New York, 1956), esp. pp. 3-41, 271-297.

fest are their conflicts, and the more distant they are from one another), the less likely they are to adjust and settle them. At the same time, it is hard to imagine cultural divergences in politics that involve no disagreements, or sharp segmental cleavages that have no cultural overtones.

If, then, the business of democracy is to produce cohesion out of division ("from many, one"), we can construct from these hypotheses two polar models of democracy, one for the most, the other for the least, stable case. The most stable democracy is one in which men disagree, without intensity and within a narrow range, on specific issues, widely share basic orientations, and have politically weak segmental identifications. The least stable case has the opposite characteristics: extensive and intense disagreements, flowing from highly divergent orientations and strong segmental cleavages. These models are, of course, close to being ideal types, that is, unlikely to exist in pure form (although, if they were undiluted ideal constructs all probabilistic adverbs and adjectives, such as "sharing widely," "weak," "highly divergent," would be replaced by absolute ones, such as "sharing universally," "nonexistent," "completely divergent"). They describe imaginable extremes that actual cases should approach concomitantly with the degree of stability or instability they manifest. Norway, for example, being a highly stable case, should approach closely to, even if not correspond absolutely with, the polar case of stable democracy.

The task now is to describe Norway's political divisions in some detail, using the concepts I have proposed, and, having described them, to see what they imply for the propositions and polar models that have been sketched.

2. Norway's political divisions have been charted with such tender care by her historians and political sociologists that one can sketch them summarily with only a minimum of caveats.[6]

---

[6] Some cautions are nevertheless advisable. They will be stated at the end of this section, when their significance can be better appreciated.

Meticulous work has been done on past as well as current divisions, applying to historical materials, as far as possible, rigorous contemporary methods of analysis. This is particularly fortunate because it enables one to trace changes and continuities in political divisions through the long history of Norway's stable democracy, rather than drawing merely a static picture of the present situation.[7]

From the time Norway first achieved virtually full self-government in 1814 until the advent of parliamentarism in 1884, her political divisions centered on one marked social cleavage, that between the official estate (Norway's aristocracy *manqué*) and the other estates of society. The labels conservative and liberal, Right and Left, often used to describe the political forces of that period, did not as yet stand for anything "manifest," any articulated political organizations, but simply for those who somehow supported one side or the other. It is very important to realize, however, that the supporters of the two sides were not odd and diverse mixtures of men, but men sharply divided by social characteristics, and that these characteristics were associated with marked cultural divergences and

---

[7] In constructing the sketch of Norway's political divisions that follows I have relied particularly heavily on Stein Rokkan's superb article, "Geography, Religion and Social Class," prev. cit. This article is in essence much the same as Rokkan and Valen, "Regional Contrasts in Norwegian Politics," and overlaps considerably with Valen and Katz's book, which, however, is the most comprehensive study of current political divisions. Some other instructive works are: Andreas M. Hansen, *Norsk folkepsykologi* (Christiania, 1898), an old but influential work that curiously blends racialism and, for its time, systematic electoral study and that has had much impact in Norway since it first appeared; Edvard Bull, sen., "Die Entwicklung der Arbeiterbewegung in drei skandinavischen Ländern," *Archiv für die Geschichte des Socialismus*, 1922, 329-361, which is useful for its portrait of the impact of early industrialization on political divisions; Rokkan and Valen, "The Mobilization of the Periphery," *Acta Sociologica*, VI (1962), 111-158, and Ulf Torgersen, "Sosiale klasser, politiske partier og politisk representasjon i norske bysammfunn," *Tidsskrift for samfunnsforskning*, VI (1961), 162-181, both especially useful for their discussion of certain regional contrasts; and Rokkan, "Numerical Democracy and Corporate Pluralism," prev. cit.

disagreements on widely ramified social, cultural, and constitutional issues.

Given the nature of the preparliamentary political system, a division between the official and other estates was bound to seem, on the surface, primarily a matter of consitutional disagreement and to involve, secondarily, questions of national identity. Constitutional law and practice instituted a separation of representative and the executive apparatus, which, incidentally, greatly favored the latter. The Storting, in the manner of parliaments of the time, met only infrequently (until 1869 every third year, for no more than three months without special royal consent, annually thereafter). Its decisions were subject to the king's veto, and this was exercised in about one eighth of all cases, particularly projects proposing major reforms. Financial grants were made to the king in lump sums, their specific uses—except for pensions granted by parliament to individual civil servants—being determined by the executive.[8] The king's ministers, although sometimes taking an independent line, were in the main his own creatures, were usually selected from the most senior *embedsmenn*, and normally held office until death or at any rate old age, when they were individually replaced. In view of this separation of the executive and representative structures, conflicts between the official estate and other segments of society, whatever else they may have been about, naturally revolved around the broad issue of the place and power of the monarchy. Because the monarchy was Swedish, that constitutional issue raised questions about Norway's national identity as well. And since the officials had not only a special legal power base outside of parliament but a strong position in parliament itself (due to the relative over-representation of the cities and continuing, although declining, deference in certain sections of the electorate), issues con-

[8] The power of parliament to grant or withhold pensions and to fix their amounts undoubtedly served as a means of limiting the independence of officials, while, however, scarcely being a full equivalent of formal accountability to the legislature.

cerning the extent of participation in the representative system also arose out of divisions over the officials' political role.

Who were the officials and what was their position in society? They included all royally appointed administrative and military officers, the state clergy, and certain members of the professions. Jointly they constituted the highest level of the formal status system. They were, in background and spirit, urbanites, particularly identified with the administrative center of Christiania in the East (Oslo since 1924). They had been instruments of the Danish domination and had been mainly trained in Denmark, for Norway had no university until 1811; subsequently they had appeared to many as the servants of Swedish masters. They were, by and large, a rationalistic intelligentsia, to some extent secularized even when serving as priests, since the church was to many of them little more than a department of state. They were, generally speaking, cosmopolitan in outlook, urbane in manner, sophisticated—and very Danish—in speech, dutiful rather than austere in morals, men of "condition." They regarded themselves as a distinct social segment and fancied themselves as a kind of superior caste, abetted by the fact that they often were members of families that had produced officials for centuries.[9]

The officials' manifold characteristics served to crystallize in basic constitutional issues a large complex of sociocultural differences and conflicts. These differences had, in the first place, a regional dimension. In nineteenth century Norway West and East were very much divided and at odds. The depth of their separation is most dramatically shown in Hansen's *Norsk*

---

[9] This is, of course, a composite, hence simplified, description. Not all officials fit it, nor did general officialdom fit it equally well at different points of time. Many officials located in the country, during a time of poor communications, took on the hues of rural life, despite their continued identification with the administrative center. And there is reason to think that in the course of the nineteenth century the cultural differences between the officials and other Norwegians gradually declined— as did political conflict between them. A contrary "composite" description, however, would be ludicrously wrong—would depict the deviant rather than the typical.

folkepsykologi (*The Norwegian People's Psychology*), a book
that aroused much excitement around the turn of the century
by arguing nothing less than that East and West were populated
by different races.[10] The aboriginal, short-skulled, small-statured,
dark-haired Norwegians were, according to Hansen, concentrated in the West, especially along the coast, and an alien race
of conquerors, fair, tall, and long-skulled, predominated in the
interior, the East, and the South. Hansen, moreover, while far
from having the naive prejudices which the German occupation
authorities later tried to implant through his work, connected
the geographic types with variations in culture patterns and
social structures and with political divisions, including voting
behavior. In this, if not his racial outlook, modern analysis has
to some extent confirmed his thesis, or at least failed to invalidate it. Torgersen, for example, has shown through a close
study of the recruitment of electors that the stratification patterns of Bergen and Christiania were markedly different in the
late nineteenth century, Rokkan and Valen that the Right was
particularly strong in the East, especially in the capital and
surrounding country.[11]

Much more clearcut, however, was a territorial difference, not
strictly regional in character: that between urban and rural
districts. Next to the occupational and status cleavage between
the official and other estates, the separation of town and country
was the strongest theme of division in the nineteenth century.
Indeed, to a large extent, the two cleavages were two sides of the
same thing, given the largely urban character of the officials, the
fact that the city in nineteenth century Norway was still largely
an administrative center, and the concentration of the officials'
supporters in urban centers. Hence, Rokkan, whose work
stamps him as anything but a *terrible simplificateur*, has identified the whole pattern of political division until 1884 as one of

[10] See also Axel Olrik, *Viking Civilization* (New York, 1930; originally Copenhagen, 1907) and Hansen, *Oldtidens normaend* (Christiania,
1907).

[11] See works cited in note 49.

"officials" versus "peasants."[12] At first—in the truly national intoxication following the events of 1814—the latter voted mainly for their "betters." But from the 1830s, coincident with and accelerated by the introduction of substantial local self-government, the peasants were mobilized in politics as a constantly more cohesive and independent force, and soon became the chief opposition of the ruling caste.

Urbanites and countrymen were separated by a large cultural gulf, no less than by difficult terrain and inadequate communications facilities that inhibited easy contact and power and status differentials that promoted conflict. The countryside was provincial, the city cosmopolitan; the peasants tended to be rude, religious, superstitious, egalitarian; the urbanites cultivated, worldly, rationalistic, hierarchic. Above all, their cultural divergence was manifested in religion and in a cultural issue that became the visible summit of a veritable mountain of assorted cultural antagonisms, the language issue. For the latter, the Norwegians have a special word, *språkpolitikk*, a fact that alone indicates its salience in their political consciousness.

The religious conflict was the less salient of the two, but is worth describing for its still greater importance later. It was not a conflict between competing sects, for practically all Norwegians were, and are, Lutherans and nominal members of the state church. Rather it concerned the role of religion in social and personal life, the very tenor and meaning of religious experience. The lead in the conflict was taken in the West and Southwest, where the Hauge revivalist movement, in rebellion against the shallow formalism of the established church, had effects comparable to that of Methodism in Britain. A large lay priesthood developed there, preaching fiery doctrines of sin and hell, of personal salvation, of the need to foil the devil's malice more than to assume God's grace, and, to underline the conflict of town and country, inveighing especially against the degraded

---

[12] "Geography, Religion and Social Class," pp. 5-14. (This *is* a simplification, of course, but a highly defensible one.)

morals of city life, drinking most of all. The countryside, in any event, was of a far more mystical and credulous bent than were the cities. The pagan inheritance of trolls, giants, huldre, water-spirits, witches, ghosts, still loomed large and provided minds highly susceptible to the superstitious, especially the threatening, elements of Christianity. In the East, per contra, especially in the capital, the church was more concerned with rational theology and more regarded as an official facility for baptism, confirmation, marriage, burial, and conventional prayer. Since it was in fact an arm of government, and its priests officials, the conflicts that the church engendered could hardly fail to be political or to become associated with basic constitutional questions.

Almost all the divisions that have been sketched—constitutional, status, territorial, religious, and moral conflicts—coalesced in the language question. No one has managed to summarize that emotion-laden and ramified issue (in some ways reminiscent of the language conflicts of countries like India and Ceylon) better than Stein Rokkan. "During the Danish hegemony," he writes:

> Copenhagen became the centre of higher learning and acquired a monopoly of printing: Copenhagen controlled the process of linguistic standardization within the two-nation realm. The spoken dialects of the Norwegians were reduced to the level of provincial vernaculars and the Copenhagen elite set the rules and the standards of orthography and grammar and, at least among the officials and the burghers of the cities, even influenced the pronunciation in day-to-day discourse. The Reformation was a major factor in this development: the translations of the Bible and the accelerated dissemination of tracts, catechisms and educational texts gradually acquainted most of the peasant population with Danish in its written form and set it apart as a language of prestige and power. This did not change overnight with independence in 1814. The country continued to be ruled by

the officials and they all had their training in Copenhagen and saw no possible alternative to written Danish as the official language of the new state. The Danish standards of spelling and grammar were simply taken for granted: it was a language for writing and printing and had its own separate functions, completely distinct from the functions of everyday speech. Danish was, after all, not a foreign language: Norwegians might not readily understand it when spoken by Danes, but the city people, at least in the East and in Bergen, had few difficulties with written Danish as an expression of the "high" language of Church and State. The discrepancies between the written language and the spoken dialects were much more marked in the countryside, particularly in the inner valleys and in the West, and these regional differences in the conditions of communication were gradually to produce important cleavages in the politics of the new nation.

The cultural ties with Denmark were bound to weaken after 1814: the development of an independent university in Christiania divorced the new elites from spoken Danish and made them more aware of the discrepancies between the written forms and what they considered to be standard educated Norwegian. By mid-century, a movement of gradual reform got under way. More and more of the literary and the cultural leaders began to alter the spelling to conform more directly to the speech of the educated classes in the cities and an increasing number of distinctly Norwegian words and phrases found acceptance in the official language. The result was the development of an independent *riksmål*, a distinctly urban language which during the first half of the twentieth century found general acceptance in the commercial and the industrial centres throughout the country and, at least numerically, became the dominant one.

Such a gradual process of accommodation between the written and the spoken language was hardly possible in the countryside, particularly not in the regions of the most isolated peasantry in the inner valleys and in the West. In these regions the gradual mobilization of the peasants finally led to a *linguistic revolt*. More and more of them came into contact with the culture of the cities and many a peasant's son tried to enter this new world by establishing himself in a trade or by acquiring an education. Some succeeded but many felt awkward and inferior in communicating with officials and city folk and felt the need to establish their cultural identity through a language of their own. A young peasant's son, an autodidact of genius, Ivar Aasen, saw this need and saw what was to be done. He undertook a detailed study of Norwegian peasant dialects and constructed on this basis a *standard rural language,* the *landsmål.* This may have had its elements of arbitrariness, but it had one decisive advantage: it gave the majority of peasants a distinct cultural identity, a language they could recognize as the nation's own. Aasen took his point of departure in the Norse of the old sagas and simply asked himself: what would standard Norwegian have looked like in his day if it had been given a chance to develop independently, if in fact the Danes had not taken over the control of the administration and the church in 1536?[13]

Aasen, Rokkan goes on to say, was not a mere antiquarian. On the contrary, his purpose was to fashion a common language as a tool of national reform, an instrument of efficient national communication that would promote the country's cultural integration and national identity. Hence his artificial language became known as *nynorsk* (new Norwegian) as well as *landsmål* (the language of the countryside). Ironically, however, he succeeded rather in fashioning a symbol around which, pro and con, the country's chief divisions could coalesce and in terms of which many latent conflicts could become concrete. Norway has never been quite free of *språkpolitikk* in some

[13] *Ibid.,* pp. 10-12. For another useful summary, see Castberg, *The Norwegian Way of Life,* pp. 71-73. For the link between *språkpolitikk* and territorial cleavage, see Derry, *Short History of Norway,* pp. 190, 205.

form since a national language was so summarily created for her.

In one major way depicting the pattern of division before 1884 as an unqualified rural-urban cleavage and cultural divergence may be misleading. With the growing political mobilization of the countryside coalesced a certain romantic nationalism and a nascent socioeconomic radicalism in the cities. The country became increasingly solidary vis-à-vis the city, but the city was not undivided. Yet the very influx of peasants' sons into urban life, as well as the vague identification of the intellectual nationalists with the undefiled rural Norway, accommodated the urban divisions themselves to the preponderant urban-rural conflicts. Even in city politics constitutional and cultural issues therefore predominated over the economic class conflicts usually associated with the growth of urban life. The country was not perfectly represented in city radicalism, especially not among the dissident intellectuals, but it was not until much later that it sought political organizations uniquely its own.

3. By 1884 the constitutional issues had been resolved in favor of the Left. Parliamentarism had been established, the franchise reformed, and the allocation of political power and authority decisively altered by these changes. But since the constitutional issues had been epiphenomena of other divisions, their resolution could hardly entail a sharp reduction of conflict. If anything, the opposite was the case. Through the constitutional question, especially through its nationalist overtones, a number of divergent forces had been aggregated in a single political movement, but after 1884 these no longer had any strong political cement to bind them. In the years following 1884 the old salient divisions persisted, tenuously united forces split, new divisions were added, and all divisions, old and new, became more "manifest," finding expression in a gradually developing, relatively unaggregative party system rather than being merely unorganized tendencies in political life.

Constitutional reform, although not complete as long as the Swedish-Norwegian Union endured, implied a considerable change in the political role of urban-rural cultural divergence. Cultural divisions had been heretofore an undercurrent in political conflict. Deprived of their superstructure, they were bound to become more directly points of contention. Certainly after the officials' constitutional defeat the peasantry and their urban allies were not left with much common ground. In many ways the urban segment of the Left, the radical nationalist intellectuals and nonofficial professionals, had culturally more in common with the officials than with the peasantry; remember that the nationalist poets, dramatists, novelists, and essayists were developing *riksmål* to unprecedented heights of achievement at the very time that *nynorsk* was to provide a linguistic basis for national cohesion. The urban radicals were most distant of all from the countryside's firebrand preachers of traditional moral and religious values. Hence, as the "defense of the rural counterculture"[14] became (after the resolution of the conflict with Sweden in 1905) a primary rather than subsidiary source of political division, a split in political alliances ensued, creating in effect three coherent, although not entirely undivided political forces: urban conservatives, urban radicals, and the countryside. This did not reduce the urban-rural cleavage, but accentuated it.

Constitutional reform also helped bring to the forefront a new cleavage, one along strictly economic lines. Economic modernization was creating in Norway, as it had in other countries, a workers' political movement. But the Norwegian workers' movement had from the outset an unusual political significance, due to the fact that rapid industrialization coincided with the rapid growth of a highly participant political system.[15] Through the concurrence of structural reforms in government, electoral reforms, the growth of organized parties,

----

[14] The term is Rokkan's. See *ibid.*, p. 36.

[15] For comments on the early significance of politics in the Norwegian labor movement, see Galenson, *Labor in Norway*, pp. 56-63.

and, through parties, the increasing political mobilization of "parochials," political divisions could, and did, more rapidly assume an economic cast in Norway than in most other countries. The result was not merely to introduce into urban politics a new conflict between plebes and patricians; this conflict also had considerable repercussions in other spheres. Once economic conflict intruded into the pattern of political division, it threatened the cohesion of the countryside no less than that of the cities by setting at odds smallholders and larger farmers, agricultural workers and employers, i.e., rural plebes and patricians. The former were, after all, tied by sympathy and indeed a vast network of blood relationships to the urban workers. There had, in any case, always existed a basis for conflict in certain subcurrents of the rural culture, for the intensity of the rural counterculture varied among different areas, for example, between the highly fundamentalist coastal communities (especially in the southwest) and the somewhat more broad-minded communities of the inner fjords and the more northern regions. The fact that the Norwegian workers' movement, constituted to a large extent from uprooted peasants, had itself a considerable tinge of country habits, speech, and morality both put it more deeply at odds with the urban patriciate and made easier its penetration of the less fanatic rural areas. Thus in the new urban cleavage some currents of the old rural-urban cleavage lingered, and in parts of the countryside some currents of the new urban cleavage found ready access.

We get here a new basis for political aggregation in place of that provided by the old constitutional issues, and such aggregation in fact occurred—up to a point. The workers made their first political breakthrough early in the twentieth century not where their organizational strength was concentrated, in the capital and central East, but in the far North, where there was a large rural proletariat of small farmers, cottars, and fishermen, dependent on a patriciate that owned and exploited indispensable port facilities. But if this was aggregation, reconciling urban to rural elements, it was aggregation at the price of a new regional cleavage—one between the "center" and the "periphery"—that has persisted and become more marked ever since. At the same time, the old Right, faced by a combination of urban and rural plebeians, was able to respond during the first two decades of the twentieth century by wedding to the old officials' toryism the more liberal values and goals of business and industry, from which the Right had previously got some support. The two shared, after all, a common urbanism and common status interests, as well as interacting more frequently. But if this also involved aggregation of a sort, it could never involve a great deal of it, for the urbanites simply could not carry into the conservative camp any large segment of the culturally divergent countryside. The Right Party (*Høyre*) remained what it had been heretofore: urban almost exclusively and Eastern predominantly; and what is generally called Liberalism in Norwegian politics, the Left Party (*Venstre*), became even more pronouncedly rural, Southwestern, and culturally isolated. The extreme contrast between this and the aggregative achievements of British conservatism hardly needs underlining.

In summary, the aggregation of Norwegian political forces after 1884 and after the dissolution of the union with Sweden was always highly restricted, and certainly never produced the sort of polarization that the old constitutional issue had created —except in the cities themselves and in the North. The Labour Party was able to an extent to penetrate the countryside, mainly around the center and in the previously parochial periphery. In it were amalgamated three divisions, two economic and one territorial. The Conservatives were able to penetrate the urban commercial patriciate, but could not break out of their territorial limits. The old Western, rural *Venstre* remained unassimilable, perpetuating the old lines of territorial and cultural cleavage.

In fact, the *Venstre* could not even remain cohesive—could not retain those who conceived themselves to be predominantly economic agrarians and those who were first and foremost religious and moral fundamentalists. In 1918, there split off from it the Agrarian Party, essentially an economic pressure group that contests elections; in 1933 the fundamentalists, long a distinct element in the Liberal Party, also founded their own electoral organization, the Christian People's Party, leaving the *Venstre* a party that now was neither distinctly rural nor distinctly urban, but still concentrated in areas where ruralism was the essential fact of political life—with what results we shall see. In these party splits narrow territorial cleavages within broader ones were manifested, the Agrarians being concentrated in the *Trøndelag* and, to some extent, the Southwest, the fundamentalists in the extreme West.

4. By 1933 the Norwegian pattern of political division had fully evolved and become closely reflected in the most manifest form of competition in democratic politics: competition among organized political parties. Describing the pattern as it now exists and is expressed in party conflict will entail some repetition of major themes already brought out, but also requires some additional data and interpretations.

The first point to stress is that Norway's political divisions today still involve pronounced cleavages rooted in the most manifest segmentation of any society, its regional and territorial differentiation. Over the years regional and territorial divisions have become more complex, with cleavage emerging within cleavage, with some lines of alliance developing among the segments and clear differences thereby becoming somewhat blurred, and with previously insignificant sectors becoming more important. But overall, the geographic divisions are still quite clearcut. The greatest contrast exists between, on one hand, the South and West and, on the other, the East and North. This primary regional contrast is still deeply associated with the old rural-urban split. In this split, agricultural policies as such do not seem to be all that is involved; if they were, the Agrarians would surely be stronger in the South and West than they are. Issues of cultural defense, which are better represented by the old Left Party and the Christian People's Party, still seem to be central; note that in 1957 these two parties together polled 37.3 per cent of the South-West rural electorate, compared to less than half as much for the Agrarians (15.6 per cent).

In fact, of course, the pattern of division is a good deal more complex than regional and territorial tendencies alone can indicate, above all because of the intrusion of economic considerations. Much of what the geographic dimension exaggerates or fails to indicate is accounted for by socioeconomic cleavage. Socioeconomic division underlies not only the urban polarization of forces into Conservatives and Socialists, but also helps account for the fact that the issue of cultural defense does not pervade to the same extent all rural areas. In general, the forces of cultural defense are rural everywhere in so far as they exist, but they exist, as we have seen, much more in the South and West than elsewhere. A major reason for this would seem to be socioeconomic. Southern and Western agriculture differs from Norwegian agriculture elsewhere in its economic aspects, and Southern and Western agricultural communities, as a result, differ in social structure, especially stratification, from other such communities. There is, for example, little forestry in the South and West, and forestry workers are proletarians who vote predominantly Labour. Again, in the South and West smallholdings are typical and variations in the sizes of farms relatively small; elsewhere local variations in farm size are much larger, ranging from part-time smallholdings to considerable estates worked by laborers. In consequence, the South and West consist of relatively egalitarian communities, marked by little class resentment. These communities have been markedly impervious to political movements premised on economic class conflicts—in contrast especially to the North, where rural life has a character considerably more assimilable to urban divisions due to the number of men dependent on the money economy in rural pursuits.

While cultural divisions over language, moral persuasions, and religious experience correspond significantly to regional, territorial, and socioeconomic cleavages, they also operate to some extent independently. That is to say, much of what a geographic and socioeconomic analysis of the Norwegian pattern of political division oversimplifies or leaves unexplained can be accounted for by a cultural dimension per se. For example, the relatively great appeal of the Christian People's Party as an instrument of rural cultural defense in the Western coastal communities seems unrelated to objective characteristics but due simply to religious fundamentalism. The Christian Party is the most independent of socioeconomic status among all Norwegian parties.[16] And throughout the country the various parties appeal to certain voters even where they are weak overall, depending on the voters' cultural dispositions. Thus workers in the East are relatively more conservative than elsewhere, having been more thoroughly imbued with urban culture, while workers in the South and West are relatively more favorable to the "middle parties" since, to a degree, they share the dominant culture of that section of the country.

The Norwegian party system has not managed to aggregate these divisions to a very great extent. A marked left-right polarization of political conflict may be found in some areas, but is not typical in most of the country. The party system includes, first, two major parties that express very closely the primacy of the rural-urban split. One is the extremely urban Right Party, which, in the last two national elections (1957 and 1961), polled about 25 per cent among urban electors but only about 10 per cent in the countryside. The other is an even more predominantly rural party, the Agrarians, who polled about 11 per cent in the country, but only 0.3 per cent in the urban centers. A third major party, the Labour Party, is mixed urban-rural. It aggregates across cleavage lines more than any other Norwegian party and is for that reason alone much the largest unit in the system. During the last two elections it was supported by about 40 per cent of urban voters and 36 per cent

[16] Valen and Katz, p. 184. For further confirmation of this point, see Johan Galtung, "Social Position, Party Identification and Foreign Policy Orientation," PRIO publication 16-2, mimeographed, table 14.

in the countryside. As we have seen, however, the Labour
Party attracts rural votes rather selectively, drawing support
mainly from those peripheral areas where primary occupations
have been especially vulnerable to penetration by industrial
economic and typically urban conflict patterns. Two other significant parties represent especially closely the cleavage between the South-West and other parts of the country. They are
also mixed urban-rural, but on a much more restricted level
than Labour, drawing urban support mainly from towns in
which the cultural influence of the countryside is still pronounced. The Left Party polls about 7 per cent of both rural and
urban voters, mainly in the South-West; the Christian People's
Party is in size and ecologically very similar, but rather more
manifestly rural and still more geographically concentrated in
sections of the South-West.[17]

As well as being rooted in cleavage, the parties (and the
regions with which they are highly identified) are, as one would
expect, markedly divergent culturally. For example, church-
going (low overall in Norway) is considerably more common
in the South and West than in the North, East, and inland regions, and while well over half of all members of the *Indre-
misjon* (Inner Mission) organizations and other fundamentalist
bodies vote for the middle parties of cultural defense (about
one third for the Christian People's Party), in the Labour
Party the great majority of voters are ordinary Lutherans or
"dissenters" and the Right draws particularly dismally among
the fundamentalists—only about 5 per cent of them.[18] Furthermore, those workers who have religious associational memberships vote much more heavily for the cultural defense parties
than those who do not, while farmers and fishermen who are
not members in such associations vote considerably more socialist than those who are.[19] Similar patterns exist with regard

[17] Party strengths are expressed here as percentages of *registered*
voters. The figures come from Rokkan and Valen, "Regional Contrasts in
Norwegian Politics," table 1.1.

[18] *Ibid.*, tables 4.3 and 4.6.1. See also Valen and Katz, table 6.16.

[19] *Ibid.*, table 4.6.2. See also Valen and Katz, table 6.17.

to language preferences (in fact the language differentiation is even more striking, since practically nobody prefers *nynorsk* to *riksmål* except a heavy concentration of people in the rural areas of the South and West), morals (there were in 1923— the last year for which the *Statistical Yearbook* provides figures —94 teetotallers out of every 1,000 adults in the West, compared to 18 in the Oslofjord area and 34 in the North), and cosmopolitanism (with opposition to joining the EEC particularly great in the South-West middle parties and only the Right, the old cosmopolitan party, heavily in favor of the step).[20]

These cultural divergences, as might also be expected, have led directly to some of the most knotty and passionate disagreements in Norwegian politics. The supreme example occurred in 1954 when an extraordinary series of public and parliamentary debates, culminating in a commission of inquiry, took place over the question of whether there is a hell and, if so, what sort of place it is. A British writer, George Mikes, has argued that these debates occurred because, having no real problems, the Norwegians have to invent artificial ones. Mikes is a humorist, but he is also British and in this case, I think, did not have his tongue in cheek. Either way, deliberately or otherwise, his argument is ludicrously wrong. To Norwegians, an argument over hell must seem almost super-real, since it contains for them intimations of all that divides them: geographic divisions between center and periphery, urban-rural ones, socioeconomic ones, and cultural divergences. Only the alcohol question in some areas, and the language question everywhere, seem to generate more heat than religious issues. During my stay in Norway I found that any flagging conversation, any tepid interview, could be warmed up by the mere mention of *nynorsk*. In Bergen I was told that an intrepid agent for the Right, recently come to make converts among the prosperous farmers of the region, had started off by entertaining them at a meeting that included drinks—an enormous cultural gaffe that

[20] *Ibid.*, tables 4.4, 4.5, and 6.1. See also Valen and Katz, table 6.18.

immediately and permanently queered his pitch. A few years ago Donald Duck comic books, which happen to be extremely popular in Norway, were banned from the Oslo municipal libraries through pressure from indignant language crusaders, because one series of cartoons dealt with a strange country of square people who happened to speak *landsmål.* To Norway's language fanatics, and many others, that was a dismal joke at best.

Norwegian party leaders are well aware of the cleavages in their country and seem to have fewer illusions, or ambitions, about the scope of their potential audience than most politicians. The Agrarians, of course, see themselves as appealing to people in rural occupations and virtually no one else, the Christians almost exclusively as appealing to religious people, above all to "mission" people. Labour's horizons are heavily confined to the working class and, to some extent, white collar employees, while the Right is highly conscious of its base in business and the higher ranks of the salariat. Only the Liberals have a more diverse self-image, one more oriented to aggregation.[21] Perhaps that itself explains why they are in fact so weak in a country where cleavage and divergence lines are so politically salient. The very diversity of the Liberals' self-conception could account for the fact that their "audience" has steadily declined since their heyday late in the nineteenth century, particularly through the shedding of splinters with much narrower conceptions of their role. However that may be, the fact remains that the one Norwegian party which has the sort of super-aggregative self-image typical of British and American parties, and to an extent even of the strong post-war parties of continental Europe (the German and Italian Christian Democrats, the French Gaullist party), has also been since 1900 the principal declining political force in the country and the least capable of holding its sections together.[22]

[21] Valen and Katz, tables 8.6 and 8.7.
[22] The Liberals did, however, make a small recovery in the most re-

Concomitant to their divergent conceptions of their audience, the parties are also markedly divergent in their broad goals, their "ideological orientations," in Valen and Katz's terminology. The Agrarians' professed goals center frankly on agricultural economics, the Christian People's Party's equally frankly on religious and moral issues, the Labour Party's on economic policy, stressing social welfare, the Conservative Party's on economics, stressing free enterprise and lower taxation.[23] Only one general aspiration, among all those explored by Norwegian survey research, mobilizes over half of all party activists and voters in the same direction: the desire for lower taxes (which is probably universal anyway). On all other broad questions one gets large, in some cases enormous, differences. For example, on the question of whether agriculture needs still more than it already gets (which is a lot), 63 per cent of the Agrarian activists say yes compared to only 7 per cent in the urban Conservative Party and 9 per cent in the Labour Party. No less than 97 per cent of the Christian Party's activists want to have Christian faith and morals strengthened by public policy, but only 18 percent in the Labour Party take that position. Among Conservative activists, 89 per cent want more done to encourage private savings and 83 per cent want less interference with private enterprise, but only 18 per cent and 5 per cent respectively think similarly in the Labour Party. The one party that seems most consistently moderate on broad issues, neither as much against nor for anything as some combination of the other parties, is once again the Liberal Party. It ought, for that reason alone perhaps, particularly to appeal to

---

cent national election, which was held after the completion of this study. They obtained 10.1 per cent of the popular vote, compared with 7.3 per cent in 1961. It remains to be seen whether this is the beginning of a trend. One may suspect, however, that if the long-continued pattern of political division in Norway weakens, the Liberals, as the party with the strongest aggregative pretensions, will be the chief beneficiaries. Their future fortunes may thus provide a particularly good index to the character of Norway's political divisions, as did their misfortunes in the past.

[23] Valen and Katz, pp. 233-262.

men not distant from one another, not intense in the realm of specific issues, but is in fact, as we have seen, a weak and declining force.[24]

Finally, divergences in goal orientations seem matched by highly divergent valuations of political personalities. For example, a series of interviews with local political leaders about the characteristics that parliamentary candidates ideally should possess revealed a generally high valuation of only one quality (political or "other" know-how and experience), just as inquiry into broad political positions has revealed only one widely shared aspiration. In other respects differences in how parties ranked various personal attributes were clearcut. Labour valued party loyalty above all (61 per cent to 10-37 per cent for the other parties); the Liberals valued most a person's moral qualities (88 per cent to 32-57 per cent for the others); the Agrarians and Christian People's Party ranked representativeness of groups and areas second of five qualities examined, while the other parties all ranked it last (38 per cent to 3-14 per cent for others); the Conservatives were distinctive for their extreme valuation of competence (*dyktighet*) (100 per cent to 41-62 per cent among Labour, Liberals, and Christians, although the Agrarians came close to the Conservatives on this scale). A most definite set of divergences in the appraisal of political character emerges from these findings, although it is not in fact closely adhered to in actually nominating candidates, that process also having the construction of many-sided

[24] See Rokkan, "Numerical Democracy and Corporate Pluralism," table 4. Rokkan there shows who among the five main parties most and least supports nine "policy" positions. These do not involve specific legislative projects, but general tendencies rather similar to those treated by Valen and Katz. Happily, however, Rokkan's definition of the issues points rather more directly at specific disagreements than do Valen and Katz. The Liberal Party was "least opposed" or "most opposed" in only one area of policy: military expenditure. In general moderation the Christian People's Party runs it a close second overall, but is extreme on the highly charged religious-moral issues while the liberals take a strong position on nothing that looms as large.

lists as an aim.[25] (For relevant tables, see Appendix A, tables 4-18.)

That these divisions are reflected, to a quite unusual extent, in the country's press also speaks for their salience and resistance to aggregation. Norway not only has many avid newspaper readers, but an extraordinarily large number of newspapers. In 1957, 173 papers—82 of them dailies—were listed in the *Norsk Aviskatalog* as members of the Norwegian Newspapers Association; this in a country that has less than half the population of New York or London. The most important reasons for this proliferation of newspapers (only five of which have a circulation above 50,000) are their close political affiliations and their extreme localistic and regionalistic character. Two papers, the Communist Party's *Friheten* and Labour's *Arbeiderbladet*, are directly national party organs; numerous others are local party organs; many more are more informally, but still closely, affiliated to political parties; few even pretend to be independent —only 44 are so listed, but the majority even of these have clearly discernible party preferences and connections. Where newspapers are not owned and controlled outright by the parties, affiliation takes several forms: the frequent use of handouts by the parties' press bureaus, personal interrelations, and perhaps above all the wide use of newspaper personnel in party activities, especially the production of political pamphlets, party programs and placards. This identification of newspapers with political parties has led to a multiplication of papers through a simple mechanism: wherever a local paper with a special political affiliation has been established, others, tied to different political forces, have followed suit, although the dominant paper in most localities also expresses the views of the locally dominant party, as well being the chief organ for local advertisements

---

[25] Valen, "Nominasjonene," table 6.321. Valen himself sees little difference in how parties value candidates' personalities, but this, I think, is due to his failure to take into account differences in the ranking of the qualities he has investigated.

and announcements, hence able to command a more diversified set of readers than the other papers.[26]

5. We can now reconsider the hypotheses stated at the beginning of the discussion in light of Norway's past and present political divisions. To which polar model of democracy does Norway most closely correspond—that of the most stable case (characterized by unintense and narrow disagreements on specific issues, a wide sharing of basic political orientations, and politically weak segmental identifications), or that of the least stable case (which has the opposite characteristics)? To what extent does Norway fit the hypotheses from which these models were derived: that democracies tend to be stable where political divisions are highly restricted in extent and/or intensity, or that they tend to be stable where, regardless of the amount of specific disagreement, there is little division over cultural norms or social identifications? Does Norway bear out the hypothesis, deduced from other propositions, that segmental cleavages are particularly inimical to democracy, cultural divergences less so, and specific disagreements least damaging of all, unless directly outgrowths of cleavages or divergences?

Consider the last question first (since the others are more readily answered once it has been dealt with). No doubt every polity manifests in its structure of competition some cleavages— some relationships between lines of social differentiation and lines of political conflict. Political divisions rarely, if ever, are simply political. No doubt also, in every polity, as one of our hypotheses stipulates, some relationships exist between cleavages and politically relevant cultural divergences, and between both of these and specific disagreements. In the more stable democracies, however, political cleavage and divergence should, upon our hypothesis, be particularly weak subthemes to the major theme of political disagreements, and disagreements

[26] See Stein Rokkan and Per Torsvik, "Presse, velgere og lesere," *Valg i Norge*, ch. 19 (mimeographed), and Svennik Høyer, "Pressens økonomiske og politiske struktur," *Tidsskrift for samfunnsforskning*, 1964, pp. 221-242.

should not grow markedly out of divergence and cleavage themselves. All that has been said suggests that it is not so in Norway, anyway not to the extent one would expect in so stable a democracy.

No doubt Norway does not have, and has never had, cleavages so disruptive as those of some more recently founded nations. Nevertheless, the most manifest political cleavages run through the history of the country. Before 1884 these cleavages were particularly marked, simple, and politically potent. So they were in many other European countries at the time, but with much more explosive effects. It might be argued that Norway's political system before 1884 was insulated against the effects of cleavage by the very nature of her *régime censitaire*—by the fact that a strong executive could counteract conflict in the representative assembly and act to a large extent independently of the Storting. That would save the cleavage hypothesis at least for the period 1814-1884. But this argument is more convenient than convincing. For one thing, the representative assembly itself seemed to function rather smoothly during the period. For another, no general crisis of legitimacy of the sort usually associated with acute political division arose until the 1880's, and then was so quickly resolved that crisis may be too harsh a term for the events that occurred. Most important, Norway's cleavages were given full scope to undermine the system by the very reforms then made. But they did not do so, nor vanish quickly in the wake of the reforms, nor even gradually dissolve in the ensuing generations. Norway's cleavages did become more complex: new bases of cleavage emerged, fissures occurred in old blocs, latent segments were mobilized. But, as we saw, these developments, while in some ways blurring the old pattern of division, in others intensified cleavage by sundering old aggregates and accentuating the segmental distinctness of some political blocs. In any event, geographic and demographic divisions never ceased to be of marked significance in the system.

Moreover, Norway's segmental cleavages were from the out-

set, and have remained, closely expressed in cultural divergences. This confirms one of our minor hypotheses—that regarding the relations of cleavages to divergences—but impugns
even more the major hypothesis now under examination. Unfortunately, we do not possess "hard" data on divergences in
nineteenth century Norway, systematic survey research being a
recent art. But the soft materials that are available, such as
historical studies of the traditional sort and literary sources, all
imply that these divergences were considerable. For the present,
moreover, Norwegian political sociologists have produced a
good many hard data (such as those cited on broad party goals
and evaluations of political character) that imply either a continuation of marked cultural divergences or the generation of
such divergences while the system was, if anything, becoming
even more stable than it had been. Furthermore, today as in the
past, *Kulturpolitik* plays a large role in Norway, which would
hardly be the case if cultural differences were inconsiderable or
irrelevant to politics.

In Norway's *Kulturpolitik* we also see the translation of divergence into disagreement, again confirming a minor hypothesis
and making doubtful a major one. On specific disagreements,
regrettably, the presently available materials are weakest, but
those that exist suggest considerable differences on concrete and
widely ramified issues: procedural and structural ones in the
nineteenth century, substantive goal-orientations at present.
Strangely enough, the direct observation of political conduct
leads one to form a very different impression. The issues that
divide Norwegians when they respond to survey researchers
seem only rarely to arise in parliament or even to be much discussed in the press or, for that matter, in private. To the casual
observer, perhaps even to alert Norwegians, the system gives
every impression of being enormously consensual, on circum-
stantials no less than fundamentals. Of course, survey findings
may be misleading, particularly since surveys are ususaly designed to reveal divisions by hook or crook and since survey
researchers native to a country rarely ask about matters that

wide agreement has removed from the public domain and their own consciousness. Still, public silence need not imply public agreement. It may in fact arise from a deep sense of danger if issues are made too explicit or from a tendency, in some political cultures, instinctively, or through conscious courtesy, to suppress even harmless antagonisms. If both survey findings and casual observation are accorded some trust, then the possibility arises that in Norway many real political disagreements are somehow suppressed, somehow kept latent in political processes, except perhaps when some culture cue absurd to outsiders—a bad comic-book joke, a tactless theological article—makes them come briefly bubbling and hissing to the surface. Whether this is so or not, it would seem that the relation we stipulated between the existence of political cleavage and divergence and the extensiveness and intensity of disagreements is far from strong and universal, and that this may be so because separated and divergent men often do not communicate on certain levels or sense the perils of doing so. And a consensus of silence obviously is different from real consensus.

At any rate, the supposition that in the most stable democracies cultural divergences are inconsequential and segmental cleavages even more so is not confirmed by Norway. Somehow, a society can have a very stable democracy yet have relatively conspicuous political cleavages and divergences. Somehow also, cleavage and divergence need not obtrude much on political discourse, even if they cannot be kept sublimated altogether.

In view of all this, the hypotheses that stipulate particular dangers to democracy in political divisions centering on segmental social identifications or divergences in broad norms also seem far from satisfactory. Norway is not in that respect the sort of country Almond and Verba depict as their ideal civic culture: one sufficiently divided by specific disagreements to give point to democratic competition, but solidly integrated at its subjective and objective core. It presents, in a way, just the opposite picture.

The hypotheses that stipulate grave dangers to democracy in extensive or intensive divisions also fail to emerge fully alive and healthy from exposure in Norway. In regard to extensiveness, Norway displays several "kinds" of division, and cleavages particularly have increased since 1884 (although in this case one undoubtedly comes a little closer to what a stable democracy should be according to established theory). About intensity we must speak with particular caution. Emotional intensity per se has not been measured by Norwegian political sociologists and can at present be dealt with only on the basis of crude impressions. To raw observation it seems low. But it seems so extraordinarily low that one wonders. After all, tepidity can result from controls over emotion as well as their absence (controls that may under some conditions break down). And in the general literature on Norwegian life and politics, especially that of the most sensitive Norwegian impressionists, there are some statements remarkably incongruent with the crude observance of stoicism. Thus Castberg speaks of the Norwegians' self-assertiveness and aggressiveness ("The fiery Norwegian is scarlet of hue, the well-tempered Swede is heavenly blue"), of their craving for contradiction, of their mercurial tendencies toward sharp, unsustained efforts in work.[27] Storing also speaks of a tendency to "stand on principle."[28] Why they say these things I do not know, but what they say seems to workaday observation so far off reality that there must be some profound instinct or reason behind their statements. Norway's poets, dramatists, and novelists certainly make emotional controls and their disintegration a major theme, particularly in the politically highly salient realms of religious and moral experience.

This is speculative in the extreme due to a lack of directly relevant data. Two related points about political intensity, however, may be made from less slippery footing. Norwegian political divisions are highly manifest through a party system that does not aggregate a great deal across cleavage and diver-

---

[27] Castberg, *The Norwegian Way of Life*, ch. 1.
[28] Storing, p. 10.

gence lines. And the political parties' failure to aggregate more —especially their inability to absorb new fissures into old, to combine them in more complex structures of political competition—attests to certain insurmountable distances among Norway's political groups. These distances not even the prospect of permanent opposition has been able so far to reduce (even on the parliamentary level) in the case of the four clearly unaggregative parties that stand against Labour.

The fact seems to be that Norway comes closer to the polar model of unstable democracy than to the model one would expect her to approximate. Exactly how close one cannot say without precisely quantifying what is as yet a matter for mere approximate judgment. Norway certainly deviates in certain ways from the ideal of unstable democracy. However, the performance of the system over more than a century would lead one to expect not merely that, but a close approximation to the polar model of stable democracy, from which the deviation clearly is much greater. In view of that, all our hypotheses, save only for some of those that relate variations in political division to one another, seem to need revision, and the whole division-cohesion perspective which they express more thinking out. In this area of democratic theory even more than in those treated in the preceding section, Norway only raises profound puzzles and ruins plausible preconceptions.

6. Two words of caution are in order at this point. The first concerns any inferences about contrasts between Norway and other stable democracies that might be drawn from this discussion. No comparisons of any kind are made here between political divisions in Norway and in other countries; we have only contrasted the Norwegian case with a model that ought to fit it more closely than it does. Although that model is grounded upon plausible propositions largely developed in studies of other cases, it may well turn out, on further inquiry, that the Norwegian pattern of political division, in its broad outlines at least, is typical of other stable democracies. It may even be found that the pattern fits stable and unstable democracies both.

In the first case, all that would follow is that the propositions examined in this chapter do not even correctly state tendencies, let alone uniformities. In the second case, one would be forced to conclude that if a stable democracy indeed requires a balance of division and cohesion, it is the cohesion side of the balance that is most variable and most important; and that would be a significant finding indeed, for close empirical studies of politics have so far stressed the other side almost exclusively.[29]

Second, it is necessary at this stage not to insist too categorically on the findings of this chapter. While the analysis presented here is based on rich and relevant work in Norwegian political sociology, there are gaps in that work and in the way I have used it that enjoin caution. The pattern of division I have sketched, while far from simple, is nevertheless only a summary of major tendencies, and it may be that in the minutiae that have been glossed over evidence less destructive to our hypotheses is contained. Moreover, the data presently available are not, even in their finer details, fully adequate to an analysis of Norwegian political divisions in terms of the analytical scheme here proposed. No one has as yet conducted research specifically to get at the three kinds of political division here distinguished or to determine with precision their extensiveness and intensity in the manner these dimensions are here defined. In consequence, it has been necessary repeatedly to read into available data implications that might be negated by more directly relevant research. We particularly lack rich data in regard to specific disagreements and to political intensity.

Most important of all, one is made wary by the very nature of the researches on which this analysis is based. Some are historical researches, and although Norwegian social scientists (especially Rokkan) have shown how much can be done to analyze historical materials with modern methods, special un-

[29] Some close comparisons between Norway's political divisions and those of other countries will probably emerge from Lipset and Rokkan's as yet uncompleted work, *Party Systems and Voter Alignments* (see note 5, ch. 1 *supra*). Some initial comparisons may also be derived from Allardt and Littunen, eds., *Cleavages, Ideologies and Party Systems*.

certainties always arise in such studies. Those that are not historical are mainly electoral studies and studies of contemporary party identifications and party attitudes. As presently conducted, such studies everywhere tend especially to reveal divisions more than elements of cohesion and to relate divisions mainly to easily obtainable ecological data, thereby getting particularly at segmental cleavages, which, through one-sidedness, they may exaggerate.

Whether Norway's political divisions are typical or exotic, studies of Norwegian political life, to be more conclusive, should deal more directly and systematically with the ties that knit the system together, as well as exploring certain neglected dimensions of the fissures that divide it into competitive fragments. Perhaps if division and cohesion were a zero-sum that would not be necessary; then the amount of cohesion could be inferred from the divisions themselves. But Norway strongly suggests that in this realm we are not dealing with zero-sums. The studies that have been drawn on here no doubt are one-sided, but on the side that they explore, that of division, they are mutually confirmatory and very convincing. They reveal astonishingly great, sharp, and persistent divisions of the types one would least expect to find in a stable democracy. Hence Norway must be so stable a democracy not because she lacks divisions in general or even the more destructive kinds of conflict, but because in Norwegian society forces are at work that make even more strongly for cohesion. What these forces are, and what new hypotheses or revisions of established hypotheses they may imply, now needs to be examined.

The Problem of
Norwegian Political Cohesion

1. If a political system survives for a century and a half without serious challenge to its legitimacy and only one noteworthy modification of form, we may be sure that some powerful cement makes the system cohesive. We may be still more certain if the political divisions of the system have never even long disrupted the day-to-day working of government, particularly if the government is a parliamentary democracy which, like the immobilistic democracies of the continent, lacks a highly aggregative party system. From these standpoints, Norway's political divisions, however great and potentially destructive they may seem when considered in themselves, must be shallow phenomena, superimposed on more fundamental attitudes and behavior patterns that bind the country together. What are these attitudes and behavior patterns?

In the chapters that follow we shall try to discover and account for them. But before beginning that exploration, it should be emphasized that it takes us into particularly treacherous territory. Cohesion in Norway, as I pointed out, is a subject virtually unexplored in rigorous modern research and a topic treated with striking inadequacy in the more traditional studies. Searching through what has been written about it, one accumulates mainly a rich harvest of question-begging arguments—for example, the arguments that Norway is very homogeneous ethnically (as if social cohesion ran in the genes or ethnic antagonisms were the only conflicts capable of undermining democracies) or that Norway is a "small" country (as if conflict were less contentious for occurring in a small arena). That being so, it is in this case, even more than in the case of Norwegian political divisions, necessary to rely on implications seen in data produced for other purposes, and it is more necessary also to trust provisionally impressions that need stronger foundations.

But there are several compelling reasons for taking the risks involved. One is that rigorous research on the subject requires, as a first step, the very definition of promising lines of inquiry. Another is that a foreigner may be in a particularly advantageous position to define them, if only because he is likely to be impressed by attitudes and behavior patterns that in members of a highly cohesive society may be literally second nature, too deeply implanted to engage their questioning minds. In addition, having been impressed early in my work on Norway by the puzzles her pattern of divisions raises, I directed my attention as a "participant observer" mainly to the realm of cohesion, going into the matter more extensively than any other. Not least, in this realm too existing scholarship provides perspectives and hypotheses that can help one approach a valid position without having to construct it in all respects out of personal imagination.

2. Studies of political cohesion suggest three broadly different approaches to explaining its existence. Political cohesion may exist, most obviously, because of a relative *lack of political divisions*. That is by far the most frequently used approach, and may work very well in certain cohesive polities. This position, however, need not be further considered here since the essential point of the last chapter was that it does not pertain to Norway. The second possibility is that cohesion can be great *despite divisions*—which is the approach already recommended for the case of Norway. But before this approach is followed up, a third possibility should be entertained. It is that political cohesion may exist, not despite, but *because of political divisions* —that is to say, because political divisions, however great and of whatever kinds (indeed perhaps just where they are complex and varied) may form patterns that somehow mechanically result in cohesion without the presence of special cohesive forces. This intriguing possibility needs exploration not least

because Norwegian political sociologists, in so far as they have raised the question of cohesion at all, usually imply that it flows directly from the pattern of division that has so much absorbed their attention.

The notion that conflicts, or active counterforces, can themselves produce cohesion of a sort is not new in social thought. It entered that realm through the tendency of social theorists to think in natural science metaphors, specifically through the influence of the notion of equilibrium in classical mechanics. That notion is at the bottom of liberal social atomism, a normative political "theory," and has enjoyed the greatest vogue, and proved most powerful as an empirical perspective, in economics. It also has a considerable history as a theoretical perspective in sociology. And in politics too some empirical theory has been built upon it.

It is, of course, this view that underlies the hypothesis, derived from Montesquieu, that liberty is best guaranteed by creating formal "balances" of governmental power. The same perspective appears in a different form in the arguments that "group theorists" use when confronting the problem of stability in representative systems. The archangel (or archdemon, if you will) of that school, A. F. Bentley, saw the whole process of government as a continuous creation of "balances" among conflicting groups and interests; and while in general he used the term balance simply to denote any outcome of political activity, the very use of the word balance may be taken to suggest that he considered the outcomes produced by competitive counterforces to be benign (naturally harmonious) in some sense.[1] If Bentley is ambiguous on that point, the leading contemporary group theorist, David B. Truman, is crystal clear. Truman sees stability in representative systems as resulting from two sources. The first is the balances produced purely mechanically by groups on the system level. These balances are produced by

[1] Bentley, *The Process of Government* (Chicago, 1908). For an interpretation of Bentley along these lines, see B. Crick, *The American Science of Politics* (London, 1959), ch. 8.

their tendency to overcome "changes and disturbances in the habitual subpatterns of interaction" and thus to return to "the previous state of equilibrium," or, "if the disturbances are intense and prolonged, by the emergence of new groups whose specialized function it is to facilitate the establishment of a new balance."[2] The second source of stability belongs to the realm of personality rather than the social system. Group interactions may be played out within individuals no less than in society, if individuals belong to many different social segments—segments that, in Truman's terminology, "overlap" and "cross-cut"—the result being, as it were, balanced personalities who, through their multiple identifications, prevent large disturbances in the political order by reducing the demands groups make on one another. This, says Truman, is the principal balancing force in multigroup societies,[3] a force as clearly mechanical (not cultural) in origin as the more impersonal interplay of the groups themselves. The same view is put in much the same way in many other studies. Lipset, Parsons—not least Norwegian sociologists like Rokkan and Torsvik—all see in "cross-pressures," "cross-cutting conflicts," "overlapping memberships," primary sources of political integration, hence of political stability.[4]

[2] David B. Truman, *The Governmental Process* (New York, 1951), p. 44.

[3] *Ibid.*, p. 520.

[4] See Lipset, *Political Man*, pp. 87-89, and sources there cited. Perhaps the best published discussion of how social cohesion may grow out of cross-cutting conflicts is in Lewis A. Coser, *The Functions of Social Conflict* (London, 1956), pp. 76-81. This work undertakes a revision of Simmel's many striking insights into the ubiquity and utility of conflict in human groups (Georg Simmel, *Conflict*, Glencoe, Ill., 1955), the section on "criss-crossing" conflicts being particularly inspired by Edward A. Ross, *The Principles of Sociology* (New York, 1920). Ross' much quoted remarks on the subject are worth citing again. "Every species of social conflict," he writes, "interferes with every other species . . . save only when lines of cleavage coincide; in which case they reinforce one another. . . . A society, therefore, which is ridden by a dozen oppositions along lines running in every direction may actually be in less danger of being torn with violence or falling to pieces than one split

There is no need to argue here against that general perspective.[5] Although metaphors from physics are now somewhat eclipsed in social theory by analogies from biology and physiology (especially by "systems theories" that attribute stability to mutually supportive elements of integrated structures possessing central facilities for the maintenance of integration), the equilibrium perspective on stability still has considerable plausibility and may serve admirably in some cases and as a partial explanation in others. The question here is whether it serves adequately in cases like Norway, or is compelled for want of any more serviceable alternative. In my view, that seems very doubtful, on several grounds.

The argument that political cohesion in Norway flows out of some particular alchemy of the pattern of division itself contains, first, some historical flaws. Cross-cutting divisions may clearly exist now, but Rokkan himself has shown, in article after article, that they are rather recent, the result mainly of the impact of industrialization on old territorial cleavage lines, while stable representative government is old. Furthermore, Rokkan has shown that the initial (even if not permanent) impact of the addition of new to old divisions was not to moderate but to aggravate conflict. In view of that, it seems less plausible to say that multiplying divisions have themselves produced cohesion in Norway than to argue that the country's cohesive forces have constantly reasserted themselves in absorbing new divisions into an old pattern of cohesion. It is also hard to main-

---

along just one line. For each new cleavage contributes to narrow the cross clefts, so that one might say that *society is sewn together* by its inner conflicts" (pp. 164-165; italics in the original). Other sociologists and anthropologists who have expressed similar views are Dahrendorf, Blau, Mack and Snyder, Gluckman, Lazarsfeld, and Coleman. A comprehensive discussion of the literature is contained in Mohammed Guessous, *On the Theory of Social Change* (unpublished).

[5] For criticisms of it see Stanley R. Rothman, "Systematic Political Theory: Observations on the Group Approach," *American Political Science Review*, LIV (March 1960); William C. Mitchell, "Interest Group Theory and 'Overlapping Memberships,' " Paper delivered at the Annual Meeting of the American Political Science Association, 1963.

tain that existing countervailing forces produce stability by constantly renewing a mechanical balance where powerful new forces have rapidly entered the political arena, as they did in Norway; and it is especially hard to do so where these forces did not have the happy function of reconstituting an equilibrium that had broken down but had (as in the case of Norway's peasant and labor movements) the manifest purpose of trying to break up an existing "balance." Nor does the notion of stability by balance among conflicting forces square with the fact that Norway's modern political history consists mainly of three prolonged periods of manifest political imbalance.[6]

These doubts arising from the empirical realm are reinforced by logical ones. The mechanical balancing of countervailing forces can certainly explain the persistence of a pattern, a form, of politics, but how can it account for the substantive content of that form in Norway? How, for example, do mechanical balances produce strong legitimacy? And how do they lead to the system's pronounced decisional efficiency? Surely a balance of conflicting forces is less likely to produce active and powerful rule than what Montesquieu thought it would produce: weak government—even *immobilisme* of the sort that simultaneously paralyzed the Third French Republic, weakened its legitimacy, yet prevented the formation of internal forces strong enough to destroy it. Balance is likely to produce active rule only if it is markedly one-sided (which would be a very peculiar "balance" and one that did not even exist in Norway in the very active period of government from 1935 to World War II) or if the countervailing forces choose to cooperate rather than stalemate one another (which would still leave the sources of cooperativeness to be explained on other grounds, for closely matched forces can as "logically" take one course as the other).

Similar doubts arise when the idea of cross-cutting is added to that of multiple cleavages. Complex cross-cutting divisions are as likely to produce a large variety of antagonistic groups having different *combinations* of characteristics as a high level

[6] See above, pp. 17-18.

of aggregation and thereby stable, powerful authority. Rural Western fundamentalist plebeians might well stand against rural Western secular plebeians, both against urbanites and patricians of any kind, and so on. And they might all feel very deeply about the partial characteristics or particular combinations of characteristics that distinguish them. From such cross-cutting divisions all that is likely to follow is what Dahl says might follow: the improbability of any segmental interest becoming dominant,[7] and indeed, one might suspect, difficulties in forming any positive majority whatever and thus in conducting the business of democracy. To get majorities logically out of cross-cutting divisions, one must, after all, assume that it is the areas of overlap that assert themselves in politics, and that they do not themselves come to constitute intransigent groupings of men sharing a certain complexity of traits. But it is just as conceivable, psychologically no less than logically, that the areas most potent politically will be those of clear social distinctiveness, in which no cross-pressures are felt and unambiguous interests exist; and it is not necessary that areas of overlap will cover a majority, nor a foregone conclusion that the criss-crossing currents at the intersections of groups will produce positive attitudes toward political decision-making. One can undoubtedly construct abstract models of cross-cutting divisions that promote positive harmony, but one can as readily construct models that have contrary results: acute disharmony or merely negative agreements. All this apart from the vexing question of what really constitutes "cross-cutting" in the subunits of society: whether cross-cutting operates only in case of actual membership and active participation in organizations (rather than merely belonging to different "categoric" groupings or having nominal membership); under what conditions a variety of social identifications is actually cumulative, tending to reinforce conflict, rather than the reverse; under what circumstances political divisions on more than one axis merely multiply the number

[7] R. A. Dahl, *A Preface to Democratic Theory* (Chicago, 1956), pp. 104-105.

of antagonistic political groups (a possible result of multiple divisions to which many have attributed the fragmented party systems of continental Europe, especially of France);[8] and whether cross-cutting requires uniformly intense identifications with all the overlapping groups by their members.

In the empirical realm, the possibility that cross-cutting divisions might actually intensify disintegration is certainly borne out by the Norwegian party system, especially by the so-called middle parties, which, as we have seen, have much in common, but evidently not enough to prevent their fragmentation. The members of the middle parties overlap at least as much as the members of the Right and Labour parties, without however being even as mildly aggregative as these two parties or as prone to cooperation. This suggests that empirically as well as logically, overlaps, aggregation, and cooperativeness are only weakly related, if at all. It may be that the lack of aggregation by Norwegian parties results from a relative absence of overlapping identifications, from too much "agglutination" of different lines of division in distinct groups of men; but in that case what of the initial argument that cross-cutting identifications account for the stability of the system?

In view of all this it seems unwise to resort to so ambiguous and metaphorical an explanation of Norway's political cohesion, at least as long as any other possibility exists. And another possibility does exist. In Norway there are special cohesive forces that work not through but alongside those that divide the country and that can explain what balance theory leaves most puzzling: the system's long unquestioned legitimacy and its efficiency in workaday operation even under inauspicious conditions.

3. In *The Civic Culture* Almond and Verba suggest that political divisions (they do not say whether of any kind or

---

[8] For a fine discussion of these problems, see Sidney Verba, "Organizational Membership and Democratic Consensus," *Journal of Politics* (forthcoming).

dimension) can be "managed" by a certain "inconsistency between norms and behavior." More specifically, competitive
political "behavior" may substantially coincide with the social
or cultural segments of society, but this somehow need not
destroy the cohesion of a polity if there exists in it a norm that
this *ought not* to be so, emanating from "some higher, overarching attitudes of solidarity."[9]

Almond and Verba are squarely on the track we will follow in
the rest of this essay, but the mere two paragraphs they devote
to this absolutely crucial argument leave many essential
questions unanswered. Just what attitudes of solidarity may suffice to overcome deep cleavages and divergences? How do
these attitudes come into being, how are they maintained in the
face of political cleavages and divergences? Is it likely that norms
unmanifested in behavior can preserve political cohesion and
guarantee the effective working of governments? And if the
norms are not manifested in behavior, how can one be sure that
they exist? What sorts of behavior, then, are indicative of the
existence of overarching norms of solidarity in a polity? And
how exactly do the norms and the behavior patterns that manifest them counteract the effects of political division, make for
democratic legitimacy, intrasystem stability, and decisional
efficiency on the part of representative governments?[10]

[9] Almond and Verba, *The Civic Culture*, p. 492.

[10] The point that Almond and Verba make has, of course, been made
before and since, and in many connections, but just as tersely, if not
more so, and without attempts to cope with the questions I have put.
Thus, John Stuart Mill argues that conflicts in men's interests may be innocuous if they are agreed on "the fundamental principles of social
union" (*On Bentham and Coleridge*, New York, 1951, 123). Ortega y
Gassett points to Cicero's belief that *concordia* (agreement in "certain
ultimate matters," "basic layers of common belief") takes the sting out
of "civil dissension" (*Concord and Liberty*, New York, 1946, 15).
George Simpson speaks of the harmlessness of differences when they are
settled on a "basis of unity" (*Conflict and Community*, New York, 1937,
p. 4). But what the "fundamental" principles of social union are, what
might be "ultimate" or "basic" matters of belief and unity, these writers
do not tell us; nor do they speak specifically of the conflicts, differences
and dissensions that can, under various conditions, be rendered harmless.

Only when one has answers to these questions can one feel confident about the validity of the position Almond and Verba take, and of the thesis of this discussion: that political cohesion is, under certain conditions, compatible with virtually any kind and degree of political division. And on these questions Norway can shed considerable light, even if more wide-ranging study is necessary to make the answers definitive.

This applies also to the large number of "functionalist" writings that make value consensus the basis of social integration. (For a review and summary of that literature, see P. L. van den Berghe, "Dialectic and Functionalism," *American Sociological Review*, XXVIII, October 1963, 696-697). A notable recent example of such writing in political science is Easton's *A Systems Analysis of Political Life*. In arguing that a viable polity requires a certain balance of "demands" and "support," Easton is saying something much like Almond and Verba, for demands are what divide polities, support what unites them. Easton's analysis (about which I have many reservations) is unusual, however, in the elaborate care devoted to the treatment of his position. Moreover, in arguing for the relative independence from one another of divisive and cohesive forces he takes a position that, to anticipate a little, closely fits my own. The crucial sentences stating this position occur at the beginning of his chapter 11 (p. 171).

V

Norway as a "Community"

NORWEGIANS have a "higher, overarching attitude of solidarity" in that they in fact display in many aspects of their behavior a profound sense of community—a considerable *Wirbewusstsein*, a sense of "we-ness," as the Germans would say. Norway thus fits, even if it does not conclusively confirm, Pye's large generalization (derived from Stouffer's study of the American soldier) that "the modern formal superstructure of relationships can give an organization strength only if supported by the powerful emotional forces arising from particularistic loyalties and by the cohesive powers of the . . . diffuse sentiments that human beings can provoke in each other."[1] The Norwegian sense of community, for reasons discussed later, is, despite the country's political divisions, preeminently political, but the political sentiments and behavior patterns that constitute it express much more general attitudes and modes of acting.

Before going into the crucial and difficult questions of how this sense of community is maintained in the face of considerable cleavages and divergences and how it leads to democractic legitimacy and practical efficiency in government, we need to describe in some detail the behavior that indicates its existence. In that way we can not only support the assertion that a deep sense of community does indeed exist in Norway but also state more specifically the sentiments of which it is constituted.[2]

[1] Pye, *Politics, Personality and Nation Building*, p. 40.

[2] To use "indicators" effectively, one must, of course, specify what an "indicator" is and what is to be "indicated." For the latter purpose the phrase employed by Almond and Verba—"higher, overarching sentiments of solidarity"—can stand some amplification. In speaking of a *sense of community*, I take my cues from a variety of sociologists and political scientists, including Tönnies, Weber, Karl Deutsch, and, especially, David Easton. Some of these writers follow Tönnies in distinguishing "communities" from "societies," defining each by the sentiments operating in them. Others, like Easton, distinguish the "sense" of community from

The patterns of behavior that will be sketched in this chapter have, inevitably, been observed mainly in contemporary Norwegian life. However, much evidence (some of which will be presented in the course of the discussion) suggests that the more important of them are not peculiar to the present but have been

---

the object toward which it is directed (which, in Tönnies' terms, may be either a society or community). Nevertheless, their ideas on the nature of communal sentiments are much the same. Easton (in *A Systems Analysis of Political Life*) speaks of the existence of "affective" bonds in a structurally differentiated system (p. 173); of "affective solidarity" oriented toward the system (p. 176); of a feeling of engagement in a "common enterprise" (p. 176); of "potent psychological bonds" among the units of, and "attachment to," an "overall group"; and of "feelings of mutual responsiveness" (p. 185). For Weber, community simply denoted "the feelings of the actors that they belong together" (H. H. Gerth and C. W. Mills, eds., *From Max Weber: Essays in Sociology*, New York, 1946, p. 183). Deutsch speaks of "mutual sympathy and loyalties; of 'we-feeling,' trust, and consideration; of . . . identification of self-images and interests." (K. W. Deutsch *et al.*, *The Political Community and the North Atlantic Area*, Princeton, 1957, p. 129.) Tönnies stressed "affective" associations and "intimate feelings" toward others, as against impersonal optimizing strategies for realizing personal or corporate interests (see note 4, *infra*.).

Putting these cues together, a "profound sense of community" denotes strong sentiments toward some complex structure *and* its members and substructures that are in some way intimately emotional, lead to cooperative and trustful behavior, and involve a strong identification of the self with others and the larger institutions of a society. For all this, Deutsch's term "we-feeling," which I use in the text in its original German form, seems to me particularly apt: a sense of community is indicated by any behavior that implies sentiments of an indissoluble "we-ness" rather than a more conditional "other-ness."

While I do not use the term community in an idiosyncratic manner, many of the "indicators" used in the text may not be readily recognized as such by contemporary social scientists. By an indicator we usually mean nowadays a precisely ascertainable quantity that stands for some imprecise quality (as GNP may indicate level of economic development, or as the number of casualties in revolutionary violence may indicate its intensity). I do use such quantities in what follows. More often, however, readily observable "qualities" are used as indicators of not-so-readily observable qualities. This strikes me as both defensible and desirable, for quantitative indicators are not always as precise as they seem, nor always as "indicative" of what one wants to know as other observations, nor always obtainable. In overemphasizing quantities we

characteristic of Norway for a long time—as one would expect in view of her long history of stable representative rule. This is not to say, of course, that Norwegian behavior has been absolutely uniform since the early nineteenth century. During the last century and a half Norway has undergone large-scale and rapidly accomplished social changes that have transformed her from a backwater of European civilization into a highly "modernized" nation. These changes—especially in economic life (industrialization), in demographic structure (urbanization) and in politics (full democratization)—have certainly affected Norwegian social relationships in important ways. But even more striking are the ways in which older attitudes and modes of social conduct, uncharacteristic, to say the least, of most industrial, urban and democratic societies, have modified conduct in the more recently developed aspects of Norwegian society. Nothing, in fact, attests more emphatically to the strength of these attitudes and behavior patterns than that they have so substantially survived in, and modified the consequences of, sweeping social changes that elsewhere have transformed both the face and heart of society.

1. One of the most telling indications of a deep sense of community in Norway is that Norwegian social relations are not defined to any large extent in "economic" terms. "Economic" does not here refer narrowly to material exchange relations, but broadly to relations in which men treat others principally as utilities for their own purposes—for example, by attempting closely to control them or by negotiating or bargaining with them for one-sided or mutual advantages. Such relations may be contrasted with those that involve unconditionally affective bonds among men, bonds free of calculation, such as relations

---

sometimes miss the most telling data—in any case, data that may be reliable in their own right or used as checks on the inferences drawn from quantitative data. I conceive of all social behavior as a vast "data bank," only some of which is quantitatively aggregated in yearbooks and the like, and much of the rest of which may speak volumes to our purposes, if used circumspectly.

of freely given respect, considerateness, love, helpfulness, sympathy, tolerance, and accommodation (although affective relations may also involve unconditional hostility, or even hatred, in which case they indicate the absence not only of community but of any social bonds whatever). "Noneconomic" relations, in this sense, may characterize material exchange relations as well as any others, and "economic" relations interactions that involve no material exchanges. Even the closest social interactions can be defined economically if men are affectively indifferent toward others, either out of egotism or because of their close identification with impersonal institutions, and if they therefore always calculate how their values, personal or institutional, may be maximized in personal relations. By the same token, the most casual encounters among strangers may be noneconomic, if they treat one another without overriding considerations of utility—that is, as if they were true intimates. I use the terms "economic" and "noneconomic" to make this distinction for two simple reasons: because the calculation of advantages in human interaction was raised by the early modern economists to the level of a positive virtue and because systems of material exchange seem in fact particularly susceptible to "economic" conduct.[3] But the terms "instrumental" and "non-

[3] Three points amplifying these concepts should be added for anyone who may find general utility in the distinction. (1) The concepts economic and noneconomic are, of course, ideal constructs, unlikely to be found in pure form. To characterize behavior by one or the other term is to say that it is predominantly economic or noneconomic, or that interactions that have strong inherent affinities for being defined in one of these ways are importantly conditioned by the intrusion of contrary behavior. (2) "Economic" does not mean "selfish," unless selfish is used in a very large sense. One can treat others "economically" for the benefit of impersonal institutions as well as for more egotistic purposes. Indeed, economic behavior may well be most callous where men are intensely committed to abstract ends or institutional aggrandizement. (3) "Economic" certainly is not a synonym for "bad." It may be, by some supreme irony, that the values of all can in fact be optimized by networks of narrow utilitarian interactions. But even apart from that possibility, which is the basis of the "dismal science," economic relations at least are not relations of bitter, or deadly, animosity, which are the true opposites of communality. On a continuum from the positive value

instrumental" would serve as well, or perhaps better, to make the same distinction.

Much of what we call modernization involves, apparently, a considerable displacement of "noneconomic" by "economic" interactions[4]—which is one reason why the benefits of civilization may often seem unbearable. Nevertheless, Norwegian social relations, despite the considerable modernization of the country and despite little open display of emotional warmth toward others, still manifest strong noneconomic patterns of conduct that constantly modify, or even nullify, economic ones. To be sure, instrumental relations among Norwegians do exist, and even predominate in some sectors of social life. In an industrial, monetary, and relatively free economy and a society that also offers nonfinancial rewards on an open but limited

---

of communality to the negative value of warlike animosity, economic relations are a kind of zero point, a point of indifference toward others as persons. Indeed, they may be better placed on a different dimension altogether, for hatred, as I have said, is as personal a relation as love, and shuns utility.

[4] This point is particularly stressed in Ferdinand Tönnies' *Gemeinschaft und Gesellschaft* (1887). Pye summarizes Tönnies' view as follows: ". . . human relations in the *Gemeinschaft* (community) form of association were highly affective, emphasizing the non-rational, emotional dimensions of the 'natural will' of man which have their clearest expression in the intimate feelings of kinship, comradeship and neighborliness, while relations in the *Gesellschaft* (society) form of association were affectively neutral and emphasized the rational capacities of man by which he is able, first, to isolate and distinguish his goals of action, and then to employ, impersonally and deliberately, contractual arrangements as a part of strategies for optimizing his values" (*Politics, Personality and Nation Building*, p. 34). These, needless to say, are abstractions from reality. Concrete "communities" are certainly never so free of strategy, nor concrete "societies" so devoid of intimacy. But used to describe a tendency that occurs in social changes now generally understood to constitute "modernization" the abstractions seem serviceable, despite the fact that Pye's own work depicts a "traditional" society —equated with community—in which calculations and machinations were intense and common to the point of obsessiveness. That picture may be reconciled with Tönnies by distinguishing the true communities of kin, comrades, and neighbors from the largely nominal structures— e.g., royal realms and empires—often imperfectly superimposed on them.

basis, a considerable amount of instrumental behavior toward others is unavoidable, even on the part of men who are not especially ambitious, restless, or distrustful. But there are in Norway unusually pronounced tendencies to *modulate*—to soften—in a "noneconomic" direction even relationships inherently difficult to conduct on a noninstrumental basis in any society whatever, to carve out at least margins of noninstrumentality in virtually every phase of social life. And this expresses a value subscribed to even where it cannot be substantially attained—something central in Norwegian norms that emerges forcefully in some social relations and at least discernibly in others.[5]

One indication of this value, among many others, is that Norwegians often seem embarrassed by placing on a commercial footing interactions that elsewhere have an easy affinity for commercial relations (which are, of course, "economic" both in the present and the more conventional sense). A striking example is the general preference of Norwegian doctors for salaried positions that remove the cash nexus from the doctor-patient relationship. This contrasts sharply with the intransigent loathing of American doctors for any arrangements whatever that have such an effect. It also contrasts with the less widely known and equally intransigent antipathy of British doctors (who, as a group, have very different attitudes toward public medical services) specifically to salaried payment. Underlying the American and British doctors' attitudes is not necessarily a desire to treat patients as utilities, but unmistakably a fear that through salaried service others will exploit the doctors to narrow and selfish advantage: patients through unreasonable

---

[5] Some Norwegian readers of my first draft disputed my assertions about the prevalence of noneconomic behavior in Norway's social life. To them, and others who may think similarly, I offer a suggestion. Precisely because noninstrumentality in social conduct is so intense a norm in Norwegian life, they may be especially impressed by, and conscious of, deviations from it; an American like myself, coming from a society in which quite different norms prevail, is more impressed by the extent to which that norm is observed even in unlikely sectors of society.

demands for services, bureaucrats through excessive controls to satisfy their appetite for power. This fear of economic relations in the broad sense, which has the ironic consequence of an insistence on economic relations conventionally defined, does not seem to exist in Norway to anything like the same extent; there it seems to be generally assumed that patients and public authorities will not exploit doctors for all the arrangements will bear. In Britain and America they do not in fact do so save in exceptional instances, but the very fear that they might expresses a general lack of confidence in the willingness of men to forego narrow advantages, even empty ones, at others' expense, and this fear has deep roots in general social conduct.[6]

Even more striking in this regard is the ubiquitous corporatization of industrial and commercial activities themselves in Norway—the largely voluntary, virtually all-encompassing network of cooperative arrangements among sellers and producers (to which we shall allude again in other connections). Many of these arrangements, which either restrict or abolish brute competition and generally involve joint research, joint marketing, and the joint definition of standards, have more than a whiff of monopoly or cartel about them; yet they are not merely tolerated but have in many cases been positively encouraged, indeed subvened, by public authority. They express a widespread reluctance to engage in the sort of behavior that raw competition generally compels, a concomitant drive toward harmony among men who cannot help but interact, and above all the same sort of confidence that obviates antipathy to medical salaries, namely that arrangements suitable for exploitation will not in fact be

[6] One reason that many Norwegian doctors frequently choose salaried positions undoubtedly is professional rather than normative: most prestigious and professionally satisfying medical positions happen to be salaried. This, however, does not alter the fact that Norwegian doctors are not frightened of salaried service to the extent American and British doctors are—that they are less intent upon a cash nexus in the doctor-patient relationship, less anxious to enjoy more or less financial independence, less likely to choose practices that entail a large amount of unfettered entrepreneurship.

used unscrupulously. This is not to say, of course, that no Norwegian ever takes advantage of another. Norwegians are human. But it does mean that there is much confidence in public-spirited, other-regarding conduct. (See Table 19, Appendix B.) As a result of this confidence, Norwegians, when victimized by selfish dealings, sometimes seem extraordinarily helpless, hurt, and surprised rather than outraged or moved to take counter-measures.

These matters are noteworthy chiefly because they display the Norwegian sentiment of community in realms of social life where, on the basis of behavior in other countries, one would not expect such considerations to obtrude. There are, however, still more unmistakable expressions of that sentiment. Perhaps the most clearcut of all is the great solicitousness Norwegians display toward the weaker and less advantaged members of their society. The present Norwegian welfare state is one of the most highly developed anywhere and has an unusually long past. Indeed, the growth of a humanitarian social service state coincides largely with the growth of modern Norway itself and is consequently as ingrained in political consciousness as suspicion of public welfare measures is in ours (no doubt again mainly because of fear of institutions that may be "economically" exploited, especially since we also approve charity, which cannot be extorted). The belief that the glory of a nation is to be assessed by something other than power and wealth, but also, or rather, by the level of decency in human relations that it achieves, figures largely in the works of Bjørnson and Wergeland, who are perhaps the two greatest hero figures in a country whose modern heroes, strange to say, are mostly poets (Ferraton speaks of a Norwegian "poetocracy"), not conquerors, diplomats, or economic barons. Norway led the world in penal reform with the early building of a model Benthamite prison and the enactment of a Benthamite code of criminal law. As early as the 1870's, capital punishment fell into complete disuse; as early as 1848 insanity was treated as something calling for care and treatment rather than the mere deprivation of liberty, the first modern insane asylum, which incidentally is still serviceable today, being a Norwegian creation. Schooling was universal and free in the towns by 1848 and everywhere by 1860. Compulsory health insurance dates to 1909. And since then comprehensive schemes for minimizing virtually every disability and risk in life have been enacted.[7]

The spirit in which these developments were undertaken is as important for our purposes as the developments themselves. In fact, it is the sentiments behind reform more than reform itself that distinguishes Norway from other modern welfare states. Bismarck's early development of social services in Germany was a masterpiece of political "economy," a method consciously intended to take the wind out of the radicals' sails, even if not grudgingly conceded, as in so many other cases, to brute pressure. The British Tories, who are responsible for more welfare legislation than is commonly realized, were generally motivated in social reform by their celebrated tactic of stealing the Whigs' clothes (although, to give them their due, feelings of *noblesse oblige* toward the lower orders made Troy men highly receptive to Whiggish measures). Even the Fabians often espoused the most humanitarian causes for the most cold-blooded reasons: because, for example, social suffering was needlessly wasteful or private philanthropy likely to be irrationally applied. In Norway, however, the weak and disadvantaged have been regarded in less utilitarian, more unconditionally human terms, much as one might regard the frail and vulnerable in a close-knit family. This is reflected not merely in the extensiveness of the social services but in the atmosphere and surroundings in which they are provided. I saw in Norway none of the disdainful poorhouse settings that still characterize so many British welfare institutions, public or private, nor any condescension toward the needy by those supplying their needs; nor did anyone

[7] See Derry, *A Short History of Norway*, pp. 147, 162-163; Storing, *Norwegian Democracy*, ch. 10; D. B. Skardal, *Social Insurance in Norway* (Oslo, 1960); and Karl Evang, *Health Services in Norway* (Oslo, 1960).

ever try to justify the social services to me as regrettable public utilities. Welfare institutions seem to blend naturally into the general tenor of institutional life, if anything to be particularly friendly, cheerful, and warm.

The tendency not to treat others as utilities comes out in Norway also in the way particular vices and virtues are defined, not least in child rearing. The supreme virtue Norwegians seem generally to cultivate is kindness and helpfulness to others. Concomitantly, the supreme vice they try to discourage seems to be humiliating or otherwise hurting another person; and being themselves humiliated seems to be their most obsessive anxiety. Their fear of humiliation may even, in a way, account for the lack of openness and warmth, and particularly the shyness toward strangers, that many have observed in Norway, indeed for a tendency frequently to withdraw into isolated privacy or very narrow social networks. In any social relations hostilities are bound to arise. But if hostile expressions that might give deep offense are strongly reproved, hostilities can only be managed by withdrawal or by concealing as much as possible all strong feelings toward others. This applies even to positive feelings, for if one's feelings toward another are strongly positive one is oneself highly vulnerable to being humiliated, just as one may hurt another by strong hostilities. Thus, the suppression of hostility and its management by withdrawal is both symptomatic of a sense of community and, to anticipate a little, a basic mechanism for its maintenance.[8]

The tendency to handle hostilities by withdrawal stood out during my stay in Norway in an incident that was much commented on, with some astonishment, in the foreign press. Khrushchev had come to Oslo in the course of a Scandinavian

[8] Rodnick (*The Norwegians*, pp. 1-3, 14-15, 64) makes the emphasis Norwegians put on kindness, their obsessive fear of humiliation, and their attendant tendencies toward the repression of strong feelings and toward withdrawal the keystone and constantly reiterated theme of a book resulting from a year's "participant observation" of Norway. He is particularly instructive on the role of these patterns in child rearing. The few opportunities I had to check his impressions confirm them.

tour during which he had everywhere put on his usual exhibition. But not in Oslo, for almost no one turned up to watch, neither to applaud nor jeer. A considerable withdrawal greeted him; the streets of Oslo seemed little more crowded than usual, mainly by people going quietly about their ordinary affairs. The same treatment apparently was meted out with a vengeance to the German occupation authorities, who were usually forced to play to empty streets and curtained windows, much to their chagrin and Norway's suffering.

In this sort of behavior one can find some basis for the much-stressed notion, apparently incongruent with our emphasis on communal sentiments, that Norwegians are highly "individualistic." Most Norwegians do seem to value and indeed often insist upon personal privacy; they also engage intensely in highly isolated activities, like lonely hikes and sailing tours. But their individualism is very much restricted to such "withdrawn" activities, not manifested to any large extent in personal eccentricity in social relations, lack of cooperativeness, manifest sparkle or originality, mental daring, taking controversial positions for sheer exhilaration's sake, any kind of "showing off," or pronounced self-seeking. In public activities Norwegians conform with a vegeance, adhering to closely defined, usually cooperative institutional norms. But they indulge the less conventional side of their natures in pursuits from which "others" are deliberately shut out, including in some instances the lonely pursuits of artistic and literary creation. In this way, nonconformity does not disrupt social interaction, nor social conformity stultify personal fulfillment; and in this way too individualism, such as it is, reinforces the capacity for communal behavior.

To put the same point in technical jargon, the behavior of Norwegians illustrates on the individual level how "phase movements" in social behavior may contribute to social "equilibrium." Phase movements, in effect, consist of apparently contradictory fluctuations in social behavior that serve the function of releasing tensions or frustrations piled up while a one-sided kind of conduct is being strongly emphasized, thus neglecting, in one way or another, the many-sided needs of personal and social existence. To serve their function, such oscillations, it has been argued, must be to a considerable degree controlled and regulated in order to keep them in harmony with each other. In Norway this is done by a literal separation of the realms in which conformity and spontaneity operate most strongly, in such a way that the latter impinge little upon public social life. Isolative withdrawal in short serves a dual function for Norwegians: that of managing hostilities and that of compensating for the conformity exacted in social interaction.

In view of the dominant nonutilitarian attitudes toward "others," it is not surprising that Norwegians should have strongly positive sentiments toward institutions and objects that, so to speak, embody otherness—in other words toward public objects available to or obstrusive upon all. They care remarkably, for example, for their common lands and, as well, keep much of their land common and accessible. Littering, epidemics of billboards and neon lights, excrescences of roadside joints, are virtually unknown. Similarly, urban building is closely controlled for aesthetic and hygienic purposes, even at considerable and consciously realized hardship to private comforts. In fact, one may well get the impression in Norway that practically any kind of private scarcity is tolerated if its demonstrable counterpart is public affluence, reversing the priorities of American life. There is, indeed, some tendency actually to turn private things into public objects, or at least to treat them as if they were. To cite but two examples: most public services were nationalized in Norway long before a socialist party came to power. And private agricultural property especially is treated not as fully private but as a community concern. Thus sales of farm land are vetted by local committees of farmers, who generally try above all to see to it that genuine farmers are given preference and land speculators, who might deface the countryside, excluded. Thus also much farmland, especially the indispensable mountain summer pastures, still is, as in times immemorial, strictly communal, attached to groups of farms and difficult to alienate under the complex laws pertaining to the "commons."[9]

In these behavior patterns we get two explanations of one of the mysteries of Norway's pattern of political division: why cleavage and divergence are not reflected in more extensive open policy disagreements. One is that much Norwegian policy reflects precisely those communal values that are widely shared: caring for public things, solicitude for the weak, and a concomitant willingness to suffer certain private deprivations, including considerable material leveling—which indeed are not widely felt as deprivations. None of these values was attacked by the twenty-eight-day wonder of 1963, the short-lived government of parties long in opposition that ensued on the King's Bay incident. It is worth noting, moreover, that the spectacular achievements of the prewar Labour minority government fell almost entirely into areas of policy where communal sentiments were strongest. The second explanation of the restricted scope of policy disagreements in Norway is to be found in the general tendency to withdraw from situations of potential hostility. There seems to be a broad tacit agreement in Norwegian politics not to raise publicly matters likely to generate open antagonisms (which, of course, is sometimes impossible). As a corollary, there is a tendency to strive quietly and privately for prior agreements before public debates are conducted and not to press hard matters on which the prior soundings are unsuccessful. From this standpoint, policy consensus in Norway is both positive and negative, a vocal consensus and a consensus of silence, the first on matters of communal values, the second on divisive issues. But the consensus of silence is not unrelated to communal values. It flows from a kind of considerateness, as well as from deeply inculcated norms regarding the management of conflicts in the society's network of communal relations.

With the fact that public objects are highly valued in Norway there is connected a further expression of community that is

[9] *Ibid.*, p. 75.

specifically political. There seems to be little suspicion or fear of public or quasi-public authority,[10] but, on the contrary, both a strongly supported ideal of public service and considerable respect for actual public activity. The high prestige of Norway's officialdom substantially survived their fall from privilege, and a career in public service is still a widely held ambition among the gifted. Furthermore, membership in the Storting is treated, formally and informally, as a high duty. Men elected to the Storting are legally *required* to serve, whether they wish or not. Attendance in parliament is in fact great, especially by British and American standards, even during the least exciting debates, such as those the outcome of which is, through prior agreements, a conclusion widely known to be foregone. Furthermore, anyone present in the chamber during a division is *obliged* to vote one way or another, that is to say, is denied the comfortable private right of abstention. And this insistence on the performance of public duties is even more emphatic in local government, where local councillors and board members are positively required to attend meetings unless formally excused and to vote on all issues discussed in their presence. Norwegians elect representatives to reach decisions and insist that they do just that, as a high public duty that has priority over any private considerations, including plain indecision.

Just how far the sentiments described here go is indicated by a recent study of an aspect of Norwegian life where one might think they would certainly not be manifested—in jail. This is Thomas Mathiesen's *The Defenses of the Weak,*[11] a study of a criminal rehabilitation center. Among many other pertinent observations in that study, the following particularly underline some of the things that have been said here: In Norwegian prisons, says Mathiesen, there is in comparison to other countries an unusual lack of prohibition on close contacts between inmates

---

[10] By quasi-public authority I mean authority wielded by the governing bodies of large private organizations, such as parties, trade unions, cooperatives, employers' associations, etc.

[11] London, 1965, esp. chs. VI-VIII.

and guards (for example, they often go on the town together during the prisoners' "furloughs"), suggesting a free extension of community even to social outcasts and that Wergeland's wish for a union even of lawmaker and lawbreaker was not vain. On the other hand, among the inmates themselves, thrown close together as they are, with all the hostilities sheer proximity might entail, there is an equally unusual amount of isolative behavior, as well as an unusual lack of the sort of peer group solidarities against the prison authorities or special groups of prisoners that are common in other countries. The prisoners' chief defense against authority is not such sectional solidarity but what Mathiesen calls "censoriousness." That is, the prisoners pursue their objectives mainly by appealing to generally shared norms and principles, particularly to precisely formulated legal rules, that correspond to those of external society. Far from being in revolt against the system of which they have run afoul, they are apparently among the most zealous guardians of its rules of justice and general conduct, and trust them, rightly it seems, to provide sufficient defenses in their extremely vulnerable position.

2. The first and foremost indicators of a deep sense of community in Norway thus are a set of behavior patterns that involve unconditional "noneconomic" attitudes both toward other persons and institutions that embody otherness, and certain tendencies in behavior that prevent or suppress interpersonal hostilities. These noneconomic attitudes predominate in certain spheres, while elsewhere, in realms where economic interactions can hardly be avoided, they clearly modify relations of utility among men.

A second set of indicators of the Norwegian sense of community may be summarized by the term *"noncompetitiveness."* These indicators involve a general reluctance either to outdo others or to be clearly seen to do so—a general deemphasis of personal achievement where invidious contrasts with the capacities and accomplishments of others are likely to be made. Noncompetitiveness overlaps somewhat with noneconomic definitions of social conduct, in that some kinds of behavior can be regarded as expressing both or either. Nevertheless, it is in principle a different expression of communality. Noneconomic norms prevent affective indifference toward others, even if in certain respects they may express themselves in withdrawal and rigid control of affection. Noncompetitive norms, on the other hand, prevent the kinds of affect—envy, rivalry, jealousy, above all humiliation—that may profoundly threaten communality in all its aspects.

Again, my argument is not that Norwegians do not compete at all. Since Norway is, to a large extent, an open society in which high positions are open to talent and achievement, competition among Norwegians is unavoidable and especially likely to be intense in areas where the number of top positions, as well as turnover in them, is very small—university life being an example. But competitiveness in almost all activities—some rather surprising—is subdued and modified by noncompetitive norms, either in substance or in form, that is, either by an actual reduction of competition or by styles of interaction that confirm the norms even if behavior deviates from them.

Noncompetitive norms might be expected to be least manifested in sport, just as noneconomic norms are most unexpected in commerce; yet it is in sport that Norwegians perhaps most strikingly display such norms. For example, professsional athletes are virtually unknown in Norway, except as guides and instructors. Professional athletes are, of course, specialists in the most palpable kind of competitive achievement. Judging from the salaries and public notoriety they generally achieve, such specialization, especially great excellence in it, is highly valued in most Western societies, an obvious manifestation of a common "achievement orientation." Professional athletes are perhaps most highly valued in the United States, where achievement seems particularly esteemed if a man's feats are readily measurable against those of others. Hence our tremendous record consciousness, which is at its most absurd extreme in baseball, where the most trivial achievements are measured and, if unprecedented, lovingly cataloged—and in which, incidentally, some very nasty behavior is positively applauded if it gets results. To outdo others in sporting competition many Westerners cheerfully undergo privations that would have appalled a stylite, and think of both the ascetic preparations and their consummation in not-so-symbolic conflict as "building character," that is, the kind of character that most of them value. Norwegians, by and large, value a different character.

This emerges also in the Norwegians' preference for those sports, some extremely arduous, that do not directly involve invidious contrasts. Most Norwegians prefer isolated sports like swimming, hiking, climbing, sailing, skiing, rowing, fishing, and hunting—sports that involve pitting oneself against non-human adversaries, not other men. They have, of course, competitive sports, including team sports. But, significantly, their fiercer instincts emerge in such sports mainly when they compete against other nations—that is, members of other communities —especially if the other nation happens to be Sweden. During my stay in Norway I saw two soccer matches in Oslo's Ulleval Stadium. One was between local teams and generated about as much partisanship in the crowd as an academic lecture (and some visible withdrawal symptoms among the players). The other was between Norway and Sweden, on which occasion many rude things about Norwegian savagery were quite rightly said in the Swedish press. But the Norwegians' international performances are much handicapped by their lack of competitiveness at home and a style of play that stresses grace and subtlety rather than toughness and aggression. They seem generally to expect to lose, and generally do. Boxing, the most starkly competitive and humiliating sport of all, is virtually unknown; and even in the sports in which Norwegians have few peers, ski jumping and speed skating, they coddle their aces less than other countries, emphasizing wide participation over individual excellence. Besides, ski jumping, despite the competitions conducted in it, is a lonely sport too, as well as one that pits men starkly against the elements. And speed skating competitions are conducted on a basis that pits the participants more directly against the clock than against one another, while the public's undoubtedly great interest and partisanship in the sport are attributable in large measure to the great role of international competition in it. It is no accident that it was five Norwegians (and one incongruous Swede) who went on the immensely lonely, uncompetitive, and arduous Kon-Tiki expedition and, what is more, emerged on speaking terms.

Equally suggestive in this respect is the relative internal non-competitiveness of industry and commerce that has already been commented on. The Norwegians' recent prosperity and extremely high rate of capital formation evidently have motivational roots, whatever they may be, other than fierce competition for profit. The economy, moreover, has long been underpinned by a remarkable development of shipping, a fact which also bears upon our argument, although in a more subtle way. No doubt the large role of shipping in modern Norway's economy is connected with a long sea-faring tradition, but any tradition long maintained depends on powerful forces to sustain it. In this connection, note that shipping is an enterprise highly suited to competition against other nationalities by a society deficient in most physical resources and, still more pertinent, one that particularly requires capacities for handling both close proximity to others and extreme isolation. Shipboard life, to which an unusually high proportion of Norwegian youths take as a matter of course, is community distilled to a microcosmic core, which is why it has become a hackneyed literary vehicle for portraying both processes of community and of the most painful estrangement. It makes large demands on cooperativeness, on the ability to retreat into oneself as a mode of managing hostilities, and most of all on team spirit, the capacity to play closely defined individual roles in a cohesive whole, where there is not even an opposing side to help one define the identity and purpose of one's own team. It thus is suitable to highly communal societies and, as a socializing influence on youths, itself contributes to the formation of cooperative norms.

In the Norwegian economy that self-contained team spirit—

team spirit in itself, not in opposition to competing teams—is writ small; in politics it is writ large. Norwegian politicians display it, first, in great party cohesion, which as previously pointed out does not greatly depend on the sort of leadership sanctions to which it is often, perhaps erroneously, attributed in Britain. The Norwegian constitution does not equip the cabinet with the weapon of dissolution, and there appears to be little central control over nominations (except perhaps in Oslo, where the national leaders live and can exert direct personal influence).[12] One gets the impression that Norwegian parliamentarians and candidates could take eccentric positions rather more freely than their counterparts in Britain, but the fact is that they rarely do, due to their own norms and the probability that local party organizations expect them to be good team members.[13] The

[12] See Valen, "Nominasjonene," *passim.*

[13] This is not to say that party leaders and their organizational apparatuses have no powers at all over the members of parliamentary groups, or that the powers they possess never are or never need to be exercised. Per Stavang, in a recently published work, *Parlamentarisme og maktbalanse* (Oslo, 1964) argues that contemporary party discipline in Norway rests, to an extent, on sanctions and methods available to leaders through modern party organizations, the most effective of which is, of course, the exclusion of recalcitrant individuals or groups (see pp. 148-154). Stavang admits, however, that precise information about how often that sanction has been threatened is not obtainable, and he is able to cite only four cases in point—none of which occurred after 1931, one of which involved a collaborative arrangement between two parties rather than a strictly internal dispute, and at least two of which were followed by speedy reconciliation. Furthermore, only two parties were involved, and only one of them, the Liberals, employed the sanction while in power—in one case while the rather atypical Gunnar Knudsen was prime minister. These things considered, it is difficult to quarrel with Stavang's conclusion (not fully compatible with his introduction) that party leaders have handled the power of exclusion with "great forbearance."

Among their other weapons, Stavang gives pride of place to control over nominations. But about the effectiveness of this instrument he says, rightly, that opinions are divided. More specifically, they are divided between Valen, "Nominasjon ved stortingsvalg," *Statsøkonomisk tidsskrift*, 1956, pp. 115-152, and T. Greve, *Nominasjon ved stortingsvalg* (Bergen, 1953), pp. 35-37; and of these, Valen's study, which argues that control is, on the whole, loose, strikes me as much more solidly based on em-

parties also take pains to safeguard their team discipline by much consultation and friendly bargaining, among leaders and with the rank and file, and set great store on at least a public show of unanimity. In the course of their national conferences, for example, "experimental votes" (*prøvevotering*) are sometimes taken deliberately to establish winning positions in apparently informal processes, followed by formal votes without dissent, "so it shall be unanimous."[14] This is like the acclamation of successful presidential candiates in the United States, but with two crucial differences: in America the practice is confined to the presidential nominating process, and everyone knows very well that it is the next to the last vote that really counts.

If such political team spirit were confined to the parties it would hardly bear out our thesis regarding the expression of community in noncompetitiveness, for parties themselves are instruments of competition; nor can one expect stable democracy readily to ensue from a fragmented system of highly cohesive, highly oppositional parties. But party discipline expresses a more general set of attitudes in social relations—agree if possible, appear to be fully agreed, act as if you were agreed even if you are not, and if you can neither agree nor appear to agree ignore the whole thing—that operates also on the more general parliamentary level. The Storting itself acts as a team, in which the party team plays a smaller role than in the British House of

---

pirical research, a position that Stavang himself seems to take.

More important still than these considerations is that party cohesion being highly variable among modern democracies, cannot be adequately explained in particular cases through factors that are highly common to such political systems. The weapons inherent in modern party organization are surely factors of that kind. They either cannot account for party cohesion at all, or they can do so only where other considerations also operate.

(It might be of interest to note, parenthetically, that the two most unambiguous cases of leadership sanctions cited by Stavang involved the language issue and a question of cosmopolitanism—which attests to the special divisiveness of such cultural matters in Norwegian politics.)

[14] Torgersen, *Norske politiske institusjoner*, sec. 7.5.

Commons. It also contains many subsidiary cross-party teams in its specialized committees. On the general parliamentary level, the tendency to seek broad agreement prior to debate has already been mentioned. That tendency held even when Labour had an absolute and cohesive majority (1945-1957) that could have been used simply to railroad decisions through the Storting. It is this search for broad majorities, and its tendency to succeed, that obviates as much overt insistence on party discipline, on "three-line whips," in the Storting as in the Commons. The same practice works even more noticeably in the parliamentary committees. "One of the most important demands [committees make] is that an attempt be made to be fully agreed"—the Norwegian word actually is *enig*, at one— "to overcome disparities in positions. This is a duty that presses both on the chairman and the members in like degree."[15] Moreover, in the party groups and leaderships the recommendations of committee members who have participated in such attempts are normally adopted without serious question. (The Agrarians alone seem exceptional on this score.) Their special expertise, their reliability as members of the party team, and the desirability of cross-party teamwork even in special sub-parliamentary bodies are alike respected; were they not, the cohesiveness of the interlocking teams of party, parliament, and parliamentary committees would be alike imperiled.

Many have suggested that parliamentary seating arrangements closely reflect certain basic aspects of political culture. Their argument is based on France, where deputies sit in a hemisphere divided into segments that distinguish all shades of opinion from left to right and make small movements in one direction or another easy and virtually imperceptible. It is confirmed by England, where MP's sit in two sharply divided sections facing one another like football teams across a line of scrimmage, and one that makes "off-sides" particularly visible. Norway may be added to the list. The Storting is shaped, on a more diminutive scale, much like the French National As-

[15] *Ibid.*, sec. 8.2.

sembly, but with a difference. The members do not sit according
to party membership, their attitude to the reigning cabinet, or
ideological bent. They sit according to constituency, so that
party memberships and political persuasions are highly inter-
mixed. This symbolizes both the teamlike character of the
whole Storting and the essential fact of territorial division—as
well as the ease with which the two can be compounded into
one. Among parliamentarians there is in fact much cross-party
hobnobbing, not least in the restaurant (which is, again not
insignificantly, an ordinary cafeteria much like Norway's many
ordinary cafeterias), and, I was told, many cross-party friendships as strong as friendships within the parties. Thus,
physically and in personal interactions, no less than in its decision-making processes, the Storting manifests just that noncompetitive team spirit we have stressed.

The Norwegian aversion to outdoing others comes out also
in the absence of some of those personal characteristics that
others associate with individualism: sparkle and force in public
speaking, mental daring and trap-setting in argument, satiric
wit, and so on. The fact is that Norwegians silently, but
severely, rebuke any kind of showing off, any scoring off others,
any unnecessary argumentativeness (norms that American
academics, myself included, have been particularly slow to
grasp). They play down success and talents of any kind,
especially their own, and make a kind of cult of modesty. In
human affairs, success is treated more often than not as a
matter of *fortuna* rather than *virtu*, something that happens to
one despite one's just deserts, and is never ostentatiously displayed, except by misfits.[16] Concomitantly, as Rodnick points
out, others, while gently and generously treated, are rarely
praised, lest they get exaggerated opinions of themselves. A Norwegian teacher told Rodnick that "only a few [young people]
can assume the responsibilities of leadership. The pupils respect

---

[16] Note in this connection the remarks of Ferraton on the modest,
popular ways cultivated by trade union leaders (*Syndicalisme Ouvrier
. . . , p. 121).

those who are more articulate than themselves and generally elect them to offices *if they are modest and appear to show that they are not interested in getting these positions.*[17] "I have never," says the humorist Mikes, "seen people who are so fond of disparaging themselves as the Norwegians. This healthy dislike for one another is symptomatic of a deep inner harmony."[18] That is an unintentionally profound observation in an intentionally shallow article.

A society so uncompetitive, so intent upon avoiding invidiousness, must be unusually egalitarian and unusually tolerant of material leveling. Norway, in fact, is both. Riches are confined to a very few wealthy shipowners and manufacturers, and no abject poverty exists, only shabbiness. This results in part from the much subdued achievement orientation we have described, in part from an extortionate system of taxation and redistribution that is, as we have seen, not widely approved in principle in any segment of society nor very vehemently opposed in detail. At any rate, the great network of public services and subventions that makes necessary such taxation is not in question.[19]

Status stratification is as mild as economic stratification.[20] Status respect tends to be accorded "specifically" to functional roles, especially those connected with public objects and authority (including academic roles) rather than "diffusely," and more invidiously, to persons as such. To this generalization there seems, however, to be one signal exception—at least if I read correctly some of the dimmer signals that emanate from Norwegian social life. Those who belong to old officials' families tend to an extent still to think of themselves as a cut above other Norwegians and to stress their breeding as the basis of their superiority.[21] These people seem also still to have a consider-

[17] Rodnick, *The Norwegians*, p. 37 (my italics).

[18] Mikes, "The Largest Little Country in the World," p. 39.

[19] A recently published study on income distribution in Norway is Lee Soltow, *Toward Income Equality in Norway*, (Madison, Wis., 1965).

[20] See, for example, G. Gathorne Hardy, *Norway* (New York, 1925), p. 10.

[21] See also Rodnick, *The Norwegians*, pp. 65-66.

able hold on certain high-prestige institutions with which they were historically associated (parts of the bureaucracy, the University in Oslo, the clergy, and the army), and, so it was alleged to me on several occasions, but without concrete evidence, to conspire subtly against intrusions into their sphere by men of lesser ancestry. They certainly seem to intermarry, to push one another along in their careers, and to stick a great deal to themselves. On occasions one gets the impression that they are still a kind of modified colonial elite that survived the achievement of independence in a country lacking a fully indigenous elite. But they are a small segment of society; their influence has become progressively weaker and more indirect; their status defenses have been widely encroached upon; and, as was pointed out in another connection, they do not get the sort of diffuse deference, especially political deference, that they would like. Hidden beneath its egalitarian surface, Norway may have an Establishment, but that Establishment, in marked contrast to Britain's, has been politically unsuccessful since the inception of parliamentarism and increasingly forced to conceal itself in isolated groups and subtle, often ineffectual machinations. It forms a minor discordant element in a society pervaded by an unusual noninvidious egalitarianism—again, apparently, even in its prisons.[22]

No doubt there are numerous people even outside of the Establishment who are frustrated, more or less consciously, by the egalitarian norms they act out and the small material differentials they accept. Man's appetite for stratification has not been eradicated in Norway, only subdued, and foreigners not infrequently hear gripes and insinuations rarely expressed among Norwegians. That very frustration, however, arises from the fact that the egalitarian norms operate effectively. In Britain, by way of contrast, men are more often exasperated by the steep stratification of society, although in both countries the

[22] Mathiesen, in *The Defense of the Weak* (ms. page 172) remarks that in Norwegian correctional institutions stratification among inmates is less pronounced than, for example, in the United States.

majority do not sullenly act out the operative norms but un-questioningly accept them.

All this gives added meaning to the fact that Norway's national heroes tend to be not only men who preached decency and unity, but, so to speak, noncompetitors, lonely men—ex-plorers and adventurers and, above all, artistic creators—and that her pantheon of Greats is sparsely populated.

3. A third general indicator of Norway's strong sense of community (again related to, but distinguishable from, those already discussed) is what might be called the extreme *organi-zability* of the country. This refers to the existence of an un-rivaled network of voluntary associations that, on the whole, have great density of membership, are highly centralized and cohesive, and play a most important role in all aspects of social life. Norwegians may frequently seek isolation but do not mani-fest any intense individual or familial atomism in a larger sense; on the contrary, they take with unparalleled ease to cooperative associations. To call them individualistic could, in this sense, hardly be farther off the mark. Rather, their organizability further supports the argument that their isolative behavior is a functional response to latent threats to communality.[23]

The proliferation of associations, while at a peak today, was coincident with the early growth of Norwegian democracy. Al-ready in the nineteenth century, especially from 1840 on-ward, large numbers of associations came into being, "providing training in self-government, loyalty, objectivity and cooper-ation."[24] Associations are also intimately connected with Nor-

[23] A comprehensive register of Norwegian associations is now being compiled by Jorolf Moren at The Chr. Michelsen Institute in Bergen. I am grateful to him for letting me look over his rich stock of materials, which could provide a virtually inexhaustible source for researches addi-tional to Moren's own, particularly since Norwegian associations pro-duce an impressive amount of documentation: basic laws, journals, an-nual reports, official histories, and so on.

[24] Lauwerys, *Scandinavian Democracy*, pp. 142-144. For a review of the growth of Norwegian "organizations," see Thomas Chr. Wyller, *Nyordning og motstand* (Oslo, 1958), ch. 7.

wegian economic development, due to the early and continuous growth of cooperatives, unions and craft associations, and employers' and trade organizations.[25] Today their number is astounding. In 1963 the *Oslo Adressekalender* listed 458 organizations with the word "Norwegian" (or equivalent) in the title, and there are in addition a good many national organizations that do not use that term or do not have their headquarters in Oslo.[26] This in a "small" country of three and a half million people, and omitting entirely local organizations which, even in the smaller cities, reach into many hundreds. Even the smallest interests have their formal associations; it is difficult indeed to think of an occupation or purpose that is unorganized. For example, the Federation of Norwegian Whaling Companies has all of six members, but an annually elected council, a secretariat, and an administrative director. There is even a *Norsk Literaturkritikerlag*, a Norwegian Literary Critics Society (the word *lag*, interestingly enough, means "team" as well as "society") which had 61 members in 1963 and an annual conference, executive council, and secretary. Before discovering that organization, as well as a Theater and Music Critics Society (42 members) and Film Critics Society (28 members), I would have thought that of all people, "critics" were least likely to constitute organized occupational associations.

The ubiquitous tendency to act through associations is implanted in the young through an impressive network of youth organizations. A report made by the Ministry of Religion and Education in 1961[27] estimates that in 1957 there were 607,000 memberships in youth organizations, not counting those that are local or informal in character, out of a youth population of 641,000. Even taking into consideration that this estimate was based on the claims of the organizations themselves, and therefore probably somewhat inflated, and that many Norwegian

[25] See Galenson, *Labor in Norway*, p. 78 sqq.

[26] Moren's count of national organizations is at present around 600.

[27] Kirke-og undervisningsdepartmentet, "Om offentlig støtte til ungdomsorganisasjonene" *St. meld.*, nr. 64, 1961.

youths have memberships in several large organizations, that is still a striking figure. The Ministry estimates that altogether about 60 per cent of Norwegian youths belong to one or more large organizations, a figure made credible by the fact that it corresponds closely to the proportion of adults (about two thirds) who are members of associations. The organizations surveyed by the Ministry ran the gamut from athletics, outdoor life, and tourism to politics, occupations, religious work, and social and cultural activities of various kinds.[28]

That a great many of the members of such organizations are not merely nominal members but very active and that the organizations themselves are cooperative and egalitarian, emerges from a survey of 11,000 nineteen-year-olds conducted in 1952. This showed that 4 per cent had been chairmen (we would probably say presidents) of organizations, that 13 per cent had served on their executive councils, and that 22 per cent had served them as officers of one kind or another. These numbers are hardly surprising, considering that there are about 15,000 youth and athletic societies of every kind, large and small, in the country, most of which have executive boards (*styrer*), various committees, and representative councils (*ut-valg*). The Ministry's report estimates that about 75,000 Norwegian youths are at any one time active as officers of associations, that the associations hold about 150,000 meetings per year, and that memberships in them tend to be continuous and stable.[29] Among adults a similar pattern seems to exist: a recent poll of a large national sample found that no fewer than

[28] Some titles of the organizations surveyed are: The Workers' Youth Array (*fylking*), The Norwegian Teetotalism Society's Youth Association, The National Association for Youth Hostels, The Norwegian Gymnasts Society, The Norwegian Christian Student Movement, The Norwegian Bands (*Musikkorps*) Association, Norway's Young Left, The Norwegian Air Club, The Norwegian Gardeners Association's Youth Commission, The Norwegian Girl Scouts Association, The Norwegian Youths' Travel Association, The Socialist Student Association.

[29] *St. meld.*, nr. 64, 1961, p. 3.

58 per cent had served on the governing boards of associations and organizations.[30]

The sheer number of Norwegian organizations is all the more impressive in view of the fact that density and concentration of membership tends to be high. Density in this case refers to the proportion of "eligibles" who are actually members, concentration to lack of competition for the same clientele by different organizations. The total of Norwegian associations is not swelled by numerous organizations that competitively seek similar members for similar ends (such as the competing farmers' organizations in the United States) or by associations, familiar in many developing countries, that are "all head and no body." For example, the trade unions include about 90 per cent of industrial workers[31] (compared to about 50 per cent in Britain, which is usually regarded as highly unionized), and 99 per cent of these are in the LO, the national union federation. The figures for farmers, teachers and *lektors,* and a myriad other occupations (including, apparently, literary and artistic pundits) are similarly impressive.[32]

To the facts that associations are numerous, densely populated, concentrated, and important in basic socialization processes it need only be added that they also play a most significant role in adult social and political life. They not only exist; they matter. Two examples may bring this home with particular emphasis to Americans. In Norway, 90 per cent of all industrial research is done by associative institutes, only 10 per cent by individual firms. This illustrates a general tendency in industry and commerce, already commented upon, to act in such close concert with others that in many cases it is difficult, if not im-

[30] PRIO, "Public Opinion and the Consequences of Disarmament," Program 16, mimeographed, item 32.

[31] Galenson, *Labor in Norway,* p. 33. For the whole "working class," the percentage is between 70 and 75. See Sverre Lysgaard, *Arbeiderues syn på faglige og politiske spørsmål,* Oslo, 1965.

[32] For comments on the tendency of members to be "concentrated" in Norwegian associations, see Torgersen, *Norske politiske institusjoner,* 10.7-10.8.

possible, to tell where a trade association ends and an individual firm begins. The associations seem to run the firms more than the reverse. And this is, if anything, even more true of primary occupations, such as farming, dairying, and fishing. In Norway's countryside, one sees no splendidly individualistic farmers' stands offering produce directly to passers-by; produce is distributed only through tight little cooperative arrangements, encouraged and subvened by the government—a fact which attests to the significance attached to them. Such arrangements make much functional sense in a country where agriculture is exceedingly difficult and arable land itself unusually scarce. But the associative and cooperative patterns of the countryside, compelled by harsh conditions that make mutuality indispensable, are typical also of the rest of society, where such compulsions do not exist.

It is, in fact, the trade union movement that epitomizes the Norwegian tendency toward large, cohesive, functionally salient organizations. Not only is the proportion of unionists, practically all of whom are affiliated to the national labor organization, strikingly high; even more impressive is the fact that the larger bodies of the movement have unusually great authority vis-à-vis the smaller: the general labor federation (LO) vis-à-vis its constituent national unions, the national unions vis-à-vis the local unions affiliated to them. The general federation plays a decisive role, in law and fact, in determining the general policies to be followed by the unions, not least in political matters, and an important role in collective bargaining and industrial disputes. The national unions, in turn, are in all respects labor's principal agencies for industrial action: their affiliated "syndicates" cannot ask for a new collective contract or conclude or denounce one without their authorization, or ask for changes in wages or labor conditions without sending a proposition to the federation, or announce a strike or return to work on their own initiative. In these respects, says Ferraton, the Norwegian union structure is one of the most centralized in the world—although "cohesively organized" or "unitary" might be better terms, since "centralized" may suggest a one-sided flow of power from the top, a lack of responsiveness and accountability of hierarchic power, which certainly is not characteristic of Norwegian unions. In this fashion labor matches the highly collective organization of the employers, and labor relations, in consequence, involve mainly encounters between broadly cohesive and cooperative employers' associations and union federations.[33]

4. Much that has been said in this discussion of the Norwegian sense of community and its indicators is strongly supported by Herbert Hendin's comparative study of suicide in Scandinavia. In the first place, Norway has a strikingly low suicide rate (about one third that of Sweden and Denmark, and lower still in certain social categories). This one would expect on the basis of Durkheim's theory of suicide, which relates its incidence to lack of strong integration into groups ("egoistic suicide") and the disintegration or lack of well-defined, accustomed norms of social behavior ("anomic suicide"). But even more important is Hendin's discovery that Norwegians

[33] For details see Ferraton, *Syndicalisme Ouvrier* . . . , pp. 117-119, and Galenson, *Labor in Norway*, pp. 38-46, 78-96. It might be noted that the powers of national unions mentioned in the text are the minimum that they exercise over locals, but much greater in many cases (Galenson, pp. 39-40). As for the Labour Federation's role in industrial disputes, note the following: wage demands of more than purely local significance need approval by the LO's secretariat (at any rate, if the Federation's support is desired); the Federation is generally represented at mediation proceedings before the conclusion of labor agreements; the Federation conducts negotiations where several national unions are involved and leads and settles any multiunion strike, or any strike that affects the livelihood of workers outside the national union directly concerned; and any union hoping for financial support from the Federation in a strike must first obtain its approval for that strike.

The influence on collective bargaining of the trade union federation and the national employers' federation, as well as the existence, since 1915, of a national labor court (the members of which are nominated by the unions and employers, but appointed by the government), have been held responsible for the unusual industrial peace that has long characterized Norway. See Steve M. Slaby, *The Labor Court in Norway* (Oslo, 1952).

who do commit suicide, or attempt it, do so for reasons strikingly different from Swedes and Danes. Swedes, for example, seem typically to commit "performance" suicides, "based on rigid performance expectations with strong self-hatred for failure." Norwegians, *per contra*, tend to commit a "moral" form of suicide that "stems from aggressive antisocial behavior and strong guilt feelings aroused by such behavior." Indeed, Hendin found in Norway not merely a primacy of moral expectations over achievement values, but a general absence of or revulsion against impulses toward competitive struggles, and a fear of success itself. In his own words:

> Norwegian patients did not have the dreams of competitive struggle that were characteristic of their Swedish counterparts. However, one dream did occur many times with the Norwegian patients, and it involved winning small fortunes in the Norwegian *tipping* or money lottery by chance or sometimes through a "system." . . . The recurrent theme was that either money or material wealth was acquired without effort. . . .
>
> There were, indeed, indications that thoughts associated with too much success aroused anxiety because the envy or hostility of others were fearfully anticipated. . . . As to the anticipated fears, they were not totally irrational, because the general attitude is to envy and belittle anyone who stands out too much or is too successful.
>
> The majority of Norwegian patients were not pressured by a particularly successful or ambitious father (or mother) in the direction of great achievement. The obsessional type of father could be exacting toward his children, but was ritualistic in the expectation of good or obedient behavior rather than outstanding performance.

Subsequently, Hendin argues that Ibsen's *The Master Builder* epitomizes, in fact and symbol, both the conquest of success and the fear that conquest arouses in Norwegians: Solness, conquering his fear of heights, climbs the church steeple—and falls to his death. Hendin confirmed the aptness of that image among his Norwegian patients, who themselves tended to symbolize achievement by heights and the anxieties it aroused by fear of them.[34]

5. The brutal Nazi occupation of Norway, and the bonds forged in the Norwegian resistance, undoubtedly welded the country strongly together. But the transient unity of war only confirmed and reinforced a more permanent sense of community that stands above and qualifies the conflicting interests and persuasions of politics. No society could have faced so seductive and so coercive an invader with so virtually unbroken a front without a powerful preexisting cement that made its many segments one. Confronted by an external enemy, the gentle Norwegians turned savage and implacable fighters, among whom very few "withdrew" or broke ranks. And those that did, the Quislings, were, on the whole, punished with remarkable leniency when the war was over, despite the bloody vengeance meted out to a few of their leaders. After all, they too were Norwegians; one would have to live with them; one could not make permanent outcasts of one's neighbors; one had somehow to make peace with them. Today they are hardly spoken about, and then only with visible embarrassment.

That the Norwegians have a single word, *samfunn*, that means both society and community, and the first syllable of which denotes "being together," "the same," "cooperate," "cohere," "union," "gather into one" (*sammen, samme, samarbeide, henge sammen, samband, samle*) is perhaps not empty of meaning. Nor is it insignificant that Bjørnson's name is linked above all others with that of Norway itself. It was Bjørnson who said, in a eulogy to his fellow poet Wergeland, delivered on May 17, 1864:

If I should express a wish for Norway on this our freedom's birthday, then I know of nothing finer than that all the dreams for its future, which took shape in the vast spirit of

[34] Herbert Hendin, *Suicide and Scandinavia* (New York, 1965), esp. pp. 127-128, 131, 133-134, 146-147.

Wergeland, might come to pass. For he willed a union of workman and king, lawbreaker and lawmaker, the wise man and the fool. And Norway's woods and mines and factories, her plowlands, fisheries and shipping—right down to the beasts and birds, *he included them all.*[35]

[35] The patterns discussed in this chapter—noninstrumental relations, noncompetitiveness, and organizability—not only indicate jointly the existence of strong communal sentiments, but also reinforce one another; each, at any rate, is functional to the others. For example, the tendency to join organizations and the ability to make them work are related to noneconomic relations through the fact that feelings of mutual trust, fostered by the latter, seem essential to operating cooperative structures. (For an extreme case in point, see Pye's treatment of Burma, *Politics, Personality and Nation Building*, ch. 8-18, esp. p. 126). At the same time, a complex and active network of organizations undoubtedly helps engender social trust, among other ways by providing a great many institutional contexts within which conflicts of all sorts may be adjusted and animosities reduced. Readers can easily work out similar relationships between the four remaining combinations of the "indicators."

VI

The Origins of Community:
A Speculation

HAVING established, admittedly in a manner compelled by the lack of "hard" data, that there exists in Norway a profound sentiment of community despite the country's considerable political divisions, we need to ask some questions about that sentiment. What are its sources—that is, how did the Norwegians' communal attitudes originate and what has maintained them in the face of the society's political divisions? Precisely how do these attitudes account for the performance characteristics of the Norwegian political system? Not least, how can one explain the existence of the Norwegian pattern of political division, long maintained in its essential outlines, alongside such very strong overarching attitudes of solidarity? For if the Norwegian pattern of division makes puzzling how her political system can be so cohesive, the communal sentiments we have described make no less puzzling how the system can be so divided. Even a provisional interpretation of Norwegian democracy can come to rest only when these questions have been answered.

1. The origins of the Norwegians' sense of community are, to me at any rate, mysterious in the extreme. Perhaps the mystery defies solution, since conclusive data on a matter so far removed and deeply buried in a society's history are unlikely to be found. But the very nature of the Norwegians' attitudes of solidarity suggests a not too implausible speculation about their foundations.

At every turn, these attitudes, and the behavior that expresses them, remind one of the typical patterns of what might be called "primordial" societies—or, to use a more common but unnecessarily pejorative and question-begging concept, "primitive" societies.[1] Is it not possible, then, that the Norwegian sense of community might result from a quite unusual survival of primordial attitudes and behavior patterns throughout the long process by which the modern Norwegian nation was formed, the successful displacement of these attitudes from typical primordial structures onto the nation itself, and the maintenance of the attitudes even throughout the relatively recent process of thorough "modernization" in political, economic, and many other aspects of social life?[2] Certainly Viking society, although already rather "developed" when we encounter it in the more reliable sources (which, incidentally, are far from absolutely trustworthy),[3] seems to have had many of the

---

[1] The term "primitive" is unnecessarily pejorative because many societies so labeled are far from rude and lacking in what we often think of as the graces of civilization. It begs questions in that a disposition toward social evolutionary theory is virtually inseparable from its use: the term usually implies a rudimentary social structure that constitutes an early episode in a uniform process of social development. Validated theory may come to sustain that view, but does not yet exist; in its absence, it seems preferable to use a more neutral concept for the social structures involved.

[2] An alternative argument would be to posit a gradual development of communal sentiments and behavior patterns out of the modern structures themselves. It is not inconceivable that a sense of identity in, and strong attachment to, modern structures (like nation-states) might result in increasingly affective, considerate and cooperative attitudes among the members of those structures. Abstract institutional loyalties, if shared, could certainly beget concrete personal bonds. (See, for example, Easton, *A Systems Analysis of Political Life*, p. 186). But it seems unlikely that such "secondary" bonds could be as strong and comprehensive as they are in Norway, and there is separate evidence indicating that Norway's communal patterns antedate full modernization—which, after all, is recent. Hence, it seems more probable that in Norway old attitudes animate new structures rather than new structures begetting still newer attitudes.

[3] Much of what we know about ancient Viking society comes not from Scandinavian sources but the works of foreigners, in Latin, Russian, Greek, Persian, Arabic, and Anglo-Saxon. Such foreigners had at most a partial and biased view of the Scandinavians, and saw them at their worst. Their "histories," in addition, are not histories in our sense, but chronicles. The more useful Scandinavian sources, like the Icelandic sagas and the *Heimskringla* of Snorri Sturluson, date to a rather late period (circa 1200), and, however enlightening, are also far from ade-

typical characteristics of primordial societies everywhere, and some of these characteristics are still intimated in contemporary Norwegian attitudes, if not in objective social structure.

Take first the tendency toward unconditional, "noneconomic" social relationships. In most other modern societies such relations are typical mainly of interactions within narrow kinship units or intimate networks of love and friendship. In primordial societies, however, they are far more pervasive, simply because the chief ties that bind men one to another in such societies (that determine fundamentally their conception of a "fellow man" and of social collectivities) are chiefly those of kinship itself—not, as in modern societies, impersonal territorial ties, or equally impersonal bonds arising from joint participation in the performance of a social function, or freely assumed, and therefore contingent, associational or contractual bonds. In primordial societies a large variety of social functions is generally performed by extended families of blood relations; in some, indeed, social ties otherwise defined are virtually nonexistent. Primordial societies also demonstrate how kinship relations and attitudes can be imputed to quite sizable and complex collectivities that are not kindreds literally speaking. Kinship notions can be extended beyond actual blood lineages, first of all, by imaginary kinship beliefs: by the myth of a common and remote ancestry. (An example is the Jewish myth of common descent from the house of Abraham.) Or they can be extended to larger collectivities by symbolism, either by rituals like those of voluntary brotherhood or adoption or in that men,

---

quate histories. As well, Viking civilization, despite shared characteristics, was far from uniform, thus making any general account of it itself a kind of abstraction. For a good discussion of difficulties in early Scandinavian studies, see P. H. Sawyer, *The Age of the Vikings* (London, 1962), pp. 1-47. Among the more pertinent modern treatments in English are: G. Turville-Petre, *The Heroic Age of Scandinavia* (London, 1951); A. Olrik, *Viking Civilization*, prev. cit.; and Mary W. Williams, *Social Scandinavia in the Viking Age* (New York, 1920)—to my knowledge the only general scholarly account in English of both the broad outlines and small details of Viking social life.

while recognizing a lack of genetic connection among their lineages, treat one another as if they were kin, and often solemnize that fact by ceremonies and slogans, such as by addressing one another in kinship terms (father, brother, sister) or by referring to one another collectively as "the children of," "of the house of," "the descendants of" some symbolic father figure. (That notion is also contained in the Jews' belief that they are the "children" of Israel, insofar as Israel is equated with God.)

Viking society was, from this standpoint, a typical primordial society.[4] The kindred appears to have been of enormous significance, for example economically, through the attachment of land not to individuals but large extended families and the responsibility of men for any needy kin, and in the enforcement of norms and laws, especially through the right and duty of kinsmen to avenge wrongs done to any one of them and their collective responsibility for any wrongdoing by a relation. As well, symbolic kinship (e.g., voluntary brotherhood) was common and helped to knit kindreds together. Is it not possible, then, that the contemporary Norwegians stress noneconomic behavior patterns because the ethos of their ancient kinship-centered society somehow survived that society's gradual transformation into a quite different form?

One special aspect of contemporary Norwegian life may lend credence to this admittedly intricate and untestable conjecture. This is that kinship ties seem still today to play an inordinately large role in Norwegian social life—inordinate at least for highly modern societies. There are unusually frequent interactions and strong feelings of mutual responsibility among relatives; personal ease and intimacy, in many cases, is restricted to one's kin; and frequent, festive ritual gatherings of kinsmen take place. In these senses, the most typically modern

[4] The term "primordial" for kinship-centered societies is justified by the fact that kinship relations are, quite literally, relations of the "first order." They exist in all societies; they perform the most indispensable functions of continuous social existence; and they alone can constitute by themselves fully self-contained social collectivities.

of all social ties, "associational" ties, are grafted in Norway upon a primordial base still unusually vital, while, simultaneously, attitudes typical of primordial relationships are reflected in more modern forms of interaction.

Or consider the fact that contemporary Norwegians at some times, even if not frequently, display unusually marked contradictions in their behavior toward one another and toward members of other societies, particularly in competitive activity. This also is highly characteristic of primordial societies, including that of the ancient Norwegians. The contradictions in the internal and external behavior of primordial men have two main sources. One is the very intimacy and functional salience of kinship bonds, which make men who stand outside those bonds seem particularly remote and irrelevant to one's life. The other, and much more important, one is that the norms of primordial society, highly valued (indeed sanctified) and rigidly enforced, are typically treated as attaching, like the material bases of life, to the particular society rather than as abstractly, and therefore universally, moral or prudent. In encountering men who are not fellows, primordial men are in consequence likely to be as hostile, arbitrary, and brutal—in other words, normless—as they are cooperative, gentle, and disciplined among themselves. In relations to other societies, primordial societies tend to be, if they possess the required capacities, warrior societies, adventurers, plunderers, and booty seekers. Among themselves, for the same reason, they tend to make outlawry the most serious of all punishments, for being expelled from an intimate society that recognizes no abstract fellowship of man implies being outside of all constraining and protective norms—being, in fact, dehumanized, for one's humanity, even on the most basic material plane, lies in one's membership in a primordial unit, not in oneself.

Thus the Vikings' violent raids and relatively peaceable domestic society, their reputation for honesty, faithfulness, and minute observance of rules among themselves but for perfidiousness, rapacity, and blood lust toward others (both richly deserved), and their common use of outlawry for serious crimes are characteristically primitive. So also is the fact that Viking slaves (thralls), obtained partly in expeditions abroad, partly from local "aboriginal" populations (like the Lapps), and partly through criminal punishment of Norsemen themselves, were generally treated with the utmost callousness, as nonhuman chattel, although they were sometimes emancipated and indeed adopted into the closer and gentler bonds of society.

Contemporary Norwegians are not, of course, human among themselves and inhuman to others. Their principles of conduct have become "modern," that is, abstract and universal, like those of other societies. Still, in relations with outsiders they tend often toward considerable unease and, at times, lapses from standards of conduct that they would hardly tolerate among themselves. While their frequent unease and occasional animosity toward outsiders is far from peculiar to Norwegians, the combination of these with their "domestic" behavior *is* unusual. Again, is it not possible that in this also they intimate, in much-subdued form and modified by universalistic norms, the spirit of their ancient culture?

Take, third, the high degree of egalitarianism in contemporary Norway. A considerable egalitarianism is also typical of primordial societies—and very much in the nature of "families." Men in such societies are, of course, stratified, but in very special ways. Their status is generally determined by qualities involving kinship criteria, such as age or special position in a lineage or group of associated lineages; or by functions connected with the knowledge and interpretation of the society's sanctified norms (e.g., in the cases of priests, law speakers, judges, councillors); or by special prowess in war and adventure; or by the possession of lands, animals, and slaves acquired in war. More important, however, is the fact that stratification and egalitarianism are in such societies somehow compatible (that is, low in tension), in that role-playing, strictly defined and hierarchically conceived, is not afflicted with invidiousness. Persons differ in age, sex, lineage, function, prowess, possessions, and ceremonial status, but are not regarded as better or worse, dependent or dominant.[5] This, of course, involves attitudes that also are confined to the concrete members of central kinship units rather than being based on abstract principles of human equality; hence, one often finds attached to primordial societies voluntary or conquered "immigrants" who are treated with the utmost invidiousness.

Viking society displayed that stratified and limited egalitarianism in all its aspects, at least among the freemen, the full members of the community. Closely defined hierarchies there were, based on the possession of land, religious functions, schooling in the laws, and prowess in adventure. But kings and farmers were separated by little more than formal and ceremonial distinction, and the backbone of society was not any nobility but a numerous class of yeoman farmers. These were men not attached to or dependent on superior persons but united in a community of equals that found its chief expression in the many local, provincial, and national "things" (*ting*), assemblies that all free men could attend, in which the more prestigious were—shades of modern Norway—required to participate, that made laws in so far as laws were made, and adjudicated serious judicial questions. "We have no chiefs, we are all equals," the Norse invaders are said, by an old French poem, to have proudly replied when the French king sent a mes-

---

[5] An analogy to this pattern is provided by the hierarchic distinctions among cohorts at universities: those between underclassmen and upperclassmen, or among freshmen, sophomores, juniors, and seniors. These distinctions denote rank and often involve privileges, but are certainly not invidious nor widely felt to be inegalitarian.

The kind of noninvidious stratification I have in mind is not confined to primordial systems, although typical of them. It is well-described in Bryce's study of nineteenth century America—and may, in fact, be the utmost that equality can mean in any society. A man, says Bryce of America, may be greater than others in possessions or capacities, "but it is not a reason for bowing down to him, or addressing him in deferential terms, or treating him as if he was porcelain and yourself only earthenware" (James Bryce, *The American Commonwealth*, London, 1889, vol. 2, pp. 606-607).

senger to ask for their chief.[6] Once more, is it altogether unlikely that modern Norwegian egalitarianism is somehow a derivative of that more ancient, more limited equality?[7]

2. But to keep saying "somehow" in arguing for a derivation of modern Norwegian from ancient primordial social patterns is not very satisfactory. The real puzzle is just how that derivation might have occurred. After all, as I have indicated, there is in the broad outlines of ancient Norwegian society nothing peculiarly Norwegian, or even Scandinavian. In the ancient histories of practically all modern societies primordial social structures can be found, and these structures do tend to run to type. What is remarkable about the case of Norway, if my speculations are correct, is the apparent persistence of many primordial attitudes long after the structure of society had undergone profound transformation and the displacement of the old attitudes upon the new structures. In other cases primordial attitudes have been progressively restricted to narrowing circles of kinship and friendship in the process of social transformation, while at the same time the kinship structures have become gradually drained of all but certain minimal social functions. Where this has not been the case, the primordial orientations have been sources of acute friction, even of violence, among tightly cohesive units in larger and at most loosely integrated societies, identification with which has been impeded

[6] Koht and Skard, *The Voice of Norway*, p. 2. See also Eric Graf Oxenstierna, *Die Wikinger* (Stuttgart, 1959), ch. 7.

[7] The generalizations about primordial society in the preceding pages are based, needless to say, on anthropological studies, although, surprisingly enough, anthropologists have not, to my knowledge, developed a general ideal-typical model of what constitutes a "primitive" social structure. The following comparative works are particularly useful if one is interested in the general outlines of primordial societies in their political aspect: Lucy Mair, *Primitive Government* (Harmonsworth, Middlesex, 1962); M. Fortes and E. E. Evans-Pritchard, *African Political Systems* (London, 1940); I. Schapera, *Government and Politics in Tribal Societies* (London, 1956); M. G. Smith, "Segmentary Lineage Systems," *Journal of the Royal Anthropological Institute* 86 (pt. 2), 39 sqq.; and, of course, Sir Henry Maine's classic *Ancient Law* (London, 1861).

by the intensity of the primordial ties themselves. Either structural changes in society have greatly narrowed the realm of the primordial attitudes or the persistence of the attitudes has greatly obstructed or modified structural changes. In most cases, therefore, the concepts "associational" and "communal," often used dichotomously, are in fact antitheses. But Norway suggests that they are not inherently, not necessarily, antithetical—that under certain (unlikely) conditions the primordial attitudes can be preserved in, and come to animate in special directions, modern structures of state and society.

What then preserved communal attitudes during the long process by which the Norwegian nation-state was formed? Any answer to this question must be highly conjectural, but my own guess is that two complementary factors were involved. The first is that the sense, and to an extent the fact, of nationhood evolved very early in Norway, compared to other European, but not Scandinavian, countries. And this historical process occurred through an aggregation of narrower communal identities, but without destroying these identities. A royal realm, both modeled upon pettier local and provincial structures and leaving these structures largely intact, had been fashioned by the end of the ninth century. This realm was never disrupted by feudalism or prolonged struggles for local autonomy against monarchs and priests inspired by dreams of empire such as those that lingered where the Imperium Romanum had existed. On the contrary, the rudimentary sense of nationhood that was developed in the ninth century was reinforced by the constant obtrusion upon Norway of external powers in contradiction to which Norwegians could define, with increasing affect and precision, their larger social identity: first, a general Scandinavian union (dominated by Denmark) in which Norway was but a term; subsequently, after Sweden's breakaway in the sixteenth century, the still more one-sided Danish hegemony; thereafter the less unequal partnership with Sweden. The Norwegian nation thus developed with little tension between the whole and its segments, and with considerable tension between the nation and external societies. The first helped preserve attitudes characteristic of petty communalities, the second facilitated, through the particularly strong bonds of shared animosity, their projection upon the larger society.

Between this pattern and that exhibited by most contemporary post-colonial societies one finds an important similarity and two even more important differences. In the latter cases, a unity of shared animosity has also universally existed. But as often as not, it has proved transient, due to two factors. Rarely does one find in these societies an ancient, spontaneously developed sense of national identity which that unity could reinforce. And the timespan during which self-definition in contrast to outside powers could proceed has been in these societies, compared to Norway, extremely brief. Had they been colonized longer, by powers with a greater capacity for enduring domination, they might today be a good deal more cohesive.

Much more germane to our purpose, however, is a question that lies closer to modern times and our central problem. Even if one can explain how Norway's communal sentiments survived in the gradual forming of the nation out of its primordial units, what has maintained them throughout the thorough modernization of society that began in politics early in the nineteenth century and became more rapid and all-embracing after the turn of the century? The long-preserved Norwegian sense of national identity itself undoubtedly helped in some measure to do so. Yet it hardly sufficed to accommodate ancient definitions of human interaction to the waves of transformation that full modernization implies. Here we must turn from the question of the origins of Norway's communal sentiments to a much more important problem. How have these sentiments been, and how are they still, maintained in the face of forces that nearly everywhere have produced, as if by functional necessity, quite different forms of conduct, and that have had highly divisive effects in Norway itself?

VII

The Maintenance of Community:
Social Interconnections

THE PATTERNS of conduct that display the Norwegians' sense of community are, of course, instilled through all the usual "socialization" processes—in the home, in schools, and in other contexts that shape the attitudes of the young. But to say this is, once again, to raise questions rather than to answer them. We want to know, above all, what there is, in the politically divided and socially very differentiated world of modern Norway, that sustains the Norwegians' emphasis on communal norms in the shaping of attitudes and conduct, and how these norms survive the Norwegians' encounter as adults with their highly divided and differentiated society. While orientations are to some extent self-sustaining from generation to generation, they are unlikely to persist if out of tune with the concrete structures of society, unlikely also to be acted out in adult life if these structures are incongruent with them. Norms, to be successfully implanted and to persist, must be relevant to objective conditions in social life.

What aspects of society, then, provide support for the Norwegians' attitudes of solidarity in the same way that geographic, economic, and cultural differences provide a basis for their political divisions? What, other than the norms themselves, knits the society together? There are, in my view, two answers. The first involves certain links between the most salient and persistent cleavages in Norwegian political life, the second a particular social and political homogeneity that cuts across all divisions and, more than anything else, gives Norwegian social life a unitary form and political life an unchallenged democratic cast.

1. The most persistent and basic divisions in Norway's po-

litical life since 1814 have been, as we have seen, territorial, with particular emphasis on a cleavage between town and country. Since the nineteenth century, when lines of political division were relatively simple, that cleavage has become less clear cut, due to the appearance of new divisions in both town and country and some tendencies toward urban-rural aggregation. But it remains at the heart of Norway's pattern of political competition.

In cold statistics and at first sight the urban-rural cleavage would seem to be acute, a rift rather than mere difference. About half of the Norwegian population lives in rural, about half in urban, areas. The party system, the main channel of competition in modern democracies, reflects the division between these areas to a considerable extent—and, in view of their cultural divergences, perhaps inevitably so. Yet whatever the political differences between them, on the deeper levels of men's consciousness town and country in Norway are far from absolutely divided, indeed are closely linked. Although the more apparent aspects of politics do not reflect the fact, there is between them, both spiritually and concretely, a close interconnection that is unusual in modern societies and that silently and subtly bridges vocal and obvious divisions.

The interconnection of town and country arises mainly from an unusually high valuation by city dwellers of rural life and manners. Cities in Norway, says Mikes, are widely "regarded as painful and unavoidable necessities in modern life; but [the Norwegians'] hearts belong to the sea and the forests."[1] In politics, that fact is expressed, among other things, in the remarkable solicitousness of urban radicals for the welfare of farmers, their tender protection of the countryside against urban contamination, and a certain contempt not so much for industrialists as for all the trappings of industrial life. The great radical Martin Tranmael, who early in the twentieth century tried to capture the national trade union organization in order to direct it on an openly revolutionary course, used to refer to some

[1] Mikes, "The Largest Little Country in the World," p. 39.

radicals contemptuously as "asphalt socialists" and had a reputation for selecting his lieutenants for their teetotalism and love of ski tours. In his idolization of rural life, he shared one of the most pervasive tastes of the more "refined circles" of earlier Norwegian society, who, according to one author, displayed in the nineteenth century an "unnatural infatuation for the peasant's rusticity."[2] That infatuation wavered from time to time as the peasants became politically more militant and challenged urban power, but it never ceased to be a strong theme in intellectual life; indeed, it was at its peak shortly after 1837, the year in which the peasants had first administered a vital defeat to the official estate over the issue of control in local government. Nor was it an infatuation confined to intellectual spheres, to the folklorists and national romantics. In recent decades it has been expressed especially in large material concessions by labor governments to farming interests, who have thereby become, if anything, more comfortable and prosperous than most urbanites, despite the harsh conditions of Norwegian agriculture. It has also been manifested in an unparalleled defense of the countryside against urban despoiling, even at the price of the severe constriction of cities and, consequently, acute housing shortages; in the Labour Party's tendency, despite its socialism, not to take a strong position on religious questions (a point that applies to the trade unions as well); and in the fact that many Labourites are still drawn to typically rural moral positions, including a preference for teetotalism (or at least the close control of liquor sales), which was once indeed regarded by many Norwegian socialists as a vital means for "liberating" the working class.

Labour's adherence to rural values may account for its success in achieving a limited amount of political aggregation, no less than the political attitudes engendered by the character of agriculture in those parts of Norway that the Labour Party has permeated. In contradistinction, the culturally least rural party,

---

[2] Oscar J. Falnes, *National Romanticism in Norway* (Ph.D. thesis, Columbia University, 1933), p. 64.

the *Høyre*, has never, as we have seen, managed to aggregate significantly across territorial lines. But even most Rightists participate in a set of nonpolitical behavior patterns that best display the general Norwegian valuation of the countryside: the preservation of rural ways not only in people's "hearts" but in city life itself.

That people live in cities does not necessarily make them urbanites. Cities can be simply large aggregates of people who maintain, as much as possible, rural ways. That is in fact to a large extent the case in Norway. Even in the largest Norwegian cities, the countryside is extremely accessible, not only because it is relatively easy to reach but because it is open when one has got to it. And the country is in fact eagerly sought out; at every opportunity—on weekends and holidays, for example— a kind of mass exodus from the cities occurs. Extraordinary numbers of people own or rent summer huts. In the cities, moreover, most people cultivate to a remarkable extent, at least by American standards, the rural graces: by private gardening and fruit growing, large amounts of and great care for public greenery, and the preservation of alleys and walking paths. The favored recreations of Norwegian city dwellers, as we saw, are also essentially rural (as well as noncompetitive); in unparalleled proportions they walk, hike, climb, ski, camp, sail, row, fish, hunt, and, above all, go gathering the countless berries that redeem the barrenness of their land.

These values and behavior patterns bridging town and country have a special foundation. Most city dwellers—three quarters of Oslo's population—are only one to three generations removed from the land and still maintain more or less close ties with kin in rural areas. Until very recently rural families tended to be large and to export most of their offspring to the towns. At the same time, however, they rarely abandoned the family farms altogether for the opportunities of urban life. Normally, in modern as in ancient times, the eldest son has stayed on to maintain the family seat, paying off the siblings' share of his inheritance, while these, in turn, continued to regard the farmstead as their true home and to have certain normative claims upon it. Thus, during World War II about half of Oslo's population were able to supplement their meager rations with supplies from kinsmen on the farms. Even today it is normal for many townspeople to obtain large quantities of meat and vegetables from relatives on the farms and thus to supplement by sizable perquisites their wages and salaries. The common kinship ties between town and country are even protected by one aspect of Norwegian law, the *odelsrett*, which assures kinsmen first preference in the sale of lands.

American and British urbanites may often go to the country for fresh air, sport, or a change of pace; Norwegian townsmen as often go there to be at home, in spirit and in fact. The coddling of farmers by the Labour Party has aided the maintenance of that easy interconnection by helping farmers so to keep pace with, even to outstrip, the urban standard of living (the possession of cars, television sets, etc.) that materially invidious urban-rural contrasts hardly arise. And that coddling becomes more understandable when one bears in mind that many Norwegian trade union and Labour Party leaders have been, and still are, themselves the sons of farmers. The first Labour government of 1928 was, in fact, headed by a farmer, the government of 1935 by a cottager's son, Nygaardsvold, whose memoirs teem with sentimental rural reminiscences.

In one sense there is in Norway an even more concrete interconnection of town and country. In many cases no sharp line between industrial work and farming exists because many workers are also part-time farmers on a small scale, while many farmers engage part-time in road building, construction, or factory work.[3] In that way sizable numbers of smallholders have been able to maintain their possessions, while industry has been supplied with much manpower, *in the countryside* rather than at its expense. To tap that manpower, a large amount of scattered, small-scale rural industry has been developed in Norway, a fact that further interconnects town and country by bringing

[3] Lauwerys, *Scandinavian Democracy*, p. 114.

urban occupations to the land while rural ways are adhered to in the cities.

Norway's farmer-workers and worker-farmers display "overlapping" as it is usually conceived by theorists of social integration. But such literal overlaps in politically divisive roles are not usual in Norway, and even more abnormal in other modern societies. In the main, the interconnections of Norwegian society do not consist of multiple roles and memberships, nor does the cohesion of Norwegian politics and society involve some purely mechanical balance resulting therefrom. The interconnections I have described involve two things that make less abstractly for cohesion and, strangely, do not figure in theories of social integration: let us call one overlapping (but not, of course, identity) in general lifeways rather than in concrete roles; the other, overlapping identifications not in individual persons but in close-knit groups of men whose affinities arise from particularistic, diffuse and affective ties, despite great differences in their functional roles. Specific roles seem to entail in Norway differences in interests, purposes, and group identifications that are great enough to furnish a basis for persistent political divisions. But the far from mechanical ties of lifeways and personal affinity prevent the divisions from being so deep and absolute that they will break down social unity and political cohesion in its larger aspects. That is why these ties are best denoted by the term "interconnection." They do not "balance" in tenuous equilibrium different and divided men, but bind them —"connect" them—to one another in small collectivities and larger ones based on the small.

That such ties can act as strong bonds between political opponents, perhaps stronger even than the bonds of political agreement and cooperation, is brought out in a striking passage in de Tocqueville's *Recollections*. "Although the French nobility have ceased to be a class," he writes,

> they have yet remained a sort of freemasonry, of which all the members continue to recognize one another through

certain invisible signs, whatever may be the opinions that make them strangers to one another, or even adversaries. This bond which still exists between its members is so close that I have found myself a hundred times more at ease in dealing with aristocrats who differed from me entirely in their interests and opinions than with bourgeois whose interests and ideas were analogous to mine. With the former I was in disagreement, but I knew what language I had to speak.[4]

If this can be true of a segment of society, might it not in some cases be true also of society as a whole?

In the notion of interconnection there may well be the germ of a theory of social integration more powerful and less question-begging than in the ideas of balance and equilibrium. At the very least this notion contains an alternative to equilibrium theory that seems particularly suitable to explaining the curious coexistence of clear-cut division and great cohesion in society. The notion of cross-cutting memberships, on the other hand, seems more suitable to explaining the absence of clear-cut divisions in the first place—as in the case of those special Norwegian urban and rural segments that are in fact aggregated in the Labour Party.

One other point relevant to general social theory is suggested by this discussion: that it is necessary to give the widely used concept "urbanization" (and other such concepts that pretend to describe social life) more than a lifeless statistical content. Urbanization is a concept that makes sense only when the meaning of life in dense or scattered population aggregates is understood. The very fact of living in "cities" may, of course, entail inevitable consequences, whatever a city might mean to its inhabitants, but the specific nature of these consequences, for city folk and general society alike, depends less on how large cities are than on what they are. In this connection recall the fact that in Norway rapid industrialization had far less

---

[4] *The Recollections of Alexis de Tocqueville* (New York, 1959), p. 242.

fateful consequences than it appears to have had elsewhere, at any rate after the first trials of personal transplantation had passed over. Torgersen has attributed this to mildness toward the workers of Norwegian governments and industrialists.[5] He is probably right, but another factor might have been involved as well: that the shift to industrial employment simply did not entail in Norway so sharp a redefinition of accustomed lifeways or so absolute a separation from older structures and familiar surroundings as in many other countries. To be sure, the influx of peasants themselves into the cities helped to give Norwegian urban life its strongly rural cast—thus, incidentally, raising the strange possibility that urbanization as a way of life may have diminished in Norway with the growth of cities as physical entities. But that would hardly have been the case had there not existed some marked interconnection of town and country, and some concrete basis for its continuation, in the first place. Large modern cities have grown everywhere through the influx of rural men, but they have not, solely because of that, become less urban in their characteristic lifeways. In this connection, the infatuation of the romantic intellectuals with the undefiled rural Norway and the related fact that the cities were long considered, even by many city dwellers themselves, to be alien enclaves in Norway, centers of foreign ways and domination, take on particular significance.[6]

2. To the interconnection of town and country should be added another that bridges lines of economic cleavage within the territorial divisions. Norwegian society is not only mildly stratified in economic (and other) terms, but the Norwegian classes interact on certain levels to an unusual extent. Above all is this

---

[5] See above, pp. 22-23.

[6] Even in the nineteenth century, however, town and country in Norway were to an extent interconnected. The *embedsmenn* were bearers of urban culture in the countryside; at the same time, however, many of them, stationed for very long periods, even life, in relatively isolated areas became imbued with rural values and ties. Hence, even while Norwegian politics was dominated by the struggle between peasants and officials mechanisms that interconnected them were in operation.

true among the young. The Norwegian school system is consciously based on the principle that elementary education should be, as far as possible, uniform for the whole nation, that it should bring together children from all sections of the community, and that secondary and higher education should be available to all qualified youths, as well as involving a genuine continuation of instruction from the elementary grades.[7] These principles are largely realized. Norwegian children of all conditions do mingle to an unusual extent in schools, and through these in sports and youth associations—in other words, outside the classroom as well as in it. One also gets the impression that such interactions are sometimes continued in adult organizations cutting across class lines (although Norwegian sociologists still need to study systematically the extent to which organizational life takes place within or across class limits). Just as important, there are in Norway relatively few striking differences in the general "lifeways" of the economic classes. While differences in income, abilities, and tastes inevitably keep Norwegian life from being uniform, it would not be possible to write about Norway the sort of book that T. H. Pear has written about the English class system, sharply contrasting class patterns in regard to such minutiae of life as speaking, etiquette, clothes, eating, drinking, and leisure pursuits.[8]

Since World War II there have also been developed in Norway a series of formally organized bodies especially designed to link men across class lines. These involve a kind of voluntary industrial codetermination and associate the principal industrial classes, workers and employers. In regard to workers' participation in management, Norway has achieved on a broad scale and without governmental compulsion arrangements that in most other countries have either required public legislation or been confined to exceptional enterprises. After the war the Labor Federation and the Norwegian Employers' Federation (N.A.F.) agreed on the desirability of setting up joint produc-

[7] Castberg, *The Norwegian Way of Life*, pp. 27-29.
[8] T. H. Pear, *English Social Differences* (London, 1955).

tion committees (*produksjonsutvalg*), with the support of, but without pressure from, the Labour Party (as well as other parties)—without such pressure, because, as Ferraton points out, Norwegians are convinced that "to impose an institution of cooperation is a psychological absurdity."[9] The agreement is intended to be compulsory in businesses employing over fifty persons, optional in others. It provides for tripartite committees of management, white collar staffs, and workers, with each committee headed by a chairman and secretary, elected annually and alternately by management and personnel. The committees do not take votes but try to arrive, in the manner of "communities," at agreed recommendations to management. In relation to the latter, they serve as organs solely of consultation and information, although through their ability to publicize their recommendations (including their power to call special information meetings) and through their ability to mobilize the union organization they can, if they wish, bring pressure to bear. Management is required to furnish the committees vital information concerning the state of the business, and the committees may take up both technical matters (production and marketing) and "social" matters: health, safety, and welfare.

Despite the lack of any governmental compulsion, these arrangements have worked at least as well as they do anywhere, although, as is usual in codetermination, not as well as was hoped. The most favorable estimates are that 87 per cent of businesses employing over fifty persons have in fact organized *produksjonsutvalg* and that in three quarters of such businesses they actually "function"; that about 72 per cent of the committees meet at least four times a year, although only 11 per cent meet monthly, the frequency stipulated in the original agreement. The committees seem to work to better effect, and more frequently, in large than in small businesses, which is as it should be, since the larger firms tend to have the greater production and marketing problems and less close informal con-

---

[9] Ferraton, *Syndicalisme Ouvrier . . .* , p. 231.

tacts among their various staffs.[10] But from our standpoint, the very existence of the committees, and their undoubtedly wide dispersion throughout industrial Norway, matters more than their restricted practical significance, since we are concerned here with interconnections among social segments, not the analysis of industrial decision-making processes. It should perhaps particularly be stressed that the committees do "interconnect" members of social segments rather than produce "overlaps" among them, since their members directly represent the segments on the committees. The codetermination committees *link* representatives of divided groups in regular contact, rather than *joining* them as individuals. Only those voluntary associations that cut sharply across class lines clearly do the latter.

[10] For details on the joint production committees, see *ibid.*, pp. 230-239. A good treatment in Norwegian is by Arnold Havelin and Sverre Lysgaard, "Bruken av produksjonsutvalg i norske bedrifter," *Tidsskrift for samfunnsforskning*, 1964 (1), pp. 30-55. Havelin and Lysgaard put their figures rather lower than Ferraton—they find that 75 per cent of firms employing more than 50 men have joint committees and 60 per cent active committees, with only 3 per cent having more than ten meetings per year. They agree, however, that size of firm and effectiveness of the committees are closely related, and give several interesting additional reasons for that relationship.

VIII

The Maintenance of Community:
Social Authority Patterns— Forms

1. The interlinking of divided men through their values, through affinities in their modes of life, through diffuse personal bonds and organizations deliberately designed to associate them, explains social cohesion less mechanically and less dubiously than their mere intersection at certain points of the differentiation of society. One has a still more powerful basis for cohesion where considerable interconnections and intersections both exist. But of all explanations of social and political cohesion, the most obvious and direct lies in the notion of social homogeneity: in the demonstration that the members of a society are, in ways especially relevant to one kind of cohesion or another, broadly similar, if not identical, so that a need for special mechanisms to integrate them does not arise in the first place.

Unfortunately, that explanation rarely works, least of all in highly "modern" societies. Obviously no society is ever thoroughly homogeneous. Social life invariably entails differences in sex, age, territorial location, status, abilities, attainments, possessions, knowledge, kinship positions, networks of friendship, power, influence and authority, and functional roles; hence to say that a society is homogeneous can never mean more than that it is homogeneous in certain ways. In "modern" societies these ways are bound to be especially circumscribed, due to the complexities of functional differentiation and specialization that modernity in any form entails; due also to the generally large scale of such societies; and due to the ubiquity in them of mixtures of diffuse and specific, particularistic and universalistic relationships, of urban and rural aggregates, and of complex economic stratification. Any of these objective divisions of society, whether universal to the human condition or limited to social types, can be, and have been, sources of political division, hence also, potentially, of political instability. Moreover, what may appear to be a homogeneity at first sight often on closer examination dissolves into heterogeneity. Practically all Frenchmen or Spaniards may be, in a certain sense, Roman Catholics, but the division between clerical and anticlerical Catholics, between nominal and active members of the church, may be far greater and far more explosive than sectarian differences. In addition to that, it is often difficult to see how certain social homogeneities produce the specific political effects attributed to them in the face of all the heterogeneities with which they coexist—why, for example, a certain ethnic similarity in a population should not merely remove one of a myriad possible sources of conflict in politics but lead to a general lack of conflict. Not least, when one has probed far enough into societies, it sometimes turns out that the homogeneities supposedly explaining their cohesion consist of the very patterns that need to be explained. Thus, the much reiterated argument that Britain has stable parliamentary rule because Britons are homogeneous is hardly convincing if their homogeneity consists, as I believe it does, mainly of a nearly universal commitment to a parliamentary system in the British style.

Norway illustrates well these arguments against facile uses of the notion of homogeneity in explaining social cohesion. Norway, being modern, is a highly differentiated society, and some of her social segments, modern and premodern, find close expression in political divisions, as we have seen. Some of her supposed homogeneities, moreover, are more apparent than real. There is, for instance, no use saying portentously that 97 per cent of all Norwegians are Lutherans, if they are Lutherans in such very different, indeed antagonistic ways. Nor is it readily apparent how some Norwegian homogeneities produce political cohesion. To cite an example of which many Norwegian writers themselves make much: Norway may not con-

tain any significant ethnic minority groups, except for the
Lapps, nor any greatly different racial stocks (although some
Norwegian writings in considerable vogue suggest otherwise);
but how does one go from these facts, if facts they are, to political cohesion, when East and West, center and periphery,
city and country, fundamentalists and dissenters, patricians and
plebes, *riksmål* devotees and *nynorsk* fanatics, are in conflict?
And if Norwegian homogeneity consists mainly of those widely
shared patterns of conduct that manifest sentiments of community, in politics and other aspects of social life, we cannot
without circularity attribute these sentiments to homogeneity,
that is, to themselves.

However, these difficulties dissolve if one can show that a
social homogeneity is not illusory, does not consist of the very
patterns it supposedly causes or maintains, and is demonstrably
related to what it is intended to explain. Norwegian society is
homogeneous in at least one respect that fulfills these requirements: there exists in Norway a remarkable similarity in patterns of authority, that is to say, in the ways that superordination and subordination are organized and exercised in both
governmental and nongovernmental contexts. This homogeneity in authority relations—perhaps the most uniform of all
Norwegian lifeways—is crucially important to us for two
reasons. The first, which is the more germane at this point, is
that through their very similarity throughout society (regardless of their actual nature) authority relations provide a concrete basis for sentiments of national identity and community
and, what is more, do so in realms of experience more manifestly related to men's behavior in national politics than any
others: in areas of microcosmic politics that everywhere
powerfully shape men's general political orientations, including
their orientations toward national government. The second,
which will become apparent as the patterns are described, is
that through their actual nature Norwegian authority relations
can directly account for the fact that communal sentiments are
reflected specifically in stable democracy, rather than some

other kind of stable government. Norwegian authority patterns are in that sense keys to understanding both the sources and the political consequences of Norway's communal sentiments.

2. Describing a society's authority patterns requires attention both to their organizational and procedural forms and to the manner, or style, in which authority is actually exercised. Organizational and procedural forms are explicit prescriptions defining hierarchical relations in social collectivities and are generally found in constitutions, organization charts, codifications of customary procedures, and other kinds of blueprints for the exercise of authority. They prescribe the location of authority in special roles and bodies, the functional spheres, or competences, of the roles and bodies, the processes to be followed in recruitment to roles of authority and in authoritative decision making, and lines of accountability to higher or lower structures. "Style of authority," on the other hand, refers to operative norms of authority, that is, the way in which authority is actually wielded, regardless of formal prescriptions, particularly the way in which authority is regarded by those wielding it and those over whom it is wielded. If a culture is legalistic, not because of the very lack of customary ways of wielding authority (i.e., not because of fear of authority restrained neither by habit nor by law) but because legal precision is itself one of its customary ways of doing things, forms and norms of authority will of course tend to be largely identical. But even in such cases they must to some extent be treated separately. However detailed, forms never prescribe everything and touch rarely, if ever, on the more personal and indefinable aspects of authority relations that everywhere infuse organizational anatomies with life. Nor can formal prescriptions always be fully acted out. Not least, every society, legalistic or not, contains authority relations that are not, and cannot be, defined in organizational and procedural blueprints simply because they do not occur in formal organizations: authority relations in families, for example, or among teachers

and pupils in schools, or among members of informal peer groups—all contexts that most social scientists consider basic in forming orientations and attitudes of every kind. In Norway, as we shall see, forms and norms of authority are in fact far from antithetical, adherence to closely defined forms being an important feature of the style of authority and certain aspects of that style being closely reflected in organizational and procedural forms; but they are not so closely similar that a description of the one is also a sufficient description of the other.

3. Perhaps the most important point to make about the forms of authority in Norway is that, in most respects and in the most diverse segments of society, they are closely modeled upon the country's local government structures, which have been gradually developing toward their present form since 1837, when the "mother law" pertaining to them was enacted.[1] There is, in consequence, a remarkable congruence of structure among governmental and nongovernmental organizations, perhaps due to the conscious emulation of local government bodies in other contexts, perhaps because of an indirect connection between local government and other organizations, namely that local government embodies structural norms which operate forcibly throughout the whole of Norwegian social life. Since local government organization in its broad outlines antedates the great majority of Norwegian voluntary associations, as well as the formation of political parties and of the parliamentary system of national government, the emulation hypothesis is at least plausible, all the more so since many Norwegian organizations not only adhere closely to the hierarchic structure of local government bodies but, to some extent at least, even their nomenclature. However, such emulation would hardly have occurred widely in the first place had local government not embodied generally shared norms regarding the proper structure of authority relations.

[1] The main local government acts are those of 1837, 1921, 1938, and 1954. Those of the twentieth century have adhered closely in essential respects to the law of 1837.

Norwegian local government[2] operates on two levels, the commune and the county (*fylke*). Of these, the commune, the smaller unit, is by far the most important, since it performs the great majority of local government functions and is not in any meaningful sense subsidiary to the larger county. The communes perform most of the more familiar functions of local governments in democracies (education—mainly on the primary level—road construction and maintenance, preventive health services, fire protection, land use and building control, refuse collection, certain welfare functions, etc.); they also tend to provide many facilities that elsewhere are completely private (such as cinemas and, in a few cases, restaurants), they own public utilities (e.g., hydroelectric plants and harbor installations), and they act as the national government's agencies for administering welfare services and assessing and collecting income taxes—the last a particularly cherished function that symbolizes their importance in the whole conduct of government and their crucial role as buffers between citizens and national authority. There were, as of 1960, 732 communes in the country, 62 urban (*bykommuner*) and 670 rural (*herreds-* or *landskommuner*).

To some extent, the organization of the communes differs

[2] A good summary in English of Norwegian local government, including its evolution, is Sherman M. Wyman's *Municipal Government in Norway and the Norwegian Municipal Law of 1954* (Oslo, 1963). See also Storing, *Norwegian Democracy*, pp. 163-179, and Valen and Katz, *Political Parties in Norway*, pp. 17-19. Norwegian social scientists have paid little attention to local government, although K. M. Nordanger and Arnljot Engh, *Kommunal kunnskap* (Oslo, 1960), provides a useful general treatment of the subject. The sparseness of social-scientific work on the subject may be due to the fact that Norway is formally a "unitary" state, the local governments possessing only powers granted them by national legislation. But the unitary nature of Norway's constitution does not in itself make local government unimportant. In addition to their role as organizational models, Norwegian local governments in fact perform many vital governmental services—more than their counterparts in many supposedly federal systems—possess a considerable amount of *de facto* autonomy and, to anticipate the text, serve as the most important training and recruiting grounds for national politicians. Hence, the subject deserves much more attention than it has so far been given.

from place to place, depending on size and, almost the same thing, whether they are urban or rural. The differences, however, are minor and concern mainly the use of professional paid staffs; in regard to lines of hierarchy and accountability there are practically no differences.

At the head of each commune there is a council (*styre*), which is the final policy-making body. Its membership, ranging from 13 in the smallest to 85 in the largest commune, is elected through a system similar to that used in national parliamentary elections; its members serve for the same term as parliamentarians (four years); and the national parties contest the local elections much as they do the parliamentary elections, there being few independents or purely local parties of the sort common in American local elections. The local *styrer* in fact are in most respects miniature parliaments (in a few cases, indeed, nearly the size of the Storting) and imitate many of the procedures of the national legislature, including informal ones, such as the frequent use of party caucuses before council meetings to concert party positions on policy issues. The main differences are that, having less to decide, they meet less frequently than the Storting (from five to eight times per year) and, having more routine business to transact, they delegate more of their work, in fact most functions other than basic policy making and financial allocation. In general, however, any politician accustomed to politics on the commune level will find national parliamentary politics largely familiar, requiring the learning of few new skills and modes of conduct.

The councils each elect an executive board (*formannskap*) consisting of one quarter of the council membership and generally reflecting proportionally the party membership of the council. The board functions more continuously than the council and constitutes in many respects the equivalent on the local level of the national cabinet. Its main functions, at any rate, read very much like a list of those that the national cabinet performs. The executive board prepares policy proposals, submits draft budgets to the councils, approves appropriations, and supervises and coordinates the commune's administration, with individual members generally assuming special responsibility for particular municipal activities, particularly in those smaller communes that do not employ senior professional staffs.[3] One member of the board is elected to be mayor (*ordfører*) and serves as a rough approximation of the national prime minister—rough approximation in that his powers are rather more nominal than those of the chief minister, although the latter's formal and actual powers are also quite restricted in comparison with those of the chief ministers of the more familiar parliamentary systems. The mayor, in effect, serves principally as the chairman of board and council meetings and as the legal and ceremonial head of the commune, having no special powers save those he can make for himself, which, in fact, are sometimes considerable, but rarely approach those of American mayors.

Much of the business of the commune, however, is not fully and effectively transacted within this strictly political hierarchy. Two other sets of people also play a vital role. In the first place, there are, in the larger communes at any rate, one or more "city managers" (*rådmenn*) who, like the *ekspedisjonssjefer* of the ministerial departments, perform vital supervisory functions as well as indirect, or not so indirect, policy-making roles; as in the case of the national civil servants, their importance has increased with the growth of active, technical government. But perhaps most important of all are the standing and special committees of the commune, of which there are in every case, but especially in the larger units, an enormous number. National laws governing local activities require the establishment of no less than thirty such committees to supervise various municipal services. Given the fact that some rural communes comprise as few as a thousand people that is certainly an impressive number of specialized bodies; moreover, in the larger communes, and indeed some of the smaller also, many more committees than are mandatory are added, so that the number of local com-

[3] See Storing, p. 175.

mittees may run into the scores or even hundreds in certain cases. Like the special committees of the Storting, those of the communes are usually accorded a kind of functional deference by the boards and councils, and like those of parliament, they also tend to develop a certain team spirit, to seek agreements as near unanimity as possible across lines of party and interest; thus local committees cultivate many of the behavior patterns characteristic of national government and are accorded much the same role. They differ from the Storting's committees, however, in one important respect: on the local level much use is made not only of local councillors, board members, and functionaries but, by cooptation, of specially interested or qualified citizens who are not regular members of the communal authority. The communes' committees thus provide opportunities for wide participation in public affairs unrivaled in most other democracies—a kind of direct democracy within small, functionally circumscribed, expert local bodies. These bodies often "interconnect" men of diverse conditions and political persuasions in organized and cohesive networks of interaction and thus, like some voluntary associations and the bodies of industrial codetermination, form bridges across local cleavages. They also more often than not give particular weight in local decisions to men having special interests (that is, vested interests) in those decisions, and therefore illustrate also the tendency of Norwegians to trust men not to exploit special opportunities for one-sided advantage. In addition, needless to say, they provide special opportunities for ordinary councillors and public functionaries to exercise special influence in local affairs.

Since the *fylker* are less important bodies than the communes, they need not be described in great detail, but their basic characteristics should be briefly indicated. There are altogether 20 counties, 18 rural and 2 urban (the special city-county jurisdictions of the two largest cities, Oslo and Bergen). Each is headed by a governor (*fylkesmann*), appointed by the king in council and acting as the representative of the national government in local administration—a highly prestigious position. The main policy-making body is the *fylkesting*, which, until 1964, consisted of the mayors of the county's communes, but is now elected by the local communal councils. The *ting* meets seldom, delegating its more continuous functions to a small representative council (*fylkesutvalg*); this body makes decisions when quick action is required, elects a chairman and acts as an advisory council to the governor, who tends to be mainly an administrative functionary. The county has charge particularly of those services over which the national government wishes to exercise special control for purposes of national standardization (above all, education) and large-scale projects (forestry, hospitals, roads, etc.) on which communes must cooperate, or wish to, for the sake of using efficiently their financial resources and spreading evenly their tax burdens. The county governors, as representatives of the national executive, must also review local legislation and may veto it, but this is strictly a legal matter, ensuring that communal legislation is not *ultra vires* or in conflict with existing laws. Although analogies between the Norwegian *fylkesmann* and the French prefect have sometimes been drawn and are superficially plausible, the differences between the two are much greater than the similarities, since the Norwegian counties are little more than special functional conveniences and their governing bodies essentially frameworks within which the national government and the equally vital local communes are interlinked.

4. That there are large resemblances between local and national government is not unusual or surprising. Such resemblances are common, although, as we shall see later, they are rather more important in Norway than in many other countries because of the way politicians are typically recruited to national politics. What is less common and more surprising is the very close resemblance between local government organization and the structure of nongovernmental bodies, especially the larger and more politically significant ones, and that the

latter in many cases resemble local government organization even more than does national government. To make this point, it might be useful first to construct a kind of abstract model of typical Norwegian organizational structure, of which local government units are the prime examples, then to illustrate how that model is adhered to in other organizations, especially the political parties and the larger, more active, and more politically important voluntary associations.

Norwegian organizational structure typically has four main characteristics. Each of these will seem familiar in many other societies but, in certain respects to be discussed anon, they are uncommon, even if not absolutely peculiar to Norway.

First of all, Norwegian organizations almost invariably consist of a hierarchy of representative collegial bodies. Normally they have three strata of authority (although in some cases there may be only two because of the organization's size). The first layer is a large, infrequently convened representative council (usually *representantskap, landsmøte, årsmøte*) elected democratically by the organization's members and serving, like the communes' *styre*, as the organization's final policy-making authority. The representative council in turn elects a smaller but still sizable executive board (usually *sentralstyre* or *arbeidsutvalg*) that serves more continuously, initiates policy proposals, makes decisions in emergencies or when quick action is required for other reasons, and exercises broad supervision over the implementation of policies. The executive board, in turn, gives rise to an individual chairman (*formann*), or a very small "directorate" (*formannskap*), or both, either elected by itself or in the representative council and working closely with paid functionaries headed by a principal secretary.

Within this hierarchy authority flows upward in that the higher and smaller bodies function more frequently, more widely, and more continuously than the lower and smaller, have special influence in the latter, and always have some autonomy in decision making. On the other hand, accountability is always carefully exacted of the more active bodies by the

less active ones, and the competence and modes of accountability of the hierarchical levels are closely defined by explicit
rules. Elections always serve as the ultimate constraint on the
higher bodies and usually are frequently conducted. The lower
and more directly representative bodies tend also to constrain
authority within the organizations by retaining, and actually
exercising, the functions of defining broad policy and determining financial allocation; rarely, if ever, are they merely rallies
that endow the leaders with a kind of ritualistic legitimacy. And
the leaders are, in various closely defined and routinized ways,
"answerable" before the larger bodies, that is to say, compelled
regularly to present reports which are genuinely debated and
must be defended. In these senses, Norwegian organizations are typically hierarchical and constitutionally detailed
democracies.

A third major characteristic of Norwegian organizations is
their extreme collegiality—that is to say, the use of bodies of
equals rather than of individuals to discharge important, and
often even minor, decision-making and supervisory functions
and, concomitantly, the restriction of personal authority at
every level, not least at the top. In this connection it should be
noted particularly that neither the *formenn* nor the secretaries
really "run" Norwegian organizations. The secretary, in form,
is always a functionary, not a leader. The *formann's* position
is rather more complicated but equally restricted. He serves,
first and foremost, as a figurehead, a person who "represents"
the organization, much as the king represents the nation in the
sense of embodying it. He also acts as the chairman of the more
important collegial bodies, his role as chairman being primarily
that of a functionary, spokesman, and mediator, not that of a
specially empowered leader; that is to say, he convenes meetings, conducts discussions, sees to it, as far as possible, that discussions produce decisions, and speaks for the bodies he chairs
to those that exact accountability from them; but the organizations' *formannskap* or *arbeidsutvalg* are their major "efficient"
institutions ("efficient" in Bagehot's sense of the term), in no

sense a kind of democratic gloss on the fundamental fact of individual leadership.

The collegiality of Norwegian organizations emerges even more clearly in a fourth typical formal characteristic: the existence of a highly developed horizontal functional (and/or local) pluralism of collegial bodies alongside the vertical (i.e., hierarchical) collegial structure that has been sketched. This means simply that the typical Norwegian organization is differentiated into many smaller working groups charged with special functions; in these ordinary members, and at times outsiders, can play a highly participant role. Thus the structure of individual organizations typically reproduces on the microcosmic level the pluralism of the whole society. Members of executive boards who take a special interest in, and responsibility for, special aspects of an organization's tasks, as well as secretarial functionaries who do so, typically work through the organization's specialized committees (or, what is much the same, specialized affiliated organizations) and thus function within special collegial contexts no less than the organizations' chairmen, and in a rather similar manner. In large national organizations local decentralization generally coexists with special functional committees or affiliated organizations, adding one kind of pluralism to another.

The structure of local government will be readily recognizable in this model, as will, to a somewhat lesser extent, that of the national government.[4] To see how nongovernmental organizations also reflect the model, let us begin with the politically

[4] National government deviates somewhat from type in that the Storting meets much more regularly, and exercises more its formal powers, than the typical organizational representative council; and in that the chief minister and his "executive board" are not directly elected by the Storting but chosen in the usual manner of parliamentary regimes. An additional deviation is the division of the Storting into two bodies, the *Odelsting* and *Lagting*, which, in certain special ways, work separately, in others as a unitary legislature. Nevertheless, the general outline of the organizational model I have sketched applies unmistakably to national government. For a detailed description in English of national governmental structure see Storing, *Norwegian Democracy*, chs. 3, 5, 6.

most important of them, the parties, then proceed to organizations more remote from—that is, less directly and continuously involved in—national and local politics.

5. A point to note immediately about the parties' organizations is that formal differences among them are quite minor; in formal structure the main parties, despite the cleavages and divergences that divide them, are highly homogeneous. In fact, and for our argument not insignificantly, formal structure, defined in very detailed prescriptive blueprints, is the element they most conspicuously share. Their similarities in that respect are great enough, according to Valen and Katz, to permit giving a generalized description of party organization rather than a detailed description of the organization of each party (something that would be unthinkable in, for example, Great Britain).[5] And in such a generalized description the main outlines of typical Norwegian organizational structure will immediately be recognizable: a hierarchy of elective collegial bodies running from the constituency level to a national peak, the bodies on each successive level becoming smaller, more continuous in operation, and more powerful, but working within highly delimited competences and answerable through clearly defined channels of accountability; individual leaders who combine ceremonial and mediatory functions with the more "efficient" aspects of leadership, but are little more than *primus inter pares* on leadership teams; a considerable amount of effective horizontal differentiation, mainly along local, but also along certain functional, lines; and all this based on very detailed party statutes, or "constitutions."

The basis of Norwegian party organization is, of course, the local party organization, generally confined to a single com-

[5] Valen and Katz, *Political Parties in Norway*, pp. 52, 84. For general descriptions of party organization, see *ibid.*, ch. 3; Henry Valen, *Det norske samfunnet: Politiske institusjoner: Partiene* (Oslo, 1962), esp. pp. 42-64; Torgersen, *Norske politiske institusjoner*, ch. 7; and Storing, *Norwegian Democracy*, ch. 7. With the exception of H. Lange's study of the Labour Party, *Fra sekt til parti* (Oslo, 1962), studies of particular political parties are rather unsatisfactory.

mune, although in the larger communes a number of local party units usually combine to form the communal organization. The local organizations join in county branches, or district branches, since these correspond to the national electoral districts; each district branch is headed by a representative council (*representantskap*) which, however, meets seldom and elects an executive board to transact ordinary business. The district branches, in turn, are combined in the national party. The highest organ of the national organization is the national conference (*landsmøte*), which consists of delegates elected by the district branches plus certain other members (members of parliament, representatives of the party press, and party functionaries),[6] and is the final authority on party policy, the selection of leaders and internal organizational problems. Since the conference meets only briefly each year the parties elect a number of more continuously active committees to carry on their business: a very small directorate (called either the *arbeidsutvalg* or *sentralstyre*) that literally discharges day-to-day business and is, in effect, a sort of collegial, elected secretariat, and a larger and less active national committee (*landsstyre*) of which the members of the directorate are generally members, that may, if required, act in the name of the *landsmøte* when the latter is not in session.[7] The directorate meets generally about once a week, the national committees from one to eight times a year; the first varies in size from seven in the Agrarian Party to fifteen in the Labour Party, the second from seventeen in the Liberal Party to thirty-six in the Labour Party; both are elected by the national conferences, although in some cases, the districts, the party's parliamentary group and organizations

---

[6] The number of those attending and the basis of determining eligibility to attend does vary somewhat among the parties. For example, in the Labour Party's conference members of parliament play a smaller role than in the other parties, while the Agrarian Party's conference includes an unusually large proportion of nonelected members.

[7] Two parties, the Liberal Party and the Christian People's Party, have in addition a national committee still larger than the *landsstyre*, the *landsråd*.

affiliated to a party may also participate. Each party also elects annually a chairman (*formann*) who is the formal head of all its central organizations and, usually, its parliamentary leader as well, headship implying mainly chairmanship and being the party's spokesman and embodiment, not by any means having special individual powers. There are also, of course, party bureaucracies, headed by general secretaries in charge of the party offices, and controlled by the party chairmen and national boards, and, finally, various special functional organizations (especially press and educational organizations) and affiliated organizations (interest organizations such as trade unions, women's and youth organizations, and in some cases temperance or religious subgroups, general sports associations, and hunting and fishing associations).

6. The trade unions—which in their present form, like the parties and the parliamentary regime, date mainly from the organizationally fecund period of the 1880's and 1890's—also conform closely to the organizational model I have sketched.[8] Ferraton particularly, because he sees their structure through French spectacles, is impressed by their, to him, strange combination of "undeformed" pyramidal authority and equally undeformed democratic process and accountability, both in the general trade union federation, the LO, and the special national unions. Furthermore, Ferraton is especially struck by the organizational similarities in Norwegian trade union structures (again in contrast to France, but also to some extent in explicit distinction to Britain); by the unity of the trade union movement based on the extreme "standardization of its construction"; by the fact that there has been no "atrophy of any syndical organs, neither at the base nor at the summit"; by what he

[8] The principal sources for Norwegian trade union organization are G. Ousland, *Fagbevegelsen i Norge*, 3 vols. (Oslo, 1949). Galenson, *Labor in Norway* and Ferraton, *Syndicalisme ouvrier et Social-Democratie en Norvège*. For a brief history of trade union development, see Galenson, pp. 7-33. The constitution of the Norwegian Federation of Trade Unions may be found in Landsorganisasjonen i Norge, *The Trade Union Movement in Norway* (Oslo, 1962), pp. 24-41.

calls "the greatest organic [i.e., organizational] homogeneity at each layer," consisting in all cases of centralized authority counterweighed by pluralism and collegial democracy, especially through the existence of genuine "balances of power" among the strata of authority and between the general trade union organization and its functionally specialized segments.[9] In other words, Ferraton sees in Norway's trade unions what I claim to be the case for the larger world of all Norwegian organizations and what Valen and Katz claim for another portion of that larger world, the political parties. It only remains to add that what Ferraton singles out as characterizing the structures of the trade unions reflects closely the abstract model of organization earlier sketched.

More concretely, the supreme organ of the LO, as of the national unions affiliated to it, is an elected national congress, which is very large in scale and meets very infrequently—constitutionally, in fact, only once every four years, although special meetings may be convened if very basic policy or organizational issues arise. There is, however, a slightly more active national representative council (again, *representantskap*), which meets at least once a year but is still too large and discontinuous a body to transact regular business. That is a task performed by various secretariats elected by the congresses, consisting of fifteen members in the case of the LO (including a specially elected salaried president and three other such officers) and of five to nine members in the national unions. They are, needless to say, assisted by professional functionaries having special legal, economic, statistical, and auditing skills. Underpinning the national structures are local unions that elect members of the assemblies which in turn elect the unions' secretariats and special officers; these local syndicates are, in their turn, subjected to a great deal of national union authority, as previously described.[10] Each of the local unions also displays, on a minor scale, the organizational structure of

---

[9] Ferraton, *Syndicalisme ouvrier* . . . , pp. 107-126, esp. p. 107.
[10] See above, pp. 106-107.

model of organization quite as much as are the unions, with whose development their own is contemporaneous and whose formal structure they duplicate.[14] The Norwegian Employers' Confederation (N.A.F.) is the equivalent of the general Federation of Labor, and the various national employers' associations affiliated to it are the equivalents of the national industrial unions. Practically all employers, like almost all workers in the case of the unions, are members of the Confederation, which means that they have voluntarily renounced the right to deal independently with their workers and conduct general negotiations through the employers' associations and the Confederation. Like the LO itself, the latter is not merely a nominal umbrella for the industrial associations but directly involved in the more important negotiations; in any case, it must approve all contracts entered into by the affiliated associations. Employers thus are organized in a highly centralized structure, based on a pluralistic, active, and organizationally homogeneous set of substructures, partly consisting of geographic districts, partly, and more important, of functionally specialized industrial associations. All of these are governed by detailed statutes similar to one another and, as specifically required, to the constitution of the national federation. This, it will be readily apparent, produces relations among employers' organizations similar to those between national and local governments, and the same kind of "organic homogeneity" among employers' organizations that impressed Ferraton in his study of the unions. The further parallelism between the unions' and employers' organizational structure can be sufficiently indicated by a sketch of the N.A.F.'s basic anatomy, which consists of the usual three-layer set of elected, accountable, and collegial authorities. The ultimate authority of the employers' confeder-

[14] A good discussion in English of Norwegian employers' organizations is in Galenson, *Labor in Norway*, ch. 4. See also Norsk Arbeidsgiverforening, *Norwegian Employers' Confederation*, Avskrift HE/JS 3/9-56 (mimeographed) and *Statutes of the Norwegian Employers' Confederation* (N.A.F.), 1956, (mimeographed); and E. Petersen, *Norsk Arbeidsgiverforening 1900-1950* (Oslo, 1950), the N.A.F.'s official history.

ation resides in a national meeting (*landsmøte*), consisting of about 200 members elected by the associations and individual firms and meeting only infrequently (once a year) to deal with high policy questions. This meeting does have something of the atmosphere and functions of a rally, actual basic authority being exercised by a somewhat smaller body, the central board (*sentralstyre*), which meets four to five times a year and consists of 47 members, also elected by affiliated associations and firms. The board, in turn, annually elects an executive committee (*styre*) of 8 members who are responsible for the discharge of current daily business, assisted by a large salaried staff; it also elects a chairman who, in the usual manner, has no independent powers but serves as spokesman, figurehead, and presiding officer at meetings. The processes through which this machinery functions are closely detailed in the organization's statute and similar in all major respects to those operating in the unions.

8. Trade unions and employers' organizations are, of course, along with the principal farmers' organization, the Norwegian Farmers' Society, the most active and important of Norwegian interest groups, the most closely tied to the political parties, and the chief associational sources of national politicians. The Farmers' Society, it should be noted, also exhibits the typical characteristics of Norwegian organization in nearly pristine form. Like all the other organizations we have discussed, its work is based on a highly detailed statute;[15] like these organizations its basis is a large number of local societies (corresponding to the rural communes and associated, like the communes, in county organizations); like them also its members are obliged by their constitution to act in a solidary rather than independent fashion by joining and buying and selling through agricultural cooperatives. Its highest authority, as usual, is a large representative meeting held once a year (*årsmote*); there

---

[15] See Norges Bondelag, *Lover om Norges Bondelag* (last revision, 1956) and the official history, G. Werner-Hansen, ed., *Norges Bondelag 1896-1956* (Oslo, 1956).

is also a smaller, but still large, representative council (*repre-sentantskap*) that meets one or more times a year and exercises rather more practical authority than the annual meeting; while current business is discharged by an executive board (*styre*) of nine members, elected biannually by the annual meeting and the affiliated organizations, and including the Society's chairman, who plays the usual role of Norwegian chairmen and is further limited in power by being subject to annual election. A number of specialized organizations are, also as usual, associated in the Society, producing functional as well as geographic pluralism at its base; they include organizations for farmers' wives, youths, dairy farmers, meat producers, egg farmers, market gardeners, fur growers, and forest owners. And between the national, local, and functional farmers' organizations there is again a remarkable "organic homogeneity at each layer," a microcosmic organizational congruence of the segments of the national organization that corresponds to the larger similarity of the national organizations themselves.[16]

9. Formal organization does not make for exciting reading, and there seems little point in piling still more detail upon the details already sketched. Suffice it to say that a general review of formal organization in associations large and small, occupational and nonoccupational, for the young or adults, reveals deviations from type little more significant than the occasional addition or subtraction of a pyramidal layer or, because an organization is particularly small, functionally homogeneous, or itself a segment of a large peak organization, the lack of horizontal pluralism in it.[17] The overall picture is one of a quite

[16] See, for example, the blueprint for the county societies in Norges Bondelag, *Normallover for fylkeslag av Norges Bondelag*, Bo. nr. 41/1963 (mimeographed), and, for one of the functional associations (the forest owners' association), *Vedtekter for Norges Skogeierforbund* (latest issue, 1954).

[17] This assertion is based on the perusal of data pertaining to the formal organizations of several hundred national Norwegian organizations, cataloged by Jorolf Moren at The Chr. Michelsen Institute in Bergen. I selected from that catalog a sample of thirty organizations, twenty-three of which supplied me with their "constitutions" (*vedtekter*)

remarkable community of formal anatomy, process, and nomenclature in every phase of associational life, urban and rural.

As I have said, it is no part of my brief to claim that the forms of Norwegian organizations are exotic, in any way unique to Norway. Obviously, parallels to Norwegian organizational structure are common elsewhere, especially in other democratic societies, and most of all, not insignificantly, in the more stable ones. The point here is simply that the ubiquity of these forms throughout society provides an element of concrete homogeneity to support the Norwegians' sense of community in an area that can be readily related to political behavior. Yet the Norwegian pattern of formal organization does have some uncommon characteristics—as it should, since the sentiments it supposedly supports are themselves out of the ordinary. One of the uncommon features of that pattern is the very combination of traits of which it consists; each one singly, and each limited combination of the traits, is more common than the whole complex of its characteristics. More important still is the fact that the typical organizational pattern is so nearly ubiquitous in Norway, that it applies to organizations almost regardless of their size and purpose, their independence or subsumption to larger associations, or the nature of their memberships. In other societies one may find some, or even many, organizations cast in the Norwegian mold; but Norway is distinctive in that one can find hardly a single exception. And this is all the more important because of the ubiquity of organization per se in Norwegian social relations, that is to say, because Norwegians "organize" interactions that in most other societies would have no formal structure at all, perhaps no patterned structure of any

---

as well as, in most cases, their most recent annual reports, anniversary volumes, and other such materials, which I went over in greater depth than Moren's catalog permitted. Since most of the organizations that did not reply were of a nonoccupational character, economic and occupational groupings were rather overrepresented in the publications I was able to consult.

kind. Most important of all perhaps is a point made at the very outset of this discussion: that the organizational blueprints governing Norwegian interactions are generally observed closely in practice, so that they are not merely ideals but describe, to a significant extent, how organizations actually do their work. Particularly in regard to collegiality, departures from form tend to be considerable in other societies; but while in Norway individual leaders (*formenn, ordfører*) are generally singled out from the membership of collegial bodies, they rarely exceed the bounds formally imposed on them by the forms of collegiality.

The relatively great correspondence of organizational forms and facts reflects the legalism of Norwegian political culture, but also the fact that Norwegian formal organizations, governmental and nongovernmental, express closely certain aspects of the Norwegian "style" of authority—of widely internalized norms regarding the way subordinate and superordinate roles are to be played—rather than being superimposed on these norms according to some abstract ideal that men are incapable of acting out in their ordinary behavior. The consequent reduction of strain between prescribed ideals and accustomed behavior no doubt itself contributes to the stability of Norwegian democracy, even granted that organizational forms and facts can never correspond completely and that formal blueprints can never cover all the minutiae of social interaction. To see this more clearly, as well as to enlarge our picture of Norway's authority patterns, we turn now to a separate discussion of that style in authority relations, recognizing that the description of the "norms" will in many cases involve a reiteration of patterns previously discussed as "forms."

IX

Social Authority Patterns: Norms

RULE by the *demos*, literally speaking, is an illusion, even if a grand and useful one. Because of that, effective democracy requires, in addition to a working balance of division and cohesion in its popular and representative aspects, a certain balance of disparate norms of authority: norms of authority that facilitate rule as well as norms of democracy that make for constraints upon and extensive participation in the activities of rule.[1] Both exist in Norway, and both are reflected largely in Norwegian organizational forms, however much more noticeable and self-consciously acted out the democratic norms may be.

1. Among the "democratic" norms that characterize Norwegian authority relations, first mention should be made of the pervasive egalitarianism of Norwegian society. Some aspects of that egalitarianism—the existence of a high degree of economic leveling and a low degree of status differentiation, and the attitudes responsible for such leveling—have already been discussed among the indicators of communal sentiments in Norway. Here we are not concerned with these matters but with the manner in which egalitarianism is manifested in patterns of subordination and superordination. Equality, literally speaking, cannot of course characterize authority relations. The very essence of such relations is inequality: the existence of some sort of asymmetry in the wielding of power and influence. Egalitarian attitudes can, however, be expressed in the more tacit aspects of authority relations, particularly those that organizational blueprints rarely, if ever, reveal. They can be found, above all, in the manner that authority wielders and their subordinates adopt toward one another; in the character

[1] For a discussion of the need for such a balance, and of its actual existence in stable democracies, see Appendix B, pp. 262-269.

of the persons recruited to roles of authority; in the eschewing of titular distinctions that identify high or low positions; in decision-making styles; and to some extent also in the elaboration of formal structures and processes that circumscribe hierarchic power.

The manner in which authority, especially high authority, generally is wielded in Norway contrasts sharply with the manner in which it is exercised in highly inegalitarian countries such as Great Britain. On the whole, the British style of high authority is remarkably "upper class," that is to say, modeled upon aristocratic modes of behavior. In Norway, as in America, it tends to the opposite extreme, to a well-cultivated folksiness—granted that the Norwegian and American ideas of the common touch differ in some notable respects. There are no hierarchic differentials in the silent prohibitions on self-display, hauteur, grandiosity, personal remoteness, open power seeking, or pretentiousness. The great thing even among parliamentarians, for example, is to appear to be a regular fellow: practical and common-sensical, well-versed in dull facts, rather inelegant, unimpressed, indeed embarrassed, by success. One displays certain rustic graces, such as quiet attentiveness, amiability, a lack of cantankerousness, disrespect, or disdain; but one also displays a certain rustic clumsiness: a monotonous delivery, a bare style, a lack of "manners" (although not of courtesy). In these respects the Storting and the House of Commons are virtually polar opposites, a fact not unrelated to patterns of parliamentary recruitment that in Britain, unlike Norway, greatly favor those actually brought up, via family and school, in the ways of the Establishment (although the House of Commons, as Aneurin Bevan once plaintively pointed out, is itself a powerful agency for seducing politicians into conformity with its aristocratic mores).

The Norwegian parliament, like the British and most others, mirrors society in these modes of behavior. Norwegian bosses of any kind tend to cultivate the common touch, Norwegian subordinates to treat them as being of their own sort. One does not, for example, use obsequious modes of address to superiors, nor do superiors use condescending forms toward subordinates; and this reluctance informally to express deference is matched by a similar reluctance to use formal titular distinctions, above all the lack of honorific titles, a fact that more than anything else makes the Norwegian monarchy appear extraordinarily republican in character.[2] Norway's failure to develop a numerous and long-lived indigenous aristocracy, allowing a direct transformation of primordial into modern forms of equality, is obviously connected with these patterns of behavior.

In regard to style of decision making, collegiality—the practice of formally placing individual decision makers in companies of peers and their propensity actually to merge their activities into such companies—itself expresses a kind of egalitarianism, confined to specific hierarchic levels. The chief minister's position in the cabinet is the most notable case in point. Overbearing prime ministers are very rare in Norway, apparently not only in public but also, as far as one can tell, in the privacy of ministerial meetings. To be sure, the office is important and to an extent what a man manages to make of it. But few men have made of it as much as they could. Perhaps only Gunnar Knudsen and (more doubtfully) Christian Michelsen went far toward exploiting its potential. Prime ministers usually act out in the large what organizational chairmen do on a smaller scale; they act as mediators and advisors and try to create agreement (*enighet*) by inducing bargains and compromises or by merely coordinating attitudes, never by dictating positions to obsequious lieutenants. In public and in the Storting they rarely try to be towering figures, but tend to assume, in the way of other Norwegians, a modest, self-effacing posture. Like British prime ministers they are first among equals, but unlike them cultivate equality more than primacy.

[2] If there is an exception to this general picture it is the public service. But even in the public service, the basic distinction between higher or lower civil servants, between *embedsmenn* and *tjenestemenn*, scarcely involves the diffuse and invidious distinctions implied by being in the administrative class and other classes of the British civil service.

They also lack some formal powers tending to diminish collegiality which British prime ministers possess; for example, the division of ministerial portfolios is itself a collective cabinet decision in Norway rather than, as in Britain, a personal prerogative exercised in the sovereign's name.[3]

If collegiality were simply formal, it would hardly be so widely observed as it is in Norway, on the highest and lowest reaches of authority. Plenty of organizations display both collegial organization and uncollegial behavior. But that collegiality in Norway is a great deal more than a form is indicated perhaps most strikingly by the fact that there is a tendency toward it even when no formal provisions compel it, indeed even when they point in a contrary direction. For example, Norway's *statsråd*, the body of ministers that served the Swedish-Norwegian king, developed from the very beginning of the Swedish-Norwegian union as "a markedly collegial council,"[4] despite the fact that no cabinet or parliamentary system in the modern sense as yet existed, ministers being specialist counsellors without collective responsibility before 1884. The collegial form of cabinet government adopted in 1884 simply ratified what had been accomplished already by collegial norms, and legalistic values, after the establishment of the form, at most reinforced the preexisting values.

Collegial sentiments, if confined to small and special groups, will, of course, readily turn into cliquishness, and a self-important clique may be quite as domineering as an overbearing individual. In Norway, however, that possibility is prevented by another, quite informal aspect of the predominant decision-making style: the high valuation of very broad agreements, a kind of collegiality in a much wider sense. This involves not merely the valuation of consensus, which obviates any need for searching out common ground. More important,

[3] See Kristian Bloch, *Kongens Råd* (Oslo, 1963), pp. 37-38. The standard reference work on the cabinet is J. Debes, *Det norske Statsråd 1814-1949* (Oslo, 1950).

[4] *Ibid.*, p. 17. See also Jens Arup Seip, *Et regime foran undergangen*, p. 9.

it involves a stress upon the reconciliation of men of different interests and persuasions, a tendency to treat even opponents as colleagues. The depth of that value is reflected in the language: the Norwegian word for a body of rules is *vedtekt*, and that word derives from *vedta*, "to agree to"; a decision resulting in a rule thus is not something that a decision maker takes but something that affected parties manage to agree on. Some aspects of that valuation of comprehensive agreement, of broad team spirit, we have already discussed, especially as it is manifested in the style of party and parliamentary politics. It should be added that the same values govern the manner of cabinet decision making. The cabinet does not merely put on public displays of unanimity enforced by rules of collective responsibility and by fears of party sanctions upon independence; it also takes elaborate pains to make unanimity real through careful discussions and adjustments on many levels before official cabinet meetings: through informal interdepartmental negotiations, discussions in cabinet committees, and proceedings in two more official bodies, the government conference and the "preparatory" cabinet meeting, the result of which is to make official cabinet meetings (in the king's presence) little more than formal ratifying ritual.[5] Of course, cabinet meetings are everywhere "prepared," but more often to deal with technicalities than to avert all possible disagreements.

The valuation of wide agreement is all the more noteworthy because it exists alongside two other democratic norms: norms of individual participation and of structural pluralism. High attendance in the Storting, the enforcement of the performance of representative roles, the unusually high density of membership in organizations, the large numbers of men who are, or have been, officers and board members in organizations, the creation by Norwegian trade unions and employers of voluntary codetermination—all these reflect the former. The wide use of functionally specialized bodies and locally decentralized units—the tendency to duplicate within organizations of almost

[5] Bloch, *Kongens Råd*, chs. 7, 8, 12.

every kind the pluralism of society in the large—expresses the latter. Because of these norms, the search for general agreements is not simplified by a high degree of individual apathy or exclusion, nor by monolithic structure; on the contrary, it is deliberately complicated by the cultivation of special corporate interests and individual involvement in decision making, either directly or through the meticulous exaction of accountability by officers to members.

2. That these various aspects of the Norwegian style of authority are norms rather than mere forms can be seen not only in the fact that they sometimes operate without being formally prescribed, but also in that they characterize social relations not amenable to formal organization, for example, relations in families and schools, the chief agencies, needless to say, for implanting standards of social conduct. While, regrettably, neither family nor school authority patterns have been deeply studied in Norway, what evidence there is, and what a "participant observer" can see for himself, points to a considerable acting out of the norms sketched here in the most intimate, informal, and formative contexts of human existence.

In his short guide to Norwegian mores, *The Norwegian Way of Life*, the eminent constitutional historian Frede Castberg observes that during the development of modern Norway, presumably coincident with the gradual democratization of political life, the patriarchal family has continuously been giving way to equality of the spouses and a lessening of parental power over children.[6] The observations and more systematic studies of family sociologists fully bear him out. For example, in a recently published study by Thomas D. Eliot (and others) on Norwegian family life it is pointed out that the gradual legal equalization of men and women during the past century, consummated a good deal earlier than in other European countries in extensive franchise reform, has been matched by a considerable equalization in occupational roles and educational op-

[6] Castberg, *The Norwegian Way of Life*, pp. 19, 25.

portunities and, more important, a significant redefinition of roles in the home. Husbands and wives exhibit "reciprocal respect"; domestic decisions are normally made only after close consultations between them; child rearing in particular has become a matter of mutual agreements; and marital relations tend, in general, to be persuasive and mutually accommodating rather than highly asymmetric.[7] Rodnick also comments on the remarkable equality of women in and outside of the home, especially the fact that they are generally treated by men as intellectual equals and expected to have a great deal of personal independence.[8] Despite some subcultural differences in these respects, the typical Norwegian child is thus confronted in the home by a manifest egalitarianism and a collegial atmosphere aiming at the establishment of agreed and reciprocally accommodating behavior.

The treatment of children themselves is highly congruent with this general picture. The ideals of Norwegian child rearing are perhaps best exemplified by the most widely bought modern manual on the subject, Alfred Sundal's *Mor og barn*, which by 1950 had run through fourteen editions. Sundal puts special emphasis on persuasion, kindness, affection, friendliness, quiet demeanor by the parents, and the use of diversion when children misbehave or threaten to do so, rather than ordering, forbidding, or punishing. Similar attitudes emerge from a large spate of pamphlets and manuals issued by the Institute of Christian Education, which, if anything, might be expected to be rather on the strict side. What the Norwegians call *fri oppdragelse*—liberal or permissive upbringing—seems to be the general norm. The majority of manuals also emphasize the need to qualify permissiveness with general "rules," even if not specific orders, that provide clear definitions of rightfully expected conduct; and some stress directly the desirability of "democratic qualities" in the home.[9] Actual patterns of child

[7] Thomas D. Eliot *et al.*, *Norway's Families* (Philadelphia, 1960), esp. pp. 8-9.

[8] Rodnick, *The Norwegians*, ch. 6.

[9] Eliot *et al.*, *Norway's Families*, p. 197.

raising, as far as one can tell from available studies (which, admittedly, present some rather contradictory findings) seem to correspond closely to these ideals. Survey researches suggest that considerably more people value a mild upbringing than a strict one; only about half of all Norwegian children seem *ever* to have been corporally punished, and these mainly before school age (although surveys of children not surprisingly reveal a somewhat higher incidence of corporal punishment than surveys of adults—which still shows a considerable valuation of parental mildness, or even repression of normatively prohibited acts);[10] children, as Rodnick, among many others, remarks, are encouraged to be independent (within a mold of general rules) and tend in fact to be independent at an unusually early age.[11] Two very good studies of parental behavior, one conducted in the 1920's, the other some twenty years later, both found parents to be at least "moderately democratic" in that restrictions on children were used sparingly, in that peremptoriness was balanced by reasoning and persuasion, and in that democratic forms were often deliberately resorted to vis-à-vis children and dictation restricted to cases where essential requirements of the child and home might have been endangered.[12] In addition, Rodnick makes much of the existence of highly cooperative and mild peer group relations among children, especially the absence of the sort of pecking-order violence with which Americans are all too familiar.[13] Children, of course, learn from peer groups as well as from older people and, as well, reflect in peer group relations what they observe among adults, even if at times in a caricatured form.

The typical modes of child management, remarks a Norwegian psychoanalyst, "may help account for the notable ease, freedom, and relaxed independence shown by Norwegian youngsters as they grow up, despite some patterns of school

[10] *Ibid.*, pp. 198-203.   [11] See also *ibid.*, p. 205.

[12] Eva Nordland, *Sammenheng mellom sosial atferd og oppdragelse* (Oslo, 1955), pp. 234-272.

[13] Rodnick, *The Norwegians*, p. 28.

discipline that do not seem to have outgrown regimentation and traditional methods."[14] Yet one may question that school life really contrasts so sharply with family life. To be sure, in Norwegian teacher-student relations elements of strong authority are highly visible, although much less so in primary than in secondary schools. Teachers, especially in the latter, command considerable respect; they engage in little hobnobbing even with their older students but tend to keep their distance; their views or the tasks they set are rarely questioned. On the other hand, pupils are rarely *gehorsam* in the German sense (now, apparently, passing out of style even in Germany) or, as the counterpart of *Gehorsamkeit*, maliciously rebellious. They do what is asked, but are rarely intimidated or obsequious. Their obedience consists rather of careful role-playing toward the teacher, and by the teacher toward them. This is reinforced by teaching methods that stress learning by rote, especially memorizing, and thus prevent ambiguities and arbitrariness in student-teacher relations (as well as serving to suppress talents and idiosyncrasies that would ill fit the constricting communal norms of Norwegian life). And in the schools, too, Castberg points out, authoritarianism has been constantly declining[15] and is, in certain ways, legally circumscribed, e.g., by a prohibition on corporal punishments.

The main reasons for the still relatively authoritarian character of Norwegian teacher-student relations will be more apparent when we come to discuss norms of authority, rather than democracy. Here, however, it is particularly necessary to stress that authority relations in schools involve more than teacher-student relationships in the classroom. They also involve, and at least as importantly, relations among the students themselves. These mitigate the influence of teacher-student relations no less than domestic influences, and indeed become more manifestly congruent with the predominant Norwegian style of authority as teacher-student relations become less free

[14] Trygve Braatøy, *Psykoanalyse og moral* (Oslo, 1949), pp. 16-22.
[15] Castberg, *The Norwegian Way of Life*, pp. 25, 31.

and indulgent, that is, as students progress through secondary school. Most important in this respect is the fact, previously stated, that large numbers of students, especially from age fifteen or sixteen on, join large numbers and many types of student organizations, and that these are conducted closely along the lines of adult organizations. They are highly collegial bodies (note the previously cited figures on the number of nineteen-year olds who have had responsible positions in youth organizations), highly participant, and, of course, pluralistic. Moreover, their pluralism tends to be an integrated pluralism in that the various student organizations generally elect delegates to a general council of *tillitsmenn* that meets frequently, makes general social arrangements for the student body, and at times speaks for the students before the school administration. Student government is thus based on student organizations rather than directly, or "populistically," on the body of individual students. It should also be noted that the student organizations normally include counterparts of the national party organizations which discuss and debate political news and issues among themselves, and that in many schools, especially the gymnasia, students regularly conduct debates, with teachers as observers, in which they take the roles of the various parties and act out the style of national political debate, sometimes directly imitating national politicians as well as the procedures of parliamentary discussion. This is, of course, in addition to external youth organizations, including political schools for younger people run by the parties.

Political socialization in the schools is particularly important, intense, direct, and congruent with the general norms of the system in the so-called folk high schools, modeled on institutions founded in the mid-nineteenth century by the famous Danish bishop Grundtvig. These are continuation schools to which young adults come for protracted periods on a voluntary basis, mainly in the rural areas. Their purpose is not vocational training or continued education in strictly academic subjects. Originally intended to enable men newly mobilized in politics to hold their own against the longer entrenched political classes, they still concentrate on inculcating a spirit of citizenship and on teaching political skills (for example, debating skills), awareness, and ambition. Particularly for the middle parties and, more generally, the local communes, they long served as nurseries for political leaders and activists, occupying in Norwegian political life a position analogous in some respects to the British public schools. But while aloofness, hauteur, authority, stylishness, "manners"—aristocratic norms—are the main fare in the latter, in the folk high schools norms of reasonableness, moderation, cooperative participation, and detailed knowledge have been most strongly stressed.[16]

3. All this constitutes one side of the Norwegian style of authority and of its roots in formative experience, the "democratic" side. The Norwegian political system could hardly function well, however, if there were no other. After all, among the norms that have been sketched, only one is concerned with arriving at decisions, the value of searching out wide agreements. But this in itself could hardly make democracy decisionally efficient; indeed, it could very well have the opposite effect. If one will settle for nothing less than very wide agreement; if wide agreement must be fashioned out of a highly pluralistic universe of highly participant interest and purpose organizations; if it must be achieved by means of egalitarian, collegial behavior within and among decision-making bodies; then it is only too probable that decision-making processes will, in the great majority of matters, come to nothing at all except decisions not to decide—particularly if even outright majorities are not resolutely employed. Restraint can immobilize a polity no less than irreconcilable fragmentation. What then gives the Norwegian system energy? What are its authoritative elements, and how are they reconciled with the system's democratic norms?

[16] An excellent analysis of the folk high schools, covering all of Scandinavia, may be found in Erica Simon, *Réveil national et culture populaire en Scandinavie* (Paris, 1960).

The most important of these elements, in my view, is a kind of deference, namely deference to specialized functional competence in a society that emphasizes functionally specific role playing to a remarkable extent. That kind of deference contrasts sharply with the diffuse social and political deference which Bagehot first identified as the key to authority in the British parliamentary system. Functional deference leads to a particularly high valuation of the expert and the specialist (who need not technically be an expert, but may simply be someone with a special interest in an area of policy), while the British type of deference accords prestige to the generalist, the broadly educated, stylish dilettante and, what is frequently of course the same, the man of good social background. But just as British deference has its roots in the days of aristocracy and squirearchy (and the relative lack in America of any kind of deference, diffuse or specific, in our early populism), so the respect Norwegians accord to functionally specific roles has historic roots in the realities of the *embedsmannsstat*, for the norms involved are typical of bureaucratic structures.

Norwegians tend to define in highly specialized terms a remarkable variety of social roles and to recruit men to such roles on the basis of formally acquired qualifications, particularly special schooling. Special functional training is, of course, typical of modern societies, for functionally specific relations play a large role in all of them. But the Norwegians go much farther in this direction than others; they even insist on considerable special schooling for such people as postal or cafeteria workers (at any rate, on the higher, more skilled levels), as a result of which much of Norwegian life has a remarkably uniform cast, and as a result of which also there seems to be relatively little cross-occupational mobility.[17] One's occupational role, in fact, is virtually part of one's name, hence, in-

[17] This is merely my impression, although it would also seem to follow logically from the stress on special schooling for virtually every major occupational role. The precise extent of cross-occupational mobility in Norway would make an excellent subject for sociological research.

important, particularly so if functional specificity is itself a strong value. But the specific roles of teacher and students inevitably entail asymmetries: expectations of respect for and conformity to the teacher, as well as certain disciplinary powers on his part and a certain personal distance between teachers and students. Only thus can systematic learning take place and arbitrary favoritism or animosities be avoided. The teacher consequently can command considerable functional respect, but only as a teacher, a role player, not as some sort of exalted being. Furthermore, norms of functional deference will make for conformity with him in accordance with well-defined rules and within unambiguous limits, rather than for a more general submissiveness. The authority patterns between Norwegian teachers and students thus make not only for functionally necessary asymmetries, but keep authority from being exceeded or being made arbitrary and personal; and this is true of all authority based upon and limited by functional specificity.

In political life as well as in the structures of large organizations, the norm of functional deference is manifested in a large number of behavior patterns, to some of which we have already referred. One example is the considerable influence of the Storting's specialized committees in policy making and the tendencies of the parliamentary parties to defer to the views of their representatives on such committees. Another is the great proliferation and consequence of specialized committees in communal administration. In ministerial discussions there also seems to be a tendency to leave a great deal to the special views of individual department heads. Most interesting of all, the public bureaucracy, which is based upon specialized expertise, is itself an unusually significant source of high-level politicians in Norway. Civil servants have always been greatly overrepresented in the Storting, where they can serve while on leave from their bureaucratic positions; and they are even more overrepresented in cabinets. Since 1884 only about half of Norwegian ministers have had backgrounds mainly in the Storting, and during the almost continuous rule by Labour since 1935 only some 40 per cent have had mainly "political" careers.[18] From that point of view the victory of parliament over the *embedsmenn* in 1884 was as pyrrhic a triumph as that of British democrats over the squirearchs. In both cases, changes in political forms could not deeply alter the effects of political norms.

Functional deference clearly narrows the range of groups and men among whom agreements must be sought—even the range of men and groups that have any strong views at all on various public issues—and helps identify men who can speak and act authoritatively in special areas of policy.[19] This enables the system to act with some ease even in many nonconsensual areas (that is, those not governed clearly by communal norms) although of course not in all, since special interests and knowledge do not always tend in agreed directions. At the same time it is a kind of deference highly consonant with democratic norms, since it does not militate against diffuse egalitarian sentiments, restricts authority to highly limited fields, disperses it among many men and structures, and compartmentalizes it in such a way that ambitious men can function easily as colleagues; and regarding men in positions of diffuse leadership, it militates against their being more than chairmen, spokesmen, and coordinators. In a still larger sense it is a sentiment highly appropriate to a society in which community is often expressed in leaving personal interests and preferences unstated, for functional criteria readily define the areas in which one ought to be silent or to make oneself heard.

A second value making for authority in Norway might be called formal hierarchism, and this also may derive from the bureaucratic norms of the *embedsmannsstat*. Formal hierarchism involves, in essence, a limited deference to impersonal

---

[18] Torgersen, *Norske politiske institusjoner*, secs. 8.9–8.10.

[19] Functional deference thus constitutes what Easton calls a "cultural mechanism" for regulating political "wants," i.e., keeping them from becoming "demands" and thereby reducing the load of demands the political system must handle (David Easton, *A Systems Analysis of Political Life*, pp. 100-116).

and open roles that organizational blueprints place in a super-ordinate position, that is, to formal roles which are specifically hierarchic rather than technical. This sentiment supplements and counterweighs the functional dispersion of authority, but is, of course, always hedged by the exaction of account-ability to subordinate bodies. Since it implies only impersonal deference to roles it is also highly compatible with egalitarian personal norms, all the more so since the higher and lower roles often do not involve face-to-face relationships. In the nineteenth century, in fact, the bureaucratic structure, while typically hierarchic, left many officials virtually autonomous in their various local, highly inaccessible domains. The *embeds-menn* fit into a highly stratified legal order, but many, year after year, did not even so much as see a superior, and thus enjoyed considerable independence, circumscribed by the impersonal system rather than personal control. It is often said in Norway that this pattern continues, in altered form, today: that officials and functionaries, public and private, whether physically sepa-rated or not, tend to carve out for themselves islands of autonomy within the hierarchic structures in which they operate, reconciling in that way personal independence and impersonal subordination.

Men who achieve formally high positions, however, do seem to acquire thereby a kind of immunity to competitive chal-lenges, and in that sense a certain personal superordination. In most Norwegian organizations, no less than in government, leadership is highly stable; struggles for formally superior posi-tions, although they occur, are somehow not quite fully legiti-mated where there is a well-entrenched incumbent. A striking case in point is provided by the party chairmen, who generally last in office as long as they live or are physically able.[20] And the longer leaders last, the more authority they are likely to acquire, both in practical ways, through gaining experience in rule, and symbolically, through coming to embody organiza-tions in their persons.

[20] Torgersen, sec. 7.8.

Formal hierarchism is, of course, an aspect of that larger norm with which we started the discussion, the pervasive formalism and legalism of Norwegian authority relations: the Norwegians' distaste for implicitness, ambiguity, inconsistency, and arbitrariness in social relations and their consequent tendency to constitutionalize, so to speak, virtually all social interactions by elaborating in detail, and observing, explicit rules to govern them. The sanctity of the national constitution, the detailed definition of local government structure and procedure, the tendency of even small nongovernmental organizations to develop elaborate *vedtekter*, are only the most direct expression of this norm. A more indirect but equally striking instance of it is the very tendency to school men, in minute detail, in the manner of acting out even trivial occupational roles and thus to standardize the ways in which they are performed. Since Norwegian organizations are remarkably uniform in constitutional structure, and since their form invariably prescribes hierarchic stratification as well as accountability, collegiality, and pluralism, formal-legal values are no less important than norms of functional deference in reconciling norms of democracy and of authority in Norway. That should explain why Norwegian legalism has not had the dysfunctional effects attributed to the norm, perhaps rightly, in other societies, particularly Germany.[21]

It is, in fact, with Germany no less than Britain, that the Norwegian style of authority should be most closely contrasted, if only because some aspects of Norwegian and German authority seem as similar as the historic character and performance characteristics of their regimes are different (just the opposite being the case in regard to Norway and Britain). Germany has been not only a highly legalistic and formally hierarchic society, but also, like Norway, a *ständische Gesellschaft*, a society of "estates" or "corporations," in which the functional or bureaucratic expert has had great influence. Wherein then do the two societies differ? First, in the absence in

[21] See above, p. 21.

Norway of any semblance of the idea of the *Obrigkeitsstaat*—the idea of a transcendentally superior and domineering state above the social estates. Second, in the absence in Norway of a clear-cut hierarchical and invidious ordering of the estates themselves. Third, of course, in the content of the norms that constitutional provisions generally prescribe, especially the existence of powerful democratic norms that counterbalance even what H. J. Spiro calls "scientistic" norms of authority. Fourth, in the tension-reducing identity in Norway of cultural norms and constitutional forms. Finally, and perhaps most important, in the fact that Norway really is a *ständische Gemeinschaft*, a corporate community, rather than a corporate *Gesellschaft*—a society in which the strong identity of the whole balances identifications with separate corporate bodies, and in which that larger identity does not depend on being embodied in an awesome and remote national authority. In sum, legalistic and functional deference may exist quite separately from what they have been associated with in Germany—*Obrigkeit*, submissiveness in steeply graded hierarchies, society without community —and when they do, may have highly positive consequences in democracy, just as in the opposite case they may compound its ills.

4. That Norwegian authority patterns are indeed highly homogeneous, thus providing a concrete basis for communal sentiments in social experiences particularly relevant to governmental rule, should now be evident. As to the question of how these patterns are specifically conducive to stable and effective democracy, it seems almost superfluous at this stage to point the moral. But since the matter is crucial, let us do so anyway, by way of summary.

In characterizing the Norwegian labor movement, the French writer Ferraton, as we saw in Chapter II, was struck by the extent to which Norwegians regard democracy as an unquestionable moral virtue, a necessary foundation of society, "a natural element"—in short, by its extraordinary legitimacy.

Since democratic norms pervade Norwegian life in the family, in schools, in economic and friendly societies, pressure groups and parties, local and national government, one need not wonder that Norwegians regard it as both natural and moral, a general "way of living," not merely a form that has merit in national governance. One need only add that the actual existence of democracy throughout Norwegian society is buttressed by a powerful democratic symbolism: by widely implanted historical myths (perhaps truths) about the character of ancient Norwegian institutions; by the association of Norway's national identity with the Eidsvoll constitution; above all, perhaps, by the great national reverence for Norway's literary heroes (Holberg, Wergeland, Ibsen, Bjørnson, among others) who, with only a few exceptions, like Knut Hamsun, have been apostles of political liberalism, community spirit, and social responsibility. ("It is a little bit," writes the British historian Derry, of Wergeland, "as though Shelley had also been Cobbett.")

The workaday efficiency of the system, which need not follow from its legitimacy alone, stems mainly from five additional factors that have been touched upon at various points of the discussion. The first involves the system's substantive consensual norms (as reflected, for example, in the success of the minority Labour government of 1935-1940 in getting through the Storting a complex legislative program in areas where communal sentiments were especially strong). The second is the tendency, in many other areas of policy, to restrict the possibilities of disagreement and deadlock by leaving matters to functional experts, or specially interested parties, or, in some cases, incumbents of respected hierarchic roles. Third, there is the tendency, where disagreement is, or is expected to be, considerable and irreconcilable, to resort to what Bachrach and Baratz have called "nondecision making,"[22] the tendency not

[22] See Peter Bachrach and Morton S. Baratz, "Decisions and Non-Decisions: An Analytical Framework," *American Political Science Review*, LVII (Sept. 1963), 632-642.

to raise issues at all, which, while of course not making for action on these matters, does prevent conflicts, obstructions, and delays that can prevent efficient decision making in other areas. A fourth factor is the stability of formal leadership, rooted in formal hierarchism, that generally provides leaders with the time necessary to gain considerable experience and special knowledge in practical affairs.

Most important of all, however, is the fact that the whole of organized Norwegian life, and much of unorganized life, through their congruence with the national governmental authority pattern, provides constant training in the ways of government, constant political socialization that fits men for governmental roles—and the concomitant fact that men simultaneously engaged in national government, party politics, and the politics of voluntary associations, as most national politicians are, need not feel strains and ambivalence through any greatly contradictory demands among their roles. Norwegians can thus serve long and genuine apprenticeships to fit them for national government before they enter it, and most national politicians do just that. A recent study of Norwegian parliamentary candidates[23] shows that they tend to be unusually mature men, the average age of candidates being about forty-seven and of those high on party lists about fifty (compared to about thirty-eight in Britain); that they tend, to a remarkable extent, to be associational joiners; and that local government, the model of all Norwegian organization, plays an even greater role as a recruitment ground for national politicians in Norway than it usually does, about 90 per cent of all parliamentarians coming from local government backgrounds and no fewer than 43 per cent having been mayors or vice-mayors.[24] That sort of long experience in congruent organizations, generally involving a mixture of legislative and executive

[23] Valen, "Nominasjonene," in Valen and Rokkan, *Valg i Norge*, ch. 6.
[24] For comparisons with Valen's figures, see Jean Meynaud, ed., "The Parliamentary Profession," *International Social Science Journal*, XIII (1961), 513-717, and Dwaine Marvick, ed., *Political Decision-Makers* (Glencoe, Ill., 1961).

positions, clearly conduces to efficacy when men finally grow into their national political careers.

5. Of the problems raised at the beginning of Chapter VI, one more remains. It is perhaps the most vexing of all that have been posed—and the most crucial, since on its answer depends the overall coherence and completeness of the arguments developed in this study. This problem is to account for the Norwegian pattern of political division in such a way that the cohesion of the system does not immediately again seem puzzling, in other words, to find some plausible source of the considerable divisions in the Norwegian polity that is not inconsistent with the larger communal sentiments we have described and attempted to explain. Social overlapping, interconnections, and homogeneities may account for values and behavior patterns that bind the society politically despite its divisions; but why, then, are these divisions manifested in political cleavage and divergence in the first place? Why not more political aggregation? Why the stubborn persistence of old historic rifts?

I should like to offer a suggestion, which, to be sure, is at present based more on logic than empirical evidence and thus requires much further exploration. The coexistence of considerable division and cohesion in the Norwegian polity may be attributed to the operation of strong norms of cohesion not only on the national level but also on the subsidiary levels of society, in localities, economic groups, and cultural segments. There is, of course, some empirical basis for that contention. Certainly it is not only the national government that displays considerable cohesion in Norway; team spirit on a more restricted level is displayed also by parliamentary committees, the political parties, voluntary organizations, indeed practically all of organized and informal life. If that spirit were confined to the subsidiary levels of society, it would no doubt tend to make stable and effective national rule impossible. But if it operates equally on both the smaller and larger levels, it is likely to produce exactly what exists in Norway: political divisions that manifest strong and persistent loyalties to special groups, most of all perhaps among neighbors (hence in territorial segments),[25] and at the same time a tendency among the fragments to constitute a stable and efficient whole.

In short, Norway's great political divisions and its great political cohesion are perfectly consistent if both have a single source rather than being results of contradictory pulls in Norwegian life, if both result from unusually compelling demands for solidarity that operate on all levels of social life. And these demands may even account for two kinds of behavior that at first glance seem incongruent with both national and segmental cohesion: the tendency of individual Norwegians frequently to withdraw into isolation (for that can be interpreted as a way of managing personal hostilities that militate against solidarity) and the occasional fragmentation of political groups, as subgroups find it impossible to live up to demands for close solidarity in larger segments—a kind of withdrawal on a corporate basis, if that is not too outrageous a metaphor.

That so different a set of behavior patterns as national cohesion, segmental fragmentation, and individual withdrawal should all result from a single cultural imperative may be too good to be true, but is just what one would expect in a highly coherent and integrated social system. And Norwegian behavior, political and nonpolitical, does manifest all three in considerable degree, without there being between them any conspicuous destructive tensions.

[25] In this connection, note especially Rodnick's finding that there is a strong emphasis in Norway on being like one's neighbors in religion and politics, even if one might be tempted by different views. Rodnick, *The Norwegians*, p. 15.

X

Summary and Implications

THEORIES are generalizations pertaining to a "universe" of cases, case studies interpretations of one unit in such a universe, and theoretical case studies a kind of synthesis of the two. Their object is to interpret specific cases through established generalizations and, by so doing, to cast a sharper light on the cases and to confirm or modify the theories or, if necessary, to generate new ones. Since this essay has presented a theoretical case study of Norwegian democracy, we need, in this last chapter, to look beyond Norway to the larger universe of democratic polities of which it is a part. What lessons does the study suggest about such polities and theories pertaining to them, especially generalizations about the conditions of stable and effective democratic rule?

1. Raising this question entails two (possibly unwarranted) assumptions that might as well be explicit at the start. It implies, first, the assumption that the data relied on in the study are reliable and the arguments about them valid. At no stage of inquiry into any case can one be absolutely sure of this. But it is worth repeating that the present study must be particularly tentative in this respect, due to my own limited exposure to Norwegian life and due to the fact that Norwegian political studies simply have not yet produced very reliable data about many matters discussed here. Particularly in the realm of political cohesion and its sources it has been necessary, given the present state of the data, to rely mainly upon personal impressions (my own and other people's) rather than the results of systematic and thorough empirical studies. In an ideal world it might have been wiser to wait until such studies have been carried out before attempting anything like the present essay. But in the real world of research one might, in that case, have had to wait forever, for only theoretically focussed studies can

draw attention to the need for more reliable data and more trustworthy interpretations in neglected areas. Social scientists, like others, tend to prefer traversing well-trodden paths to exploring new terrain, and often it is only by raising disregarded questions and following them through their ramifications to tentative answers that gaps in knowledge are revealed. In any event, the work of gathering data and of formulating theories about them must always be to some extent concurrent, since information, however long and thoroughly compiled and processed, is never complete or absolutely accurate and theory forever turning up new paths of exploration or exposing the weaknesses of old lines of inquiry.

Consequently I am disinclined to apologize for the character of some of the data used here or the large inferences drawn from small amounts of them—but reluctant also to insist on all the specific arguments that have been presented or, so far as these are integrated, the general argument of the study. It does, however, seem reasonable to make certain claims for the study. I would certainly claim that important questions have been asked in it and apposite observations used to work out plausible, if tentative, answers. I would claim also that both the questions and answers, in many cases, point toward a need for thoroughly exploring many aspects of Norwegian politics and society about which the better empirical studies of that country are often silent and the worse ones inclined to give easy, habitual, and blatantly implausible answers. And I claim, finally, that the more reliable knowledge of Norwegian political life we already possess, however scanty, suffices to cast doubt on many widely accepted hypotheses, to emphasize a need for stating less dubious ones more precisely, and to direct attention to new and more plausible generalizations. Regarded in that manner—as an episode in continuous research and reflection upon research—this study ought to be useful, even if the first assumption underlying these concluding speculations is not entirely warranted.

A second assumption entailed in using the case of Norway

as a basis for reflection upon democracies in general is that Norway is in fact a relevant case. In one sense this can hardly be doubted: Norway *is* a democracy, by practically anybody's definition. But in another sense one may wonder: is Norway not so peculiar a society that what pertains to her can illuminate no other case? It may be so; certainly, in going through these pages one may well come to suspect that we have examined, so to speak, an extraterrestrial society and indeed arrived at unearthly results. Yet this is something that one can feel about any concrete society, once one has got far enough into the always distinctive ways it combines a multitude of general relationships. Besides, Norwegians seem terrestrial enough. Their behavior is manifestly subject to the same physiological and psychological uniformities and functional imperatives that operate elsewhere. And while their society confounds many theories, it does, as we shall see anon, confirm others, suggesting that it is not the Norwegians but the theories they confound that are out of line. No doubt the total concrete configuration of Norwegian society is something special; but this is true of any concrete configuration, be it a society, personality, organism, or inorganic object, and does not mean that the particular relations constituting the configuration are unique as well.

In any case, there is only one way to find out whether pertinent general theory can indeed be derived from Norwegian experience, and that is to try to state or restate theories about stable democracy in such a form that they can account for the Norwegian case as well as others. This is our final task.

2. Before attempting to develop the broader theoretical implications of the study, however, a summary of its main arguments is in order. The principal points made during the discussion have been these:

(1) Norwegian democracy has been highly stable and effective, in the sense of exhibiting great system and intrasystem stability, great legitimacy, considerable decisional efficiency, and few, if any, deviations from authentic democratic

rule, even under crisis conditions associated elsewhere with the breakdown of democracy.

(2) The performance characteristics of the Norwegian polity cannot be accounted for by a large variety of hypotheses that plausibly explain the performance of other democracies, including hypotheses about the effects of constitutional structure, material environment, history, and culture.

(3) Norwegian democracy bears out, as it must, the argument that stable democracy requires a balance of division and cohesion (or "consensus" and "cleavage"); but this argument is not very informative unless made more precise.

(4) One highly plausible way of making the division-cohesion hypothesis more specific (based on a number of related hypotheses stated more or less explicitly in the literature on democratic politics) is confounded by the Norwegian pattern of political divisions: namely, that democratic polities are stable and effective to the extent that they correspond to a polar model of democracy in which men disagree, without intensity and within a narrow range, on specific issues, share widely basic orientations, and have politically weak segmental identifications. While the Norwegian case does not approach very closely the opposite extreme, it departs far more from the polar model of stable democracy than the performance characteristics of the system lead one to expect, particularly through the salience of segmental cleavages and cultural divergences that, to some extent at least, are expressed also in specific disagreements.

(5) The undoubtedly great cohesion of the polity is not primarily the result of the pattern of political division itself, particularly not of mechanical balances among the segments, although through overlapping or cross-cutting memberships some "intersections" of divided groups exist and may to some extent make for cohesion.

(6) Norway, despite its political divisions, manifests in many aspects of political and nonpolitical behavior a remarkable "overarching attitude of solidarity"—a deep sense of com-

munity undiminished by the segmental cleavages, cultural divergences, and specific disagreements of its political system; and this sense of community emerges, above all, in three kinds of behavior: "noneconomic" definitions of human behavior, noncompetitiveness, and great organizability.

(7) The specific behavior patterns these involve still reflect the social structure and orientations of primordial Norwegian society, somehow transferred to the national level in the course of Norway's political history and preserved intact even during the Norwegian revolution of modernization that occurred mainly in the twentieth century.

(8) The communal sentiments of Norwegians presently have two main supports in concrete social structure, apart from the usual socialization processes. They rest, first, upon the "interconnection" of divided men and groups through affinities in their modes of life, diffuse personal bonds, and organizations deliberately created to associate them. Second, they are sustained by the remarkable formal and normative homogeneity of Norwegian authority patterns in virtually every segment of social life.

(9) The similarity of Norwegian authority patterns is particularly significant because it involves homogeneity in a realm of social experience related especially closely to political life, and because the substance of Norwegian authority patterns can account directly for the performance characteristics of the polity (especially the great legitimacy of democratic rule and its workaday efficiency) as well as supporting stable democracy indirectly through providing a foundation for more diffuse communal sentiments that facilitate the processes of democratic rule.

(10) The coexistence of great political cohesion alongside considerable political division in Norway ceases to be a mystery when one realizes that both may have a single source in strong demands for solidarity on different levels of society; and these demands for solidarity may even account for certain aspects of the individual behavior of Norwegians which, at first

glance, seem incongruent with the cohesiveness both of the national society and of its segments.

Diagramatically, the essence of the argument can be represented by the following model (the arrows indicating direction of causation):

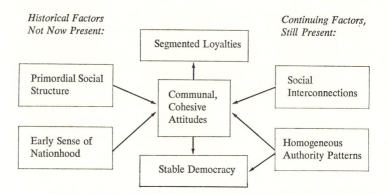

3. During this analysis many aspects of Norwegian life have been related to the stability and effectiveness of her democracy: individual values, educational structure, economic life, networks of personal ties, organizational blueprints, and so on. In trying to generalize the findings of the study, one's first inclination is to say, quite simply, that the more another country resembles Norway in any of these matters, the more likely it is to be a stable and effective democracy too. One's second impulse is to stifle the first, since it manifestly leads to untenable conclusions. So direct an imputation of the concrete characteristics of one case to others, so simple a translation of the particular into the general, is clearly doomed to failure, in the present case as in so many others.

This should be evident from what has been said about other democracies in the course of discussion. To be sure, no concerted effort has been made here to introduce comparative materials; making systematic and thorough comparisons is a task better performed when many more detailed theoretical case studies are available. But from time to time characteristics of other democratic polities were alluded to, at least in passing, and nearly always to demonstrate how Norway differs from other cases. What is most important to note about these passing observations is that, more often than not, they drew contrasts between Norway and other stable democracies, particularly Britain, not between Norway and unstable cases. And in this there was a purpose, however offhand and random the comparisons may have seemed. My intention was to elucidate the considerable variety of substantive conditions reconcilable with stable and effective democracy, even in regard to matters directly related in the present study to the performance characteristics of the Norwegian polity, and thus to create scepticism toward any direct and simple generalization of Norwegian experience. Such scepticism should be heightened by the fact that Norway also displays numerous conditions related by other writers, probably correctly and always for good reasons, to the defects of democracy elsewhere—for example, legalism, rapid modernization, a coincidence of fundamental issues in the course of political development, powerful specialized parliamentary committees, and so on—and by the fact that some of these matters too have been held to have had benign effects in the Norwegian case. Norway seems to belong to some queer and extraneous universe precisely because it seems in many respects similar to unstable democracies, and in even more respects different from other stable ones.

The contrasts drawn between Norway and Britain are particularly instructive in this regard. Frequently they involve not mere differences but nothing less than opposites. In addition to striking discrepancies between British and Norwegian constitutional provisions and parliamentary procedures, British social structure has been highly inegalitarian, Norwegian social structure highly egalitarian; the British tend to cultivate ceremonies and majesty in political life, the Norwegians matter-of-factness and the common touch; the British indulge visible eccentricities, the Norwegians suppress them; the British educational system is very heterogeneous, the Norwegian highly uniform;

Britain's development of democracy was prolonged and gradual and Norway's rather rapid, a point that applies to industrialization and urbanization as well; the Norwegians are extreme formal legalists, the British whatever may be the converse of that—conventionalists perhaps; and one could go on much longer in this vein. Concrete patterns that seem related to stable democracy in either case more often than not are missing, imperfectly developed, or reversed in the other. This is particularly so if one takes account of the long history of Norwegian democracy rather than looking at Norway only in the present. In that case, even such manifest resemblances between the two countries as their presently high levels of economic development lose significance.

If other stable democracies are taken into account, these contrasts become still more pronounced. Especially in the chapter on communal behavior in Norway, one may get the impression that it is not any unstable representative system but the United States, whose government is in no way grossly unstable or ineffectual, which provides a kind of antithesis to the Norwegian pattern. Americans certainly are not notable for "noneconomic" definitions of social conduct, for mutual confidence in one another's altruism, for much sympathetic solicitude for, and unconditional acceptance of, the weak and disadvantaged, for the suppression of hostilities in children or adults, or for highly valuing public objects or public careers. At the same time, a more competitive society, and one that values more intensely competitive achievements, not least to the manifest detriment of others, would be hard to find, or even to imagine.

Yet if democracies resemble or differ from one another in their performance characteristics, they ought, in an explicable world, to be concomitantly alike or different in other respects. In what, then, are the resemblances and differences most crucial for explaining democracy's stability and effectiveness likely to be found? How can the arguments of this study be generalized, if not in regard to such specific aspects of society, culture, and history as have been mentioned?

Given the many specific differences between Norway and other stable democracies and the not inconsiderable similarities between Norway and unstable cases, one answer seems particularly tempting, even perhaps inescapable. This is that democracies function as they do not because of any particular substantive aspects of society but because of the ways in which these aspects are generally patterned—in other words, that the performance of democracies depends on general contours of social life that can accommodate a considerable, even if not limitless, variety of specific contents. The specific attitudes, interactions, and institutions of democratic societies are after all always related and distributed in some manner. They thus constitute patterns the formal attributes of which may be compared and contrasted in their own right, and may be similar while their contents differ, in the same way that circles or squares have similar shapes regardless of their varying dimensions. That hypotheses stressing such characteristics of "form" are likely to serve our purpose better than propositions of the other kind is indicated, first, by logic (for if democracies displaying similar performance characteristics differ markedly in content, in what but form could they closely resemble one another?) and, second, by the most crucial arguments of this case study, especially the nature of the existing theories of stable democracy that these arguments support or cast doubt upon.

Most hypotheses about the conditions of stable democracy do invoke matters of specific content rather than of general pattern. They speak of specific constitutional provisions, specific attributes of economic life, specific aspects of class systems, demography, religious structure, and so on. It is just such hypotheses that make Norway seem exotic, as well as producing, in the great majority of cases, weak correlations when broad comparisons are made. On the other hand, Norway strongly supports certain hypotheses about democracies that stress the formal patterning of their contexts, raising the possibility that such hypotheses will prove more tenable when broadly applied as well.

To make this less abstract—both to illustrate what is meant by propositions about patterned forms and to point out what theories about stable democracy can best generalize the arguments of this study—let us go in some detail into the major hypotheses that Norwegian experience confirms, having already listed, especially in Chapter II, many that it makes doubtful.

4. One hypothesis about the conditions of stable democracy that Norway strikingly bears out, and that illustrates well the nature of propositions about patterned forms capable of accommodating various contents, was formulated and argued by the present writer in a monograph published some years ago.[1] This is the hypothesis that democracies (and perhaps also other kinds of rule) tend to be stable if governmental and social authority patterns are highly congruent—if they involve considerable resemblances and thus have a certain fit. The hypothesis does not require the virtual isomorphism of authority structures

[1] Vanity may be involved, but I consider this monograph so relevant to Norway and so useful for elucidating the larger implications of this study that I have attached it as an appendix. This will enable readers to see more fully developed what is said about it here. Two points about it, however, should be borne in mind. First, the monograph was written before I did any research on Norway and was constantly in my mind as I did that research; indeed, I went to Norway partly, but not exclusively, to test out its arguments in an unfamiliar setting. That Norway confirms these arguments might therefore be put down to a kind of self-interested selectivity of observation, although that is something that should be demonstrated, not assumed. Second, the monograph was written some time ago, and only as a first statement of ideas requiring further work, the nature of which is indicated in the conclusion of the piece. Some of that work, both empirical and theoretical, I have since done. But I have not yet written a more definitive version of the theory; in any case, nothing done since its first appearance entails any really basic changes in it. Hence I append it here in its original form, despite the fact that if it were being written now I would make some points rather differently as well as add much new material.

that characterizes Norway; in fact, the likelihood of such iso-morphism was explicitly held to be remote in the earlier essay. Nor does it require congruence in authority relations between government and every other segment of life (which was also held to be unlikely). Rather it stresses a special need for such congruence in regard to structures most involved in providing three crucial governmental "inputs": elite recruitment, political socialization, and overt political competition. In very stable democracies, however, one would expect on the basis of the hypothesis a relatively close approach to isomorphism of the more crucial authority structures and an exceptional congru-ence of authority patterns throughout all social life—precisely as is the case in Norway.

The rationale for the hypothesis need not be fully repeated here. In essence, it has three elements, apart from its *prima facie* plausibility. First, the hypothesis seems to fit closely the more extreme cases of stable and unstable democracy, such as Great Britain and the Weimar Republic. Second, it makes sense in terms of certain well-established theories of the effects of anomie and strains in the performance of social roles. Third, it can help explain why other theories of stable democracy hold in some or many cases, but not in all.

The Norwegian case reinforces all three elements of that rationale. It adds, of course, another conspicuous case in point. It also supports the position that the hypothesis is well-grounded upon theories of human motivation, for in saying that through the congruence of social with governmental authority patterns Norwegians become deeply committed and accus-tomed to the role playing required by government one says, in effect, that such congruence prevents potentially destructive normlessness, ambivalence, or deviant behavior in political actors. As for how Norway supports the third rationale for the hypothesis, one example may suffice. In the monograph that originally argued the hypothesis it was contended that level of economic development relates only weakly to the stability of democracies, (1) because it is not the level but the rapidity of economic development that really matters, very rapid development having particularly deleterious consequences, and (2) because some of the societies at present most highly developed economically achieved that position by relatively slow development (that is, by being early starters); and the consequences of rapid economic development were held to be deleterious precisely because of the impact of such development on the general coherence, the congruent patterning, of a society's various components. Norway, however, shows that even very rapid economic development need not prevent effective democracy (at any rate, not where the latter precedes the former), however often it may in fact have done so. It will not do so if, for whatever reasons, it does not seriously disrupt general social patterns conducive to the stability of democratic rule. This makes still stronger the position that specific conditions such as national wealth and economic growth rates impinge on democracy only in so far as they affect the general patterning of social forms.

The congruence hypothesis—like others of its kind—does not imply, as this example illustrates, that specific aspects of a society's constitutional structure, economic life, social stratification, culture, or history are irrelevant to the question of whether or not it can be a stable and effective democracy. General patterns, after all, are formed by specific contents. What it does imply is that between the performance characteristics of democracies and their specific social and political attributes lies an intervening variable that governs the effects of the specific attributes. Hence similar attributes may in some cases have different consequences, different attributes similar ones, in democratic systems. But this is not at all the same as saying that the attributes are of no import. In fact, it follows from this position that certain specific changes in a democracy, say in its constitutional structure, could in fact have quite dramatic consequences. Such consequences cannot, however, be predicted from the specific changes alone.

The congruence hypothesis readily dissolves many apparent

mysteries arising from comparisons of the specific characteristics of stable democracies. For example, take the fact that British and Norwegian authority relations, while greatly different, nevertheless seem to produce in many respects similar results. Surely that fact ceases to mystify when it is realized that the authority patterns of the two societies are in fact closely similar in form, despite great differences in content: in both cases the patterns are highly congruent, indeed highly uniform throughout society, particularly those aspects of society that matter most politically. From this standpoint Bagehot, who argues that deferential attitudes and behavior make parliamentary democracy effective, is both right and wrong. He is right for Britain, where authority relations have been remarkably congruent just because, among other attributes, they have consistently involved deference in many realms. He is wrong in raising his interpretation of Britain to the level of general theory, for authority relations obviously may be congruent without being deferential, or without having any other specific characteristics.

The range of specific authority patterns consonant with stable democracy is not, however, infinite. It is circumscribed by at least two factors. The first and most obvious is that democracies, while varying considerably in form, must, of course, have certain core elements in common; otherwise the concept democracy itself would have no meaning. Institutions that regularize political competition, as well as norms and rules making for wide political participation and for sharp limitations upon the exercise of governmental power, especially arbitrary power, would seem to be minimal requirements for democracy to exist at all; and these must somehow have bases in a society's complex of authority relations. Stable democracy, in a society whose authority patterns contain virtually no democratic elements at all, is thus, needless to say, unthinkable.

A second constraint upon the variability of authority patterns consonant with stable democracy arises from another hypothesis that Norway bears out, and that also involves what we have called a general form. This is the hypothesis that stable democracies require norms and behavior making for authority no less than for democracy—a balanced blend of disparate attitudes and modes of acting in authority relations. According to that hypothesis polities that are too one-sidedly democratic, whether in governmental structure only or in a wider sense, are as likely to be unstable and ineffective as democratic polities superimposed on preponderantly authoritarian social structures. This hypothesis, like congruence theory, involves form rather than content because there is no special mixture of democratic and authoritarian norms that alone satisfies what it requires. Norway and Britain, at any rate, satisfy its requirements very differently. Functional deference, formal hierarchism, and legalistic norms largely accomplish in one case what diffuse social deference, reverence for governmental authority, and ceremonies that clothe authority in majesty help to achieve in the other. And there may well be still other sources of authority that could operate as functional equivalents of the British and Norwegian patterns. But this is not to say that any norms and practices of authority may be freely substituted for others without altering the performance of democracies. To say that norms of democracy and authority must be balanced is to say more than that they must coexist. It is to say also that they must be compatible, in the sense of not themselves creating unmanageable strains and ambivalences. From that standpoint, the norms that make for authority in Norway are singularly well attuned to the society's democratic norms, particularly in two senses: through making authority highly impersonal, they prevent it from compromising the essential egalitarianism and collegiality of Norwegian life, and through assigning great authority to functional experts, they facilitate the search for wide agreements in a highly participant and pluralistic society. Thus, if one key to stable democracy is the congruence of authority structures in general, a second is the reconciliation of disparate elements within these structures. The various ways in which that reconciliation might be accomplished remain to be formulated, and it will probably not be easy to formulate them, since it is evident that they differ widely.

A third hypothesis supported by this case study is that stable democracy requires considerable pluralism in social life—a large number of "secondary groups," particularly organized associations, in which many members of society participate and which intervene between national authority on one hand and individuals and their primary groups on the other. Since this hypothesis does not specify what particular sorts of secondary groups stable democracy requires, but merely that it requires many, it too refers to a pattern, a form, that may have varying contents, yet similar effects, in different settings. The monograph in which the congruence hypothesis was first set out provides a rationale for the pluralism hypothesis too, arguing, in gist, that authority patterns in democracies are unlikely to be congruent unless considerable networks of densely populated and otherwise significant secondary groups exist.[2] That, of course, implies that the pluralistic structures of democracy also cannot be infinitely various; at the very least they must themselves be constituted along lines that make them congruent with governmental authority patterns. But this still leaves considerable scope for variety. And it should be noted that other uses of the same hypothesis, based on different rationales, impose still fewer restraints upon the specific content social pluralism must have. Thus, Truman's view that overlapping, or multiple, memberships are a source of moderation and cohesion in democracies requires only that individual identifications, as well as secondary groups themselves, be pluralistic and not confined to groups representing a single class or occupational interest;[3] Kornhauser's theory of mass society adds to that requirement only the proviso that the secondary groups be "strong";[4] and Durkheim's early formulation of the

[2] See Appendix B.

[3] Truman, *The Governmental Process*, ch. 6.

[4] William Kornhauser, *The Politics of Mass Society* (Glencoe, Ill., 1959), ch. 3.

pluralistic hypothesis (foreshadowed still earlier in de Tocqueville) requires nothing more than that the secondary groups exist.[5]

5. The hypotheses sketched so far concern the primary object of this case study: to arrive at generalizations about the conditions of stable and effective democracy that fit Norway as well as other cases. But the study had a secondary object too, closely related to the first. It was intended to make more informative a particular generalization about stable democracy which is, without proper elaboration, no more than a truism: that effective democracy presupposes a balance of division and cohesion (or consensus and cleavage, in others' terminology).

Since most of the case study was prompted by that generalization, our findings in regard to it deserve a separate summary. These findings, however, nicely fit the previous argument, because the most important of them surely is that the balance of division and cohesion characteristic of stable democracies is itself a form that may have various contents. This point emerges most forcibly in the argument that division and cohesion in democracies do not belong to the world of zero sums. Nothing that makes either more considerable need diminish the other. In fact, in certain cases the same conditions may augment or diminish both, in the way that pressures for solidarity in Norway, by operating on more than one level of society, simultaneously solidify the whole political system and its segmental and cultural fragments. That being so, one can imagine several patterns of division and cohesion which, in different ways, are all "balanced"—at any rate, in the sense that there exist within a polity forces capable of resolving competing political demands within stable institutions having legitimate leaders whose decisions are widely accepted, even when the demands are high in affect and when the system is subject to acute environmental stresses. No one, to be sure,

[5] Emile Durkheim, *Professional Ethics and Civic Morals* (Glencoe, Ill., 1958), pp. 62-63.

would argue that any kind or degree of political division can produce such institutions, leadership, and decisions. But Norway suggests that they can be achieved despite kinds and degrees of division widely held to be incompatible with stable and effective democracy, through integrative forces commensurate with those that divide a system. It is, consequently, vitally important that the sources of political cohesion be studied as searchingly in the future as those of political division have been studied in the past.

On the basis of the forces discussed in an earlier portion of this study as capable of producing cohesion in democracies, three types of systems in which division and cohesion are "balanced" can be distinguished. The first might be called *consensus systems*: systems in which cohesion results from a low degree (but, it should be stressed, never absolute lack) of political division. Consensus may exist even in societies in which there are marked social and cultural distinctions, indeed social rifts, but obviously the greater these are the less likely is political consensus. Similarly, the political mobilization of large numbers and varieties of people through highly organized structures of political competition clearly tends to augment political division. Hence modern societies with their complex social differentiations and networks of interest, their wide political participation and highly organized political groups, are on the face of it rather unlikely to be consensus systems. They are more likely to be what one could call *mechanically integrated systems*: systems in which cohesion results largely from political divisions themselves, either directly through their countervailing effects on one another or indirectly through the moderating effects—the tendency to scale down political demands—that Truman and Kornhauser both attribute to overlapping memberships.[6] Such systems, however, are always

---

[6] This use of the term "mechanical integration" should not be confused with Emile Durkheim's concept "mechanical solidarity" (see *The Division of Labor in Society*, Glencoe, Ill., 1949; originally published in 1893). Durkheim's concept means the inverse of what I have in mind,

likely to be more durable than effective, for the consequences of mechanical cohesion generally are to keep decisions from being taken, due to lack of pressures for them or due to the fact that pressures mutually cancel one another. The third type might be called *community systems*: systems in which cohesion exists mainly despite division, due to overarching sentiments of solidarity, whatever their source may be. Community, it is essential to note, does not make for cohesion in the same way as consensus. The latter obviates the need for searching out agreements, while the former makes for cohesion rather through norms that facilitate the quest for agreements—for example, by putting a high value on agreeing as an end in itself, even where men are manifestly divided (as happens in most societies when events, such as war, induce temporarily strong sentiments of solidarity), or by cultivating a certain political considerateness of others: deference to their expertise or experience, sympathy with their special interests, or reluctance to raise issues that might exacerbate feelings of hostility of any kind and so prevent agreements even where they might be reached. But, of course, communal sentiments tend themselves to make for certain kinds of political agreement, most of all in areas that the communal values themselves involve.

Consensus systems, mechanically integrated systems, and community systems are, needless to say, ideal types, and pure examples of them are, as always, hard to find.[7] More often than

---

since it denotes solidarity resulting from shared sentiments. In contrast, the complementary relations and balances that may exist in highly differentiated societies he labels "organic solidarity." Although Durkheim's concepts are widely familiar, I feel that it is pardonable and wise to reverse them, since they are themselves strangely inverted in terms of conventional meaning and the technical idea of mechanism in the natural sciences and modern philosophy. Talcott Parsons' use of the term mechanism ("the mechanist who denies that any sort of 'normative' control ever operates in the empirical world") is more in tune with both. (See Max Black, ed., *The Social Theories of Talcott Parsons*, Englewood Cliffs, N.J., 1961, p. 341.)

[7] It should also be noted that consensus, mechanical integration, and community are each themselves "forms" capable of accommodating a

not, elements of all three exist in the most stable cases. They certainly do in Norway. But Norway clearly is preeminently a community system, while among the other cases that have been alluded to, Britain probably comes closest to the first type[8] and the United States (at any rate if Truman's interpretation has merit) to the second. To some extent this is discernible in the decisional outputs of the three systems. These are considerable in Britain in almost all areas. They are strikingly less considerable in the United States on major issues, except when the system is temporarily "unbalanced," as it was in the early days of the New Deal, or when issues mobilize few countervailing forces or bring about ephemeral coalitions of overwhelming strength. Interest mongering is the predominant decision-making style of the system, and on major policies it seems usu-

---

variety of functionally equivalent contents. Thus, not only the *balances* of cohesion and division, but cohesion and divisions themselves, illustrate my argument. Cross-cutting divisions may certainly differ greatly in substance while remaining similar in form and effects. Consensus might exist on different matters, with similar consequences. And it is possible that there is more than one kind of "community." Here the term primarily denotes certain special relations between the self (or the intimate "we") and others, symbols of otherness, and common possessions. But it has been pointed out to me (by Samuel H. Beer) that there may also be a rather different kind of community, one of highly regulated competitiveness, in which the rules of competition confine instrumental calculations, set limits to competitiveness, and provide a non-affective basis for operating organizations. It is perhaps just this sort of "community" that may grow out of strictly "modern" patterns rather than the maintenance in modern life of primordial attitudes.

[8] Britain might, however, be more precisely described as a system of *political complementarity*—which may be regarded as a special kind of consensus. There has been, for example, a remarkable complementarity between the attitudes of the British elite and nonelite, the one expecting diffuse deference and special access to positions of political authority, the other granting both the deference and the access. This complementarity of attitudes is a kind of consensus for two reasons: it involves general agreement on the proper qualifications for political authority; and it is premised on the elite's adherence to widely shared procedural and substantive norms—including the norm, typical of "Tory democracy," that authority is a trust requiring the higher orders to govern with due regard for the welfare of the lower.

ally to take a great deal more than mere majorities to move the system toward positive outputs. In Norway, however, even minorities seem capable of achieving positive results, provided that they act in areas in which communal values or technical desiderata loom large. In other areas, Norwegians often arrive by silent repression at "nondecisions" that Americans tend to reach by hard-fought stalemates. To some extent, also, the different balances of division and cohesion in the three countries are discernible in the characteristics of their structures of political competition, especially party competition. Britain has a highly consolidated party system; America a party system consolidated in name but actually consisting of a great many overlapping fragments that seem particularly adept at producing negative majorities; Norway a fragmented party system that is, despite its fragmentation, capable of producing consistently positive outcomes in the parliamentary process. All three are stable democracies, but because the balances of division and cohesion that make them stable differ, so do many of their other characteristics, even those pertaining to the performance of their governments.[9]

6. From every point of view, then, the stability and effectiveness of democracies seem to depend on certain general forms of social and political life rather than any aspects of their specific contents. The contents, to repeat, are not inconsequential. In every case there are limitations on how widely they may vary. In every case also differences in them will lead to differences in other realms: to democratic polities that are stable and effective in more or less different ways. But as to the larger

[9] In Chapters VI-IX, I discussed the ways in which the Norwegian "community system" probably originated and the forces that seem to have maintained it throughout modern history. It would be interesting, perhaps, to ask in a more general way what produces one type of "balanced" system or another, or no balance sufficient to make democracy stable and effective at all. On this, however, my ideas, for better or worse, are rudimentary—little more than hunches—and unlikely to become more precise without much further case study and theoretical reflection.

question on which this study has concentrated—whether democracies will be stable and effective to any significant degree at all—the forms as such seem to be far more important than the specific attitudes, actions, and structures that constitute them.[10]

This may be taken as the concentrated essence of the theoretical implications of the study, distilled from a number of subsidiary propositions that are already rather broad. The subsidiary propositions, incidentally, are related to one another not only because all refer to general social patterns; they also belong together in that each adds something to those that precede it. The first, concerning the need for congruent authority patterns, is augmented by the second, which says something about the characteristics the congruent authority patterns ought to have; the third, concerning social pluralism, speaks of the generic form of societies in which the required authority patterns are likely to exist; and the fourth is concerned with the ways in which the always potentially centrifugal forces of pluralistic societies may become cohesive. What is still re-

[10] This argument is consonant even with recent work by Lipset, who has done more than anyone else to relate the stability of democracies to specific social conditions. Comparing four nations that, in a broad sense, are all stable democracies (Britain, the U.S., Canada, and Australia), Lipset finds in them considerable "value differences," which he relates to other specific differences in the four polities. (See S. M. Lipset, *The First New Nation*, New York, 1963, pt. 3.) The argument also fits Montesquieu's belief that many problems do not have *unique* solutions and the finding by the originators of the Theory of Games, von Neumann and Morgenstern, that in most cases a "multiplicity of solutions" exists, but a multiplicity that is strictly limited. "Considering solutions as 'stable standards of behavior' this . . . [means] that given the same physical background, different 'established orders of society' or 'accepted standards of behavior' can be built, all possessing . . . characteristics of inner stability." But on this point, Deutsch remarks (still consonant with my position) that "there may be more than one way to win, or to do best, but there are vastly more ways to lose or to do poorly" (Karl W. Deutsch, *The Nerves of Government*, New York, 1963, p. 55). My suggestion here is that "multiple" solutions can in some cases be transformed into "unique" solutions by being stated on a more general, and more formal, level.

quired is testing these broad generalizations in numerous cases, and, should they hold up, evolving from them narrower hypotheses that tell us not only whether democracies will be stable and effective broadly speaking, but in what specific ways and to what degrees they will fulfill the criteria of stable democracy, or fail to do so.

But before having done, let us dwell a little longer on the most general argument of this study. Even ignoring the unending puzzles that arise when specific aspects of the political structures and social settings of democracies are compared, the finding that the broad performance characteristics of democracies depend on forms capable of having various contents should not be surprising. It has a certain inherent plausibility for two related reasons. One is that democracy is itself legitimized more by its form than by its substantive outputs or specific rulers; the other that its form, while requiring certain core elements, may vary over a considerable range. That is certainly not true of all political systems, some of which are legitimated by the personalities of those that rule them, or by their success in producing specific results, or by forms of governance that offer little or no scope for variation.

What is probably more surprising is the very considerable variety of contents that the forms consonant with stable democracy seem able to accommodate, despite limits on their variability. But the fact that stable democracy is possible in many settings and through a variety of governmental structures provides no special ground for optimism about the possibility of creating it or the probability of its coming spontaneously into being. Stable democracy is in fact rare, particularly in those cases where attempts have been made through human contrivance deliberately to construct it. Why that is so, given the present argument, is surely plain. General social forms, requiring the proper articulation of many aspects of society, are certainly harder to engineer than any specific social conditions. This is particularly so since democratic government needs to be consonant with social realms little susceptible to human manipulation, unless it be backed by the potent terror and instruments of penetration of totalitarian rulers, and perhaps not even then. Moreover, the forms that appear to make democracy stable and effective require particularly delicate and tenuous balances between forces that can more easily be virulently contradictory than beneficently compatible; and the proper adjustments of these forces seem unlikely to come about without the operation of uncommon mechanisms, growing out of unusual historic sequences, like those that characterize Norway and, in different ways, other stable democracies.

Yet any study that improves theoretical understanding is bound to be instructive in regard to practical tasks, and perhaps to moral reflection as well. It can, at a minimum, help avoid gruesome mistakes. The worst of these surely is the mere transplantation of the institutions of stable democracies to other environments. Where this has been done, the institutions, more often than not, have withered or become downright poisonous. The next worst surely is to proceed from simple hypotheses about specific social attributes, such as that democracy will be enhanced by anything that increases gross national product or draws actively into politics previously passive men. But theory can do more than help prevent misguided actions. It can reveal where practical possibilities exist or are foreclosed, and direct attention to realms that must be altered or fostered if desired results are to be achieved. The present study, for example, has decided implications for constitution making in democracies, suggesting that its main task is not to embody abstract ideals in legal rules, but to harmonize the governmental structure with structures instrumental in preparing men for the performance of political roles. It does not follow, however, that democratic governments can be no more than mirrors of given social structures, since, to some extent no doubt, these structures may be altered to make them more compatible with desired governmental forms. But doing so requires a better understanding of what compatibility denotes in such a case, and what precisely it is that needs most to be manipulated.

As for moral reflection, that may have no place in a theoretical case study. Yet men are moralizing as well as perceiving
and theorizing beings; hence some very brief remarks in a normative vein may perhaps be permitted. I do not intend here to
argue any personal values; but neither do I wish to conceal
them. I confess what will in any case be plain: that I was deeply
attracted by many aspects of Norwegian life, not least because
it provides impressive contrasts to the harsher—the more competitive and instrumental, the less protective and closely knit—
features of American society. At the same time, however, it
was apparent that the alluring characteristics of Norwegian
society entail costs one might not (and some Norwegians
themselves do not) want to pay. I refer especially to the stifling
of intellectual daring, unusual talent, and useful ambitions, to
the small rewards for rare achievement, and the restricted
scope for personal quirks, dash, cleverness, and imagination.
And these costs surely are not personal alone but involve important social consequences, especially for Norway's ability to
hold her own with nations less comfortable but more restless
and energetic.

A foreigner might then be attracted by the gentleness and
strong bonds of Norwegian life or repelled by the price paid for
them; a Norwegian might choose to maintain the bonds or
loosen the constraints they necessarily impose. What seems
most important, however, is the very fact that such a choice
exists at all. Norway opened for me, and may for others, moral
possibilities that previously seemed foreclosed by the ineluc-
table essence of modern life.

It may be likely that modernized men will regard one another
chiefly as utilities; that diffuse affection should be confined by
them to ever-narrowing circles of social interaction; that they
must leave the weaker largely to their own devices, or to impersonal and grudging institutions, in order to make society
generally stronger; that their special interests, fragmented by
social differentiation, will always be reconciled by callous bargaining or mutually canceling pressures in mechanical fields of

political forces, or else not harmonized at all; that their private comforts will be bought with public shabbiness; that they must eradicate their past to live in a dynamic present. But even if these things are likely, Norway shows that they are far from necessary. There are other possibilities.

To have moral relevance, however, the possibilities realized in Norwegian life must be open to others. Are they? Probably less than one would like—for undoubtedly Norwegian society has been shaped less by choice than circumstance—but perhaps more than might be thought. At the same time it is conceivable that future choices and circumstances will change the balances and congruities of Norwegian life itself, and with them the performance of Norway's political system. A picture of any society in historic time always portrays an object moving from an obscure past to an unknown future. With a little imagination, one could, indeed, construct a formidable list of factors even now at work in Norway that contain the potential for transforming the society. But that is another matter, not germane to my present purpose.

PRINCIPAL SOURCES

(1)   Torgersen, *Norske politiske institusjoner.*
(2)   Rokkan and Valen, "Regional Contrasts in Norwegian Politics," in Allardt and Littunen, eds., *Cleavages, Ideologies and Party Systems.*
(3)   Rokkan, "Norway: Numerical Democracy and Corporate Pluralism," in R. A. Dahl, ed., *Political Oppositions in Western Democracies,* New Haven, 1966.
(4)   Valen and Katz, *Political Parties in Norway.*
(5)   Norwegian National Election Survey, 1957.
(Other sources cited where appropriate.)

Citations in parentheses identify the chapters and sections of this book to which the tables pertain.

TABLE 1 (Chapter II, 2)

THE LEGITIMACY OF NORWEGIAN DEMOCRACY

Q: Would you say that a democratic form of rule is, in general, better or worse than other forms?

	%
Better	78
Worse	2
Don't know, not interested	20
Reasons for preference:	
All can participate, express their opinion, government elected	28
More freedom, less compulsion	15
Don't like dictatorship	10
Most just	8
Has best results	7
Others and don't know	26
	n = 2,100

Source: Norsk Gallup, *Aftenposten*, 11 November 1965.

TABLE 2 (Chapter II, A, 3)

CABINET STABILITY

Period	Ministries	(*months*) Average Duration	Number of Prime Ministers
1884-1905	8	31	4
1905-1920	6	30	5
1920-1935	11	16	8
1935-1964	5[a]	70	4
1884-1964	30	32	21

[a] Gerhardsen's temporary, voluntary yielding of the prime minister-ship is not counted as a change in ministry.
Source: (1), 8.9.

TABLE 3 (Chapter II, B, 4)

LEGALISM:
LEGAL TRAINING AND THE HIGHER CIVIL SERVICE

	Fylkesmenn[a]		*Ekspedisjonssjefer*[b]	
	1900	*1960*	*1900*	*1960*
Lawyers	19[c]	12	14	37
Other higher education	—	1	1	10
No higher education	—	5	—	1

[a] Highest local government position.
[b] Highest rank in national civil service.
[c] Absolute numbers throughout.
Source: (1), 9.4.

TABLE 4

NORWEGIAN ELECTION RESULTS, 1882-1961
STORTING SEATS FOR MAIN PARTIES

	Labor		"Left" (Liberals)			Right	Total
1882[1]			83			31	114
1885			84			30	114
1888			39			75[a]	114
1891			63			35[a]	114
1894			59			55[a]	114
1897			79			35[a]	114
1900[2]			77			37[a]	114
1903			50			63[a]	114
1906[3]	10		73			36	123
1909	11		46			64[b]	123
1912	23		70			24[b]	123
1915	19		74			21[b]	123
1918	18		51			50[b]	126
		Soc. Dem.		Agrarians			
1921[4]	29	8	37	17		57[b]	150
1924	24	8	34	22		54[b]	150
1927	59		30	26		30	150
1930	47		33	25		41	150
1933	69		24	23		30	150
1936	70		23	18		36	150
					Christians		
1945	76		20	10	8	25	150
1949	85		21	12	9	23	150
1953[5]	77		15	14	14	27	150
1957	78		15	15	12	29	150
1961	74		14	16	15	29	150

[1] "Indirect" elections, 1882-1903.

[2] From 1900, small splinter parties (fewer than 8 seats) are omitted from the table.

[3] Single-member constituency elections, 1906-1918.

[4] D'Hondt PR system, 1921-1949.

[5] Sainte-Laguë PR system, 1953–present.

[a] Includes "moderates."

[b] Includes "National Liberals."

TABLE 5 (Chapter III, 2-4)

TERRITORIAL CLEAVAGE

Election results 1882-1961: differences in party strength between the cities and the rural districts.[1]

	Labour[2] Cities	Labour Rural	Left[3] Cities	Left Rural	Moderates Cities	Moderates Rural	Agrarians Cities	Agrarians Rural	Right[4] Cities	Right Rural
INDIRECT ELECTIONS										
1882			36.0	47.2					45.9	22.0
1885			37.8	49.3					45.1	22.3
1888	1.1	—	28.0	29.4	3.9	16.1			46.0	21.9
1891	2.0	—	37.9	36.9					47.1	32.7
1894			46.0	44.9					46.3	43.5
1897			45.7	44.3					42.9	38.5
1900	7.2	1.6	30.5	30.5					29.0	21.3
1903	13.7	4.4	22.3	23.7					32.6	21.9
DIRECT ELECTIONS										
1906	20.9	6.1	20.9	33.0					31.2	16.1
1909	22.7	7.9	15.3	20.3					31.4	19.9
1912	27.4	11.3	16.5	27.2					26.7	17.4
1915	27.9	14.3	16.6	23.0					26.1	12.6
1918	24.0	15.0	9.6	21.0			—	3.7	33.5	10.1
1921	29.7	16.5	8.9	17.8			—	12.5	37.4	15.9

Year	C.P. Cities	C.P. Rural	Cities	Rural	Cities	Rural	Christians Cities	Christians Rural	Cities	Rural	Cities	Rural	Nat. Soc. Cities	Nat. Soc. Rural	Soc. People's Cities	Soc. People's Rural
1924	6.3	3.3	27.8	14.9	8.3	16.4			—	13.3	36.7	16.4	2.6	1.3		
1927	4.0	2.1	32.4	21.6	8.6	14.2			—	14.3	30.8	11.4	2.4	1.2		
1930	2.2	0.9	29.0	22.1	10.8	18.4			0.3	17.4	38.8	16.5	—	—		
1933[5]	2.2	1.0	35.8	28.2	10.5	14.6	—	0.9	0.2	15.0	27.6	11.9				
1936[5]	0.8	—	40.0	33.6	10.6	15.1	0.8	1.3	—	13.8	29.1	14.6				
1945[5]	13.8	7.1	32.9	30.3	9.4	10.9	4.9	6.5	—	8.5	20.5	9.8				
1949	6.4	4.0	39.9	35.9	11.0	10.9	3.3	8.6	—	9.9	24.8	9.3				
1953	5.0	3.5	38.9	35.7	8.2	7.7	6.1	9.4	0.3	10.5	25.2	9.7				
1957	3.2	2.3	40.3	36.4	7.6	7.5	5.8	9.0	0.3	10.6	25.0	9.7				
1961	2.6	2.1	38.4	36.0	6.8	7.1	5.6	8.5	0.3	10.8	25.7	10.9			2.8	1.4

Notes to Table 5

[1] The strength of each party or party group has been expressed as percentages of all *registered* voters at the given election (registration was voluntary through 1897, from 1900 onward automatic on the basis of population records).

[2] Includes various "workers' lists" 1894-1903 and the Social Democratic Party (Labour's right wing) in 1921 and 1924.

[3] Includes the "Worker Democrats," later the "Radical People's Party."

[4] Includes the Moderate Left from 1891 to 1903 (the electoral statistics did not allow a detailed distribution of original votes by the political colouring of the candi-

date), the "Unionist" Party of 1903 and 1906 and the *Frisinnede* (National Liberals) from 1909 to 1936.

[5] A minor party, the "Society Party," in some ways similar to the Social Credit party in Canada, was nationally active in 1933 and 1936 and appeared under a new name (in Bergen only) in 1945. It gained these percentages of votes from the electorate:

	1933	1936	1945
Cities	2.4	3.1	—
Rural districts	0.6	2.4	0.4

Source: (2), table 1.1 (by permission of the authors).

TABLE 6 (Chapter III, 4)

REGIONAL CLEAVAGE

The distinctiveness of the South-West: differences in the politics of the major
occupational groups in communes at different levels of industrialization
within two contrasting divisions of the country.

Occupation of head	Community	Region	N =100%	Soc. %	Middle %	Cons. %	Unclear, non-voter %
				Intended vote 1957			
Worker	City, town	South, West	77	61	8	9	22
		Rest	230	63	7	9	21
	Industrialized	SW	31	45	30	3	22
		Rest	161	65	6	5	24
	Other rural	SW	70	35	24	4	39
		Rest	173	64	10	4	22
Farmer, small holders, Fishermen	Industrialized	SW	25	4	68	8	20
		Rest	40	32.5	30	2.5	35
	Other rural	SW	86	10	58	6	26
		Rest	228	32	35	11	22
Middle class	Cities, towns, Industrialized	SW	84	13	25	29	33
		Rest	228	26	11	39	24
	Other rural	SW	77	16	72	18	25
		Rest	108	29	18	25	28

Source: (3), table 2.

Regional contrasts in party polarization 1900-1957: data for rural districts only.

Valid votes = 100%	1900	1903	1906	1918	1921	1927	1930	1936	1945	1957
Oslofjord area	31,895	34,259	32,394	88,054	118,598	156,101	187,534	238,352	260,412	253,503
Soc. (CP. + Lab. + Soc. dem.)	—	6.8	16.2	34.2	32.3	43.3	35.9	46.5	51.8	53.0
Left (and Christians)	49.5	37.3	35.5	16.3	9.8	6.3	8.9	7.1	17.3	14.8
Agrarians	—	—	—	4.4	16.4	17.7	18.7	12.6	8.2	10.2
Conservatives	50.5	55.9	47.7	44.7	41.5	32.6	36.6	30.8+2.2[1]	22.7	21.1
Polarization score[2]	—	.63	.64	.83	.88	.92	.89	.92	.81	.83
East Inland and Trøndelag	59,357	58,984	73,840	170,186	218,849	239,945	284,370	337,604	354,282	411,241
Soc. (CP. + Lab. + Soc. dem.)	8.4	11.8	9.5	34.3	30.9	42.9	38.6	49.3	60.1	58.9
Left (and Christians)	58.7	48.6	68.0	39.1	25.6	19.9	19.8	14.9	16.6	14.1
Agrarians	—	—	—	9.2	21.4	26.2	26.4	20.8	14.8	17.1
Conservatives	32.9	39.6	21.3	15.1	21.4	10.9	15.3	11.4+1.9[2]	8.6	9.7
Polarization score	.41	.51	.31	.56	.67	.73	.73	.81	.81	.83
South and West	63,031	57,166	59,533	111,587	184,802	189,865	244,890	289,944	297,594	355,722
Soc. (CP. + Lab. + Soc. dem.)	0.4	1.3	1.7	14.8	14.0	21.9	16.7	24.1	33.9	36.5
Left (and Christians)	55.1	51.4	63.5	59.0	44.1	38.2	41.1	37.8	41.3	37.3
Agrarians	—	—	—	9.3	22.7	26.7	27.2	19.5	13.9	15.6
Conservatives	44.5	47.3	32.2	16.2	18.5	13.2	15.0	13.9+0.6[2]	9.9	10.6
Polarization score	.45	.49	.34	.34	.42	.48	.44	.51	.52	.56
North	16,658	15,096	21,040	51,217	75,582	78,604	104,174	134,972	111,441	154,448
Soc. (CP. + Lab. + Soc. dem.)	—	28.9	29.2	40.4	32.5	45.5	32.1	46.3	66.5	60.3
Left (and Christians)	73.5	47.9	55.3	54.8	26.1	22.9	26.3	16.6	13.8	16.8
Agrarians	—	—	—	1.8	13.8	10.0	11.9	8.2	3.7	8.5
Conservatives	26.5	17.7	13.2	2.3	26.9	21.6	29.7	18.7+0.6[2]	16.1	13.9
Polarization score	—	.47	.42	.44	.70	.75	.70	.80	.86	.82

[1] National Socialist vote.

[2] This gives the Socialist + Conservative (inclusive of the National Liberal and, in 1936, the National Socialist) vote as a ratio of the total vote cast for *all major party groups except the Agrarians* (dis-regarded in this context since they express another dimension of representation).

Source: (2), table 1.3 (by permission of the authors).

TABLE 8. REGIONAL CLEAVAGE AND CULTURAL DIVERGENCE (Chapter III, 3-4)

Persistent differences in language, values and politics; statistics for the rural districts of each region for:

(a) choices of language for children in primary school,
(b) membership in teetotalist organizations in 1923,
(c) votes in the prohibition referendum in 1926,
(d) votes for Moderates and Christians 1888-1961

Region	(a) Language[1] % of school districts using landsmål/nynorsk 1910	1956-57	(b) Teetotalists[2] per 1000 adults 1923	(c) Votes for prohibition[3] 1926	(d) The "Christian" share of the old Left[4] — 1888 Left + Mod.	1888 Mod. in % of Left + Mod.	1945 Middle parties	1945 Chr. in % of Middle	1961 Middle parties	1961 Chr. in % of Middle
Oslofjord	0	0	18.4	26.2	45.2	20.3	25.5	43.9	24.0	34.2
East Inland	13.5	35.7	25.9	35.4	66.0	25.1	27.3	9.8	21.5	24.2
South	28.8	48.5	79.4	74.8	68.7	53.0	47.7	—	48.7	34.8
West	47.4	94.0	93.7	76.3	82.2	55.3	57.0	34.1	51.8	38.1
Trøndelag	14.2	42.9	82.8	60.8	65.3	11.9	41.2	16.8	36.3	27.7
North	4.4	13.1	33.9	53.2	77.9	20.2	17.4	—	25.5	36.3

[1] For 1910: *NOS* V 218, table 1, p. 3. For 1956-57: *NOS* XI 344, table 14, p. 19. The 1910 table gives figures by *district* only while later statistics also indicate the *no. of children* in *nynorsk* schools. The national figures for 1956-57 were 49.0% of the districts, but only 33.5% of the children: the *nynorsk* districts are clearly less densely populated than the others.

[2] *NOS* VII 129, table 29. These statistics were unfortunately discontinued after 1923, cf. *NOS* VII 196, p. 51ˣ.

[3] *NOS* VIII 14, p. 3. The distributions for the first referendum in 1919 is of less interest in this context since the votes in the rural districts were so overwhelmingly *for* prohibition at that time:

	Cities and towns		Rural communes	
	For	Against	For	Against
1919	44.5	55.5	70.1	29.9
1926	30.3	69.7	51.7	48.3

[4] The percentages for the Left, the Moderates/Christians, and the Agrarians are calculated on the basis of *valid votes*, not on the basis of the total electorate.

Source: (2), table 4.1 (by permission of the authors).

TABLE 9 (Chapter III, 4)

REGIONAL CLEAVAGE AND CULTURAL DIVERGENCE

Membership in religious associations:
survey data for differences between occupational groups in the contrasting
regional divisions of the country.

Occupation of head	Type of locality	Sex	N = 100%	Member of State Church, no. assoc. %	Member of religious assoc.:			
					Mission societies %	Other, in State Church %	Dissenter %	NA %
EAST, TRØNDELAG, NORTH								
Worker	Total	M	281	90	4	3	2	1
		W	283	82	7	6	5	1
	Urban	M	111	91	1	3	3	2
		W	119	83	4	7	6	—
	Rural	M	170	88	6	3	2	1
		W	164	81	10	5	4	—
Smallholder, farmer		M	87	92	5	—	2	—
		W	111	60	31	3	5	—
Middle class		M	169	88	5	4	4	—
		W	167	81	7	5	5	1
SOUTHWEST								
Worker	Total	M	92	91	3	4	1	—
		W	86	74	13	8	5	—
	Urban	M	34	94	—	6	—	—
		W	43	88	2	9	—	—
	Rural	M	58	90	5	3	2	—
		W	43	60	23	7	9	—
Smallholder, farmer		M	56	82	13	—	5	—
		W	55	45	45	3	5	2
Middle class		M	69	84	9	1	4	1
		W	59	76	15	4	5	—

Source: (2), table 4.4 (by permission of the authors).

TABLE 10 (Chapter III, 4)

CULTURAL DIVERGENCE

Church Attendance and Voting
(Stavanger Area)

Vote intention:	Attending Church Seldom or Never	Attending Church Regularly	Church Attendance Not Ascertained
	%	%	%
Communist	2	—	3
Labor	41	15	34
Liberal	16	23	8
Christian	5	25	5
Agrarian	8	14	11
Conservative	12	10	3
Nonvoter, uncertain	9	5	10
Refuses, not ascertained	7	8	26
TOTAL	100%	100%	100%
N	768	187	62

Source: (4), 167.

TABLE 11 (Chapter III, 4)

REGIONAL ECONOMIC CLEAVAGE AND CULTURAL DIVERGENCE

Differences in language preference between the regions:
survey data for 1957.

Q: Which language form do you prefer to use when you write?

		N = 100%	Riksmål %	Bokmål[1] %	Landsmål, nynorsk %	Other answers[2] %
		TOTAL	NATIONWIDE	SAMPLE		
		1546	65	19	12	4
			EAST			
Urban	Tot.	359	81	14	1	4
	Workers	190	83	11	1	6
	Middle class	169	79	17	1	3
Rural	Tot.	394	71	15	7	7
	Workers	170	76	13	2	9
	Middle class	142	76	17	2	7
	Farmers, etc.	82	63	15	14	5
			SOUTH, WEST			
Urban	Tot.	199	63	24	12	2
	Workers	101	66	20	13	1
	Middle class	98	59	29	11	1
Rural	Tot.	218	33	11	50	5
	Workers	69	35	18	45	1
	Middle class	42	29	17	50	5
	Farmers, etc.	107	34	7	53	7
			TRØNDELAG, NORTH			
Urban	Tot.	84	85	14	1	0
	Workers	41	93	7	—	0
	Middle class	43	77	21	2	0
Rural	Tot.	261	54	39	5	2
	Workers	88	59	35	3	2
	Middle class	49	53	37	8	2
	Farmers, etc.	124	52	42	6	2

[1] Includes 4 respondents stating they preferred "*samnorsk.*"

[2] These were: 5 respondents, "a mixture"; 6, "both forms"; 3, "what I was taught at school"; 13, "ordinary language"; 36, n.a. and refuse.

Source: (2), table 4.5 (by permission of the authors).

TABLE 12 (Chapter III, 4)

Cultural Divergence and Economic Cleavage

Teetotalism and Voting
(Stavanger Area)

	Teetotalers			Nonteetotalers		
Vote intention:	Worker %	White collar %	Farmer %	Worker %	White collar %	Farmer %
Communist	3	—	—	3	1	—
Labour	48	14	1	63	23	13
Liberal	9	33	13	10	29	10
Christian	13	18	20	1	2	—
Agrarian	4	3	51	2	2	57
Conservative	3	16	2	6	33	8
Nonvoter, uncertain	10	6	8	9	7	6
Refuses, not ascertained	10	10	5	6	3	6
TOTAL	100%	100%	100%	100%	100%	100%
N	290	147	85	244	174	52

Source: (4), 169.

TABLE 13 (Chapter III, 4)

CULTURAL DIVERGENCE AND REGIONAL CLEAVAGE

Cosmopolitanism: Opinions Concerning EEC entry:
differences between the major regions of Norway
(data from survey carried out by Norsk Gallup, February 1962).[a]

Party	Region	% for EEC	% against EEC	% don't know
CP+ SF	Total	13	81	6
Labour	Total	44	27	29
	E Region[b]	46	26	28
	SW Region	42	30	28
	TN Region	45	27	28
Liberal	Total	33	45	22
	ETN Region	23	58	17
	SW Region	39	37	24
Christian	Total	25	36	39
	ETN Region	32	28	40
	SW Region	15	49	36
Agrarian	Total	32	49	19
	E Region	35	51	14
	SW Region	18	63	19
	TN Region	50	18	32
Conservative	Total	59	17	24
	E Region	59	13	28
	SW Region	60	28	12
	TN Region	56	17	27

Source: (2), table 6.1 (by permission of the authors).

[a] Respondents who had heard of EEC only.

[b] E=East; SW=South, West; TN=Trøndelag, North.

TABLE 14 (Chapter III, 4)

SPECIFIC DISAGREEMENTS

Differences in goal orientations among the voters for the five major parties.

Survey data for 1957

Policy area	Ranking of parties from lowest to highest per cent opposed to government policy								
	Party actives					Only voters			
	Least opposed				Most opposed	Least opposed			Most opposed
I. *Taxation*	Lab.	Lib.	Chr.	Agr.	Cons.	Lab.	Lib.	Chr.	Agr.
1. Taxes too high	58	67	77	78	93	66	80	82	90
2. Too much control of income reports (independents)	Lab.	Lib.	Chr.	Cons.	Agr.	Lab.	Chr.	Lib.	Cons.
	4	17	24	50	60	4	18	23	37
II. *Control of Economy*									
1. Too much restriction of housebuilding	Lab.	Chr.	Agr.	Lib.	Cons.	Lab.	Agr.	Chr.	Lib.
	23	37	50	67	78	29	48	51	67
2. Too much interference with enterprise	Lab.	Chr.	Lib.	Agr.	Cons.	Lab.	Agr.	Chr.	Lib.
	5	57	67	78	83	12	38	44	60
3. Too little to encourage private saving	Lab.	Chr.	Lib.	Agr.	Cons.	Lab.	Agr.	Chr.	Lib.
	18	70	70	78	89	29	60	65	76
4. Too little done to stop inflation	Lab.	Chr.	Lib.	Agr.	Cons.	Lab.	Chr.	Agr.	Lib.
	12	43	55	66	80	15	44	50	56
III. *Protection of primary economy*									
1. Too little support for agriculture	Cons.	Lab.	Chr.	Lib.	Agr.	Lab.	Cons.	Chr.	Lib.
	7	9	23	33	63	11	12	17	19
IV. *Religion*									
1. Too little done to strengthen Christian faith and morals	Lab.	Lib.	Cons.	Agr.	Chr.	Lab.	Cons.	Lib.	Agr.
	18	44	56	59	97	26	42	44	65
V. *Defense*									
1. Military budget too high	Cons.	Chr.	Agr.	Lab.	Lib.	Cons.	Agr.	Lab.	Chr.
	33	50	53	66	72	49	63	63	71
	Lab.	Lib.	Chr.	Agr.	Cons.	Lab.	Lib.	Chr.	Agr.
N=100% for each group	164	18	30	32	54	407	75	68	52

Source: (3), table 4.

TABLE 15 (Chapter III, 4)

SPECIFIC DISAGREEMENTS

Goals of Political Parties as Seen
by their Leaders
(Stavanger Area)

Q: What would you say (your) party stands for, and what is it trying to achieve?

	Party of leaders:				
	Labour	*Liberal*	*Christian People's*	*Agrarian*	*Conservative*
	%	%	%	%	%
Democracy: protection of rights of the individual	—	65	—	—	—
The best for whole society, Collapsing class differences	21	39	8	5	3
Social welfare, social justice	58	12	4	5	6
Socialism, help lower classes	40	—	—	—	—
Freedom from government regulations, private initiative	—	—	—	5	80
Protecting and strengthening Christianity	—	4	92	—	11
Equalization between farming and industry	—	—	—	53	—
Interests of rural districts	—	—	—	68	—
Other answers	—	—	—	5	9
No goal mentioned	12	12	4	—	9
Total	43	26	26	19	35

(Percentages add to more than 100 because the question called for multiples answers.)
Source: (4), 35.

TABLE 16 (Chapter III, 4)

SPECIFIC DISAGREEMENTS

Goal Orientations in Politics. Issues Seen by Party Leaders
as Matters of Principle (Stavanger Area)

Q: Can you name any examples of issues that you would consider important matters
of principle for your party?

Issues mentioned:	Leaders					
	Lab. %	Lib. %	Chr. %	Agr. %	Cons. %	Total %
Nationalization of big firms, industrial democracy	14	—	—	—	—	4
Full employment	37	—	—	—	—	11
Low interest level	9	—	—	—	—	3
Shorter working hours	9	—	—	5	—	3
Higher wages and salaries	2	—	—	—	—	1
Profit-sharing, abolition of caste	7	15	—	—	—	5
Further development of social insurance	44	19	23	—	14	23
Compulsory arbitration	—	23	—	—	—	4
Organizational freedom	—	8	—	—	3	2
Appointment of a commissioner for grievances against administrative decisions	—	12	—	—	—	3
Reduction of taxes; more just tax system	2	15	4	11	34	13
Stop inflation; encourage private saving	2	4	—	5	23	7
Denationalization: sale of state shares and firms	—	—	—	—	17	4
Improve teaching for people in agriculture	—	—	—	5	—	1
Cultivation of forests, new land	—	—	—	11	—	1
Increased prices in agriculture	—	—	—	16	—	2
Increased teaching of religion in school	—	—	73	5	—	13
Temperance	—	4	54	—	—	10
Strengthen opposition against experiments with nuclear weapons	—	4	—	—	—	1
Strengthening of defense, international cooperation	4	12	—	5	14	7
Development of public water power, road improvement, and of railroad and telephone	7	8	—	26	9	9
Improvement of educational system	14	62	—	5	26	18
Development of industries	9	—	—	11	6	5
Increased house construction	12	8	—	—	17	9
Others	19	23	16	16	11	14
No issue given	23	8	12	32	32	20
N	43	26	26	19	35	149

(Percentages add to more than 100 because the question called for multiple answers.)
Source: (4), 235.

TABLE 17 (Chapter III, 4)

PARTY LEADERS' VALUATION OF DESIRABLE CHARACTERISTICS OF
PARLIAMENTARY CANDIDATES

rty	Political or technical competence, experience, good sense %	Rank Order in Party	Appeal to voters: well-spoken, well-known, well-liked %	Rank	Moral qualities: honesty, responsibility politeness, etc. %	Rank	Loyalty to Party %	Rank	Representativeness of group interests %	Rank	Other %
bour	41	(3)	26	(4)	46	(2)	61	(1)	14	(5)	5
erals	62	(2)	23	(4)	88	(1)	27	(3)	4	(5)	4
ristians	58	(1)	38	(2,3)	35	(4)	32	(5)	38	(2,3)	—
rarians	95	(1)	37	(2,3)	32	(4)	10	(5)	37	(2,3)	—
nservatives	100	(1)	37	(3)	57	(2)	37	(3)	3	(5)	6

Source: Valen, "Nominasjonene," table 6.321.

TABLE 18 (Chapter III, 4)

"POLITICAL AGGREGATION"

Strength of Attachment to Present
Parties

Q: In many districts conditions may well be such that one or two parties
have very small chances of getting enough votes for a single representative. People in such parties will generally have *three alternatives*:
they may vote for their *own party* anyhow, irrespective of the
chances, they may vote for the *party nearest to their own*, or they
may *not vote* at all. Which do you yourself consider is right in such
a case?

	Labour %	Liberals %	Christians %	Agrarians %	Conservatives %
Own Party	59	56	56	57	37
Nearest Party	27	27	35	35	50
Abstain	9	9	2	4	7
N	618	88	106	104	188

(Totals are less than 100% because of other responses: e.g., "depends,"
"don't know.")

Source: (5).

TABLE 19 (Chapter V, 1)

TRUST IN OTHERS

Q: On the whole, would you say that you are satisfied or dissatisfied with the honesty and standards of behavior of people in this country today?

	Satisfied	Dissatisfied
Norway	77%	23%
Switzerland	64	36
Denmark	48	52
Britain	47	53
France	47	53
U.S.	37	63
West Germany	35	65

Note: The "no opinion" vote varied from 8% (U.S.) to 27% (France).
Source: AIPO, October 9, 1963.

TABLE 20 (Chapter V, 2)

PARTY COHESION IN THE STORTING
(51 roll calls)

Party	Dissenting from Party Majority	Absent[a]
	%	%
Labour	2.5	12
Agrarians	2.3	11
Liberals	6.2	15
Christians	6.7	13
Conservatives	2.8	16

[a] Absentees probably include a larger proportion of dissenters than conformists. However, the roll calls included issues that various parties do not treat as matters of principle. Hence the percentages in the dissent column are probably accurate indicators of cohesion on significant issues.
Source: (4), 49.

TABLE 21 (Chapter V, 2)

SIGNIFICANCE TO VOTERS OF THE PARTY TEAMS

Q: When you choose between the different lists at the election, what is most important to you—the individual candidates and their competence, or the party as a whole and its ability to defend the views of the voters?

	Labour %	Liberals %	Christians %	Agrarians %	Conservatives %
Individuals	5	17	13	5	10
Both	15	22	25	20	16
Party	72	50	52	62	66

Q: It is often maintained that we would get a better government in this country if we could be allowed to vote on independent individuals rather than on party lists in our elections. What do you think about this?

	Labour	Liberals	Christians	Agrarians	Conservatives
Ind. absolutely best	5	15	14	14	14
Ind. probably best	5	9	7	6	12
Lists best	58	49	40	49	45
N	618	88	106	104	188

(Totals are less than 100% because of other responses (e.g., don't know; no answer; "chaos if no party lists"; etc.).
Source: (5).

TABLE 22 (Chapter V, 3)

MEMBERSHIP IN ORGANIZATIONS OF VOTERS (V) AND POLITICAL LEADERS (L)
(Stavanger Area)

Number of memberships:	Labour		Liberal		Christian		Agrarian		Conservative	
	V	L	V	L	V	L	V	L	V	L
	%	%	%	%	%	%	%	%	%	%
One organization	42	33	34	—	38	11	35	32	30	17
Two organizations	13	33	18	27	21	27	23	16	21	17
Three or more organizations	7	28	14	69	22	62	26	47	13	52
No memberships or not ascertained	38	6	34	4	19	—	16	5	36	14
TOTAL	100%	100%	100%	100%	100%	100%	100%	100%	100%	100%
N	365	43	171	26	90	26	95	19	113	35

Source: (4), 319.

TABLE 23 (Chapter VI, 8)

EGALITARIANISM

Perceptions of Class Differences

Q: Do you think we have large class differences in this country?

	%
Very large	1
Rather large	12
Rather small	29
Insignificant	30
None	24
N	1406

(Total less than 100% because of other responses.)
Source: (5).

TABLE 24 (Chapter VI, 9)

"FUNCTIONAL DEFERENCE" ON THE CABINET LEVEL

The Proportion of new cabinet members having
a Storting background.

Period	Number of New Ministers	Proportion with Parliamentary Background	
	N	N	%
1884–1905	63	33	52
1905–1920	53	32	60
1920–1935	64	41	64
1935–1964	60	24	40
1884–1905	240	130	54

Source: (1), 8.10.

A Theory of Stable Democracy*

PREFACE

FOR AS long as men have studied politics they have tried to discover connections between political life and its social setting. In this search one aspect of social life has been strangely neglected—strangely, because it is the element of social life most obviously and immediately relevant to political behavior on the governmental level; I refer to authority patterns in nongovernmental social relationships, in families, schools, economic organizations, and the like. We have propositions about the relations between politics and geography, politics and economic organization, politics and social stratification, politics and religion, politics and child training, politics and role structure, politics and education. But, beyond allusions to the subject, we have no general propositions about the relations between politics on the governmental level and politics in nongovernmental social structures. Under any circumstances this would be a serious omission, for it stands to reason that if any aspect of social life can directly affect government it is the experiences with authority that men have in other spheres of life, especially those that mold their personalities and those to which they normally devote most of their lives. The omission is all the more serious when one considers that the propositions now available for relating society and polity are all, in one way or another, highly imperfect, however much some of them may be supported by evidence and logic. Certainly none has as yet been established so rigorously as to have led to even a moderate consensus among political scientists, nor has any line of analysis yet proved so promising that political

* Originally published as Research Monograph Number 10 by the Center of International Studies, Princeton University, 1961.

scientists can feel easy about leaving other possibilities un-explored.

There is another reason why one should be mystified by the lack of propositions relating governmental authority to other forms of social authority. For some time now numerous developments in political science seem to have been converging on just such propositions. One such development is what the political philosophers call pluralism: the belief that the state has neither a moral nor a practical monopoly upon political authority. Another is the belief that political science must concern itself with a subject matter broader than the state for methodological reasons: for example, on the ground, stated by Catlin already thirty years ago, that political science, if it is to be a true science, must have a subject matter which is simple, general, commonplace, and frequent of occurrence—the state, as we know it, satisfying none of these criteria, while the "act of control," in whatever context it may occur, allegedly satisfies them all (5, p.68).* Still another development leading in the same direction is the growing concern of political scientists with power and influence relations as such (22; 23). Finally, political scientists, and others, have been concerned for many decades now (since Mill, at least) with the possibilities of private despotism in a context of public liberty and with "informal" politics within the context of constitutional law.

These trends have in fact produced a small number of studies dealing with the politics of nongovernmental structures (8, pp. 1-3)—a surprisingly small number, considering the enormous variety of cases available. They have also produced many exhortations to political scientists to produce more such studies, by, among others, Merriam, de Jouvenel, and Dahl (28; 19; 8). But while political scientists have not entirely neglected to study nongovernmental relations as political structures, and while they have certainly not neglected the possibilites of social determination of the operation and fate of governments, no one seems

* The citation numbers refer to the references found on pages 287-288.

even to have thought of systematically linking the first interest to the second, of producing propositions which explain certain facts of public authority on the basis of certain facts of nonpublic authority. I can think of only one good reason for this omission —namely, that the modern idea of the state has so tenacious a hold even on those who disavow it that they tend not to think of private authority when they are concerned with public authority, but think of it only when they are not concerned with states at all. However that may be, propositions linking the two do not yet exist, and the present paper seeks at least to begin remedying this state of affairs.

Despite its title, it presents only an idea, not a full-fledged theory. Nevertheless, it seems to me worthwhile stating the idea now, even in an obviously rudimentary form. The main reason for this emerges from the conclusion of the paper: before the idea can claim to be a full-fledged theory, so much theoretical and empirical work still needs to be done that it might be years before one could say much more about the subject than can be said about it now. In the meantime, I hope that the present statement of the idea will provoke others to look into it, so that its theoretical and empirical elaboration will not be a job falling only to myself. There is more than enough work here for all who may have an interest in it.

I. Characteristics of Stable Democracy

A theory should always begin by defining its subject. In the case of stable democracy this might seem to be a simple matter, but the concept actually raises one or two knotty problems.

Ordinarily we mean by a stable democracy one which has demonstrated considerable staying power, a capacity to endure, without great or frequent changes in pattern. On this basis, the French Third Republic, to take a simple and familiar example, was certainly a stable democracy; like M. Talleyrand in the French Revolution, "it survived," longer at any rate than any other French constitutional order, and longer than many other constitutional orders elsewhere. Yet this example also indicates why a definition of stability as mere longevity will not quite do, even if we could agree on just how long a democracy must endure to be considered stable.[1] Taking the term in this sense, a system may be stable because of its own effectiveness or simply because of the ineffectiveness (or bad luck) of its opponents; it may persist, as did the Third Republic, for no better reason than that it never quite manages even to collapse, despite much opposition and many hairbreadth escapes. But this sort of tenuous survival surely requires an explanation different from that required by the persistence of a constitutional order because of its capacity for adapting to changing conditions, for realizing political aspirations and holding fast allegiances. The first can be explained only on the basis of particular historical circumstances (or "accidents")—the misjudgments of a MacMahon, the untimely relations of a Boulanger with his mistress, the timely realization of the Communists that helping the Fascists would not expedite the proletarian revolution. The second requires an explanation, not in terms of fortuitous circumstances, but in terms of settled social and political conditions; it is, therefore, for political science the more interesting phenomenon, and indeed the only one political science can really handle. The theory of this paper, consequently, does not concern itself with stability merely in the sense of endurance, but stability in a more complicated sense. Endurance is a part of it, but only a part.

What else does the concept imply? First of all, it implies effective decision making—"effective" not in the sense of right action on the basis of some particular scheme of values, but in the basic sense of action itself, any sort of action, in pursuit of shared political goals or in adjustment to changing conditions. The political order must not be "immobilistic," for immobility

[1] This is not a serious problem if we think of stability as a category (like wealth, length, weight, etc.) which has meaning only in a relative sense. Governments are never really stable or unstable; they are more or less stable, in more or less fundamental ways.

can lead to desired results only by inadvertence, if at all. A government must govern, whatever else it may be supposed to do, otherwise it is not a government at all; and on this criterion the Third Republic, for all its staying power, certainly comes out badly. In addition, we can hardly call a government a stable democracy unless it is genuinely "democratic," and this implies that it must satisfy at least two conditions. One is that democratic structures must not be mere façades for actual government by nondemocratic structures; the decisions of government, which make it "effective" and perhaps capable of survival, must come from the democratic process, at least in large part. On the basis of this criterion the Third Republic comes out badly again, for it was a government carried on in normal times mainly by a nearly autonomous bureaucracy ("the Republic on top, the Empire at bottom") and in times of crisis mainly by temporary dictators armed with *plein pouvoir*; it was, in effect, largely a system of democratic politics and nondemocratic government. The second condition is that elections in such systems must decide, in some basic way, the outcome of the competition for power and policies; for what else can one mean by democracy? On this basis, too, the Third Republic fares badly, for its elections decided very little, compared with the traditions of the bureaucracy, the whims of parliamentary dictators like Laval, Chautemps, and Daladier, and the irrepressible *trasformismo* of the Radicals, the party always indispensable to governments and always in power, whatever the outcome of elections.

The term "stability," when applied to democracies, thus implies three conditions: persistence of pattern, decisional effectiveness, and authenticity: and barring the sort of large good fortune which saved the Third Republic repeatedly upon the point of extinction, we may be sure that these three conditions hang closely together. The Third Republic, in fact, is the only case which does not completely illustrate this fact—it would indeed be strange if there were many others, for the sort of accidents which preserved it have only a slight statistical probability. In other cases—the Weimar Republic, for example, or the Fourth

Republic, or pre-Fascist Italy—the interdependence of all three conditions is clearly revealed. Governmental paralysis, particularly in the face of crisis, is generally a prelude to the demise of democracy. It always leads, even before the end of the formal representative system, to government by free-wheeling bureaucrats, or parliamentary dictators, or inconsequential minority leaders like Facta and von Papen. And even if a democratic system survives in form by surrendering power to its adjuncts or to a minority, it cannot in that case be said to survive in fact; nor is it then likely, on the evidence, to survive for long in form. That is why all three conditions can be sufficiently stated in a single adjective, *stable* democracy, without any cumbersome additional ones (e.g. "effective").

II. The Problem of Stable Democracy

Certain conditions obviously favor stable democracy, so obviously in fact that no decent theory ever stops with them. When someone says, for example, that democracies tend to be stable if they enjoy wide support (25, p. 77; 33, pp. 361-383), he has obviously not said very much, and probably nothing that we really want to know. Neither is it very instructive to be told that a highly integrated party system (like the British) is more conducive to stable democracy than a fragmented party system, or that a climate of moderation and pragmatism in politics is more favorable to it than one of extremism and ideological dogma (14, pp. 585-589; 33, pp. 194-210). There is in fact a well-known syndrome of conditions connected with stable democracy which is practically synonymous with the term, in that it would be difficult to imagine the one without the other; this syndrome of conditions includes, above all, consensus on the form of government, a high degree of political pragmatism, and a certain kind of party system: either a two-party system or a larger number of parties possessing to a high degree what the Germans call *Koalitionsfähigkeit* (coalition capacity, to be very literal). These conditions do "explain" the existence of stable democracy, but only in a very superficial way: the same way that the statement, "X pulled the trigger of a loaded revolver while pointing the muzzle at himself," explains how X came to commit suicide. In both cases, the explanation we really seek is one step further removed. We do not really want to know what sort of political party systems and climate of opinion favor stable democracy. We really want to know what conditions underlie the requisite syndrome of favorable conditions, whatever it may be, for only on this level of the problem are the answers not obvious.

Getting beyond the obvious in regard to the problem of stable democracy requires also that we do not dwell very long on the general functional and structural requisites of viable social systems which sociologists and general systems theorists have so far managed to establish, even though these requisites are meant explicitly to explain the stability or instability of systems (2, pp. 225-227; 24, pp. 149-197; 30, pp. 167-177). We could, of course, discuss the collapse of democracies like the Weimar Republic, pre-Fascist Italy, or the French Fourth Republic in terms of these requisites; and keeping them in mind will certainly help us to look for and to find certain important weaknesses and malfunctions in these political systems. But the use of system requisites is also unlikely to lead us to the desired level of explanation. To some extent these categories will merely help establish the fact that the political systems mentioned do indeed fit our definition of unstable democracy: for example, that they failed to "maintain" the democratic "pattern" by the surrender of power to nondemocratic adjuncts of the system. To some extent, they will only lead us to the more familiar truistic theories stated earlier: to lack of "integration" in party systems, for example, or lack of "conformity" to the norms of the democratic polity on the part of many of its members. To some extent they will lead us to certain symptoms rather than preconditions (effects rather than causes) of instability: for example, the inadequate "adaptation" of fluid social resources through faulty economic policies, as in the constantly misshapen budgets of the Third and Fourth republics; or the failure of basic mechanisms of accountability and consent, as in the virtually unchecked use of decree powers by parliamentary autocrats; or the failure of a government's structure of coercion, as illustrated by the unconstrained violence in pre-Fascist Italy by D'Annunzio's orgiastic nationalists, pillaging peasants and workers, and Mussolini's own *fascisti*. In every democratic system which has failed, we do find a failure to satisfy some of the system requisites that men like Parsons, Levy, and Apter have proposed; if nothing else, this means that their claims to have established truly general categories are not invalidated. But the fact remains that these categories simply do not get us to the level of the problem with which we are concerned in this case.

Our real problem is not to find whether system failures have indeed occurred in unstable democracies, or to link their occurrence to manifestly unfavorable conditions. We need to discover the deeper, or more remote, conditions which rule out or make possible stable democracy, either directly or by bringing into being the obviously deleterious or obviously favorable conditions discussed above.

III. The Congruence of Authority Patterns

The Universality of Authority

To solve this problem, a theory is required which, up to a point, is also a *general* theory of governmental stability. Since democracy is a special kind of government, it seems plain logic that a theory of stable democracy should consist of two parts, one stating the general conditions which make governmental stability probable, the other stating the particular conditions required to make democracies stable. These particular conditions should of course be special instances of the more general conditions which produce governmental stability. It may be that no general theory of governmental stability can really be developed, that every kind of government is *sui generis* in this regard; but at this stage of inquiry we have no reason whatever to think that this is the case. Hence the first proposition of the present theory is in fact a proposition about the stability or instability of any governmental order, whatever its special character. This proposition concerns the nature of, and the relations among, the different authority patterns in a society.

In every society we can discover numerous authority patterns, both attitudes regarding authority and, to use Lasswell's terminology, authority "practices." Certainly this is so if we use the term "authority" in its broadest and most conventional sense, to denote relationships of superordination and subordination among individuals in social formations, relationships in which some members of the formation take decisions and others treat the decisions as binding. In this simple sense of a hierarchy of wills, the state certainly has no monopoly upon authority. It may be quite possible, and even useful, to distinguish between the authority of the state and other kinds of authority; and it is easy enough to define authority in a way that will confine it arbitrarily to the state. But as the term is used here, authority in some form is a characteristic of practically any persistent social aggregate, at least in that certain actual practices of subordination and superordination will be found in such aggregates, and probably also in that there will exist in the society as a whole and in its subunits certain dominant notions as to how such practices *should* be conducted. Authority exists not only in the state itself, but in parties and pressure groups, in economic organizations, in various kinds of associations, in schools and families, and even in friendships, bands, clubs, and the like. We can discover it in any set of social relations which, in the not too happy jargon of social psychology, is "cooperatively interdependent" (11, pp. 129-152)—that is, very simply, not competitive. The only persistent social relations in which we are pretty certain not to find it are "competitively interdependent" relations, like the bargaining relations which take place in a free economic market or in international politics—granted that a certain amount of bargaining can be an aspect of authority relations as well, and a certain amount of authority set limits to the scope and content of bargaining.

I assert this universality of authority patterns in noncompetitive social relations, not because it is absolutely necessary to my theory to assert it, but because it is a palpable fact. All that is necessary to the present theory, however, is that authority should exist in *some* social relations other than those of formal government, particularly in those social relations, like the family or economic organizations, which one finds in any society; and this assertion will surely not be disputed by anyone without some sort of redefinition of authority.

The Idea of Congruence

Stated very briefly, the first proposition of the theory I would suggest is that *a government will tend to be stable if its authority pattern is congruent with the other authority patterns of the society of which it is a part.* The crucial term in this proposition is of course "congruence," and it needs to be defined, particularly since, as used here, the term is not at all self-explanatory.

Authority patterns are congruent, in the first place (but only in the first place), if they are identical (that is to say, since we are dealing not with an abstract geometric universe but real life, if they very closely resemble each other). An example of congruence in this sense is furnished by the authority patterns in British government and British political parties, at any rate if we accept the standard analyses of the latter by Beer and Mc-Kenzie (3; 27). Both patterns consist of a curious and very similar mixture of democratic, authoritarian, and, so to speak, constitutional elements; this despite the fact that British government can be traced back to the eras of medieval constitutionalism and royal absolutism, while political parties are, in almost every respect, creatures of a much later period, the era of the mandate; and this also despite the fact that the formal constitution of the Labour Party makes it seem very different from both the Conservative Party and the British governmental structure.[2] In both government and parties, the idea of the mandate is formalized and paid considerably more than lip service, in one case in the House of Commons, in the other in the Annual Conferences. In both cases, however, the leaders actually enjoy long tenure in office and a great deal of autonomy, even though the autonomy of the Conservative Leader rests on formal rules and that of the Labour Leader "merely" on actual practice; in both cases, moreover, the idea of the mandate is contravened by the fact that the leaders are widely *expected* to govern, in the sense of taking personal policy initiatives and sometimes even acting contrary to opinion in the rank and file. In both cases, too, this autonomy of leadership is mitigated by the expectation—on the part, incidentally, of both elites and masses—that authority will be exercised "constitutionally"; that is to say, that it will be exercised, if not in conformity with written documents, then at least within a framework of widely accepted and well-understood limits and rules, including, for example, the rule that authority inheres always in a collective structure, whether this structure is provided for in a formal constitution, as in the Labour Party, or not, as in the Conservative

2 We can treat this breakdown of authority patterns into democratic, authoritarian, and constitutionalist patterns at least as a first approximation toward a useful typology of authority patterns, although by no means the only one available. *Democracy* in this case refers to the rule of numbers, hence its equation with the idea of the mandate; in other words, it denotes a high degree of participation in decision making, regularized choice between competing political elites, and the transmission, usually not very precisely, of instructions from the political "mass" to the political "elite." *Authoritarianism* refers to limited participation in decisions by the mass and to a high degree of autonomy and a low degree of formal precariousness of position on the part of the elite. *Constitutionalism* refers to the subjection of the elite to a broad and highly explicit impersonal framework of rules, procedural and substantive, where this framework of rules operates as the principal limitation on the autonomy of the elite. We might say that democracy involves the rule of a dependent elite, authoritarianism the rule of an autonomous elite, and constitutionalism the rule of law; but this is such a great oversimplification that it can only serve as a shorthand to help one keep the vital distinctions in mind.

Party and the governmental machinery. In addition to these absolutely fundamental resemblances, there are also many less basic, although no less striking, similarities between British government and parties. For example, both Parliament and the parliamentary organizations of the parties have largely an advisory and exhortatory role in decision-making processes; in both Parliament and the party Conferences, the leaders are given certain traditional privileges in debates (they speak longer, for example, and more frequently); in both government and parties, bureaucracy plays an indispensable but subordinate and unusually self-effacing role, even in this age of massive government and massive parties; and, of course, government and party leaders entirely coincide, a fact which the Weimar parties show to be by no means inevitable in a parliamentary system.

The essential patterns of cabinet government, and the essential attitudes on which it is based, thus all have their counterparts in the major British parties. In fact, it has been argued, cogently I think, that cabinet government on the British model compels a certain correspondence between party structure and governmental structure, certainly while a party is in power, and therefore also perhaps while it is in opposition and presumably aspiring to power. Cabinet government could not otherwise work at all on a party basis; hence the anxieties of many Englishmen when the Labour Party strays, as it infrequently does, from the model of the cabinet system and acts as if it really believed in its formal constitution. But this argument should not be taken to mean that British parties cannot help but have a structure similar to that of British government. "Compel" does not in this case mean "cause." The argument means merely that British government can work smoothly only if such a congruence of governmental and party structures exists, not that things could not actually be otherwise. There are plenty of parliamentary systems in which the same logic holds, but few in which the same congruence can be found.

The most extreme and plainest form of congruence, then, is identity. Mixing metaphors, we might speak in this case of isomorphic authority patterns. But identity cannot exhaust the meaning of congruence when applied to social phenomena, for it is difficult even to imagine a society in which all authority patterns closely resemble each other. Certainly such a state of affairs is impossible in a democracy. Some social relations simply cannot be conducted in a democratic manner, or can be so conducted only with the gravest dysfunctional consequences. Take, for example, those social units which link different generations—families and schools. An infant cannot be cared for democratically, or a child brought up and schooled democratically. Families and schools can be permissive, but this is merely to say that they can be authoritarian in a lax and lenient manner. Families and schools can also carry on a certain amount of democratic pretense, and indeed more than pretense, and when they do so on a large scale, that fact is not without significance; but by and large they cannot carry such simulation and imitation of democracy to very great lengths, if they are not to produce warped and ineffectual human beings. One of the most basic and indispensable functions in any social system, the socialization function, must therefore always be to some extent out of tune with democratic patterns, and potentially at odds with them. The same point applies, almost as obviously, to certain relations among adults. We have every reason to think that economic organizations cannot be organized in a truly democratic manner, at any rate not without consequences that no one wants; and we certainly know that capitalist economic organization and even certain kinds of public ownership (like the nationalization in Britain of industries absolutely vital to the health of the whole economy) militate against a democratization of economic relations. The case of military organizations is even plainer in this regard, and the case of public bureaucracy just as clear. Again, there can be some simulation and imitation of democracy in firms, or public offices, or military units, but only within rather narrow limits. Precisely those social relations in which most individuals are engaged most of the time—family life, schools, and jobs (most kinds of jobs)—are the least capable of being democratically organized. To expect all authority relations in a democracy to be identical would therefore be unreasonable, and we could probably demonstrate the same thing, in other ways, for other kinds of governmental structures. In any complex society, but above all in democracies, we must expect some heterogeneity in authority patterns, even if we deal only with fundamental patterns and not circumstantial details.

In that case, however, one can still speak meaningfully of a congruence of authority patterns if the patterns have a certain "fit" with one another—if they dovetail with, or support, the governmental pattern, however indirectly. One way in which they can do this is by the partial imitation of the governmental authority patterns in other social structures. Democratic (or other) pretenses, if taken seriously and carried far, may have important consequences for the operation of the governmental structure, even though they are pretenses. Furthermore, structures like economic or military organizations may, in some cases, willingly incur certain functional disadvantages for the sake of acting out norms associated with governments in their substantive decision-making processes. For instance, capitalistic economic organizations which play a great deal at democracy and permit certain deviations from the logic of the double-entry ledger in order actually to carry on certain democratic practices may be said to be more congruent with democratic government than those which stick closely, both in ritual and process, to the economically most rational practices.

In view of this, we might be tempted to say that authority patterns are congruent if they have, not everything, but something in common. But if the equation of congruence with identity makes demands which are too great, its equation with mere resemblance, however slight, does not demand enough. On the first basis, we shall almost never find a society in which authority patterns are really congruent; on the second, we shall assuredly not find any in which authority patterns are incongruent. However, by congruence I do not mean any resemblance at all among authority patterns. Where authority relations are not all highly similar, the term refers rather to a particular pattern of resemblance among them, one which makes stringent requirements, but not requirements impossible to fulfill—a pattern of *graduated resemblances*, so to speak.

To grasp the concept of graduated resemblances, one must think of societies as being composed of segments which are more or less distant from government. Governments themselves are adult structures, and for this reason families, for example, are more "vertically" distant from them, in terms of age levels, than schools, and schools more distant from them than purely adult structures. In the same way, adult structures may be "horizontally" segmented, so that some appear close to, others distant from, government. Parties, for example, ordinarily are situated closer to government than pressure groups; among pressure groups certain types may be particularly closely involved in government or parties; and all pressure groups are located more closely to government than nonpolitical organizations. These are very rough breakdowns; in some concrete cases, moreover, it may be difficult to make unambiguous distinctions, and the same social structures will not always fall into the same positions in every society. But none of this affects the definition: that social authority patterns are congruent, either if they are very similar, or if similarity to the governmental pattern increases significantly as one approaches the governmental segment itself.[3]

On the basis of these explications of the term "congruence," we can now restate the first proposition of the theory. *Government will be stable, (1) if social authority patterns are identical with the governmental pattern,* or *(2) if they constitute a graduated pattern in a proper segmentation of society,* or *(3) if a high degree of resemblance exists in patterns adjacent to government*

---

[3] The illustration below (and it is only an illustration, of course) should help to clarify this definition, if it is not clear enough already. Assume the following segmentation of society:

$$A^1 — A^2 — A^3 — A^4 — A^5$$

Let d_n stand for democratic pattern, so that d_5 equals complete democracy and d_4, d_3, d_2, and d_1 correspondingly smaller degrees of democ-

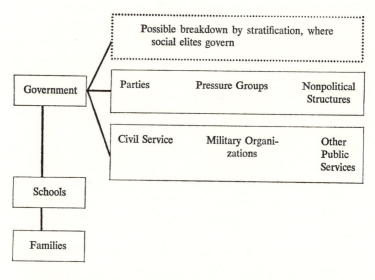

and one finds throughout the more distant segments a marked departure from functionally appropriate patterns for the sake of imitating the governmental pattern or extensive imitation of the governmental pattern in ritual practices. Conditions (2) and (3) are both, of course, looser and less demanding versions of condition (1); all refer to a basic need for considerable resemblance in authority patterns if government is to be stable, particularly in those segments of society which impinge directly on government. Condition (3) may be regarded, in this way, as the minimum required for governmental stability (and the minimum meaning of congruence), but perhaps the most that can be realized in relation to some particular pattern of government. By the same token, *governments will be unstable* (and the authority patterns of a society incongruent) *if the governmental authority pattern is isolated* (that is, substantially dif-

---

racy. Let a_n similarly stand for authoritarian pattern. Now society (1) and (2) have congruent authority patterns, society (3) incongruent ones:

(1) $A^1d_5a_1 - A^2d_4a_2 - A^3d_3a_3 - A^4d_2a_4 - A^5d_1a_5$

(2) $A^1d_5a_1 - A^2d_4a_2 - A^3d_4a_2 - A^4d_3a_3 - A^5d_3a_3$

(3) $A^1d_5a_1 - A^2d_1a_5 - A^3d_3a_3 - A^4d_5a_3 - A^5d_1a_5$

ferent) *from those of other social segments, or if a very abrupt change in authority pattern occurs in any adjacent segments of society, or if several different authority patterns exist in social strata furnishing a large proportion of the political elite* (in the sense of active political participants). In the last case, congruence with the authority patterns of a particular part of the elite —say, a particular social class—may be quite possible, but congruence with the overall authority patterns of a society is logically out of the question.

Two Examples: Great Britain and Germany

To make these propositions less abstract, let us look at two concrete cases which illustrate them: contemporary Britain and Weimar Germany.

We have already seen how closely the authority patterns of government and political parties resemble one another in Great Britain, and that this resemblance helps to make effective the processes of cabinet government. One can similarly find great resemblances in authority patterns between British government and other aspects of British social life. As one moves away from the governmental segment these resemblances do decline, but never markedly or in a very abrupt manner.

For example, there is a quite striking resemblance in the authority structures of government and pressure groups, a resemblance also required for effective cabinet government, at least in this age of the social service state (as I have pointed out in another work) (12). This resemblance is perhaps greatest in the case of groups constituted almost exclusively for political purposes (that is, in "attitude groups") (31), but it also exists to a surprising extent in functional organizations, like professional and economic organizations, which go in for politics only as a more or less important sideline. Among such functional organizations, moreover, the resemblance to government is particularly great in groups most directly involved in governmental and party affairs, e.g. trade unions, large-scale employers' organizations, cooperative societies, and the like. It is true that, on the whole, involvement by the group in non-political affairs, such as economic bargaining, tends to decrease resemblance to the governmental pattern. Also, certain non-political activities (for example, economic activities as against those of professional associations) act as inhibitions on too great an imitation of the governmental pattern. But throughout the whole universe of British pressure groups, resemblance to the governmental pattern is quite surprisingly great, even in organizations where, for functional reasons, one would least expect this.

British pressure groups tend to follow more or less closely, but ordinarily very closely, a certain ideal-typical authority pattern, which will immediately ring familiar to anyone acquainted with British government and parties. At the apex of this authority pattern, one usually finds a ceremonial figure who symbolically represents the group, perhaps presides over important meetings, and makes solemn speeches, but occupies a largely ritualistic and honorific position—although in a few cases ceremony and "efficiency" may be combined, as it is also in the leadership of the Conservative Party. Under this figure, there generally is a council or executive committee, a collective body which usually exercises the real decision-making power, at least so far as higher decisions are concerned; more often than not this body is dominated, despite pretenses of collective decision making, by its chairman and a small handful of especially powerful members. Under the Council, one generally finds a large number of other collective bodies—functional committees—with overlapping- memberships, the dominant roles on these committees being played by the more powerful figures on the council. The functional committees and council are formally considered "responsible" to large annual conventions (a conference, or representative meeting, or whatever it may be called), which are always supposed to exercise the ultimate decision-making power, but generally act only as bodies acclaiming the leaders, occasionally criticizing them, and very infrequently making substantive contributions to policy;

nevertheless, the leaders take care not to deviate too far from the public opinion of the convention and at the very least put up a show of responsiveness to the rank and file. Finally, there are a number of paid, full-time officials, a secretary and his assistants, who administer the organization's activities, play an extremely important role in regard to all affairs and an all-important role in regard to routine business, work closely and unobtrusively with the chairman and other important council members, generally get their way, but know when to stay in the background and when not to press their views. Throughout this structure operate norms typical of all public authority in Great Britain: that decision making must be carried out by some sort of collective leadership, which is both responsive to the mass of the organization and, to a large extent, autonomous of it, which is expected to behave according to some sort of code well-understood in the group but normally not explicitly defined, and which, although resting to some extent on an elective basis, enjoys great tenure of office, often for as long as the leaders want to keep their positions.

In short, in the typical British pressure group we find the same mixture of basic authority forms which characterizes British government and parties, as well as imitations of less basic British authority practices, from the ubiquity of committees to the imitation of ceremonial headship. This resemblance of the pressure-group pattern to the governmental pattern even extends to very minor matters, such as styles of debate at the annual conventions (directing remarks at the presiding officer, referring to other speakers in a florid and impersonal fashion, rarely delivering set speeches), or ways in which motions are introduced and processed, or ways in which orders of speakers are determined. We find this pattern, in almost every aspect, in a professional association like the British Medical Association (12), in a trade union like the National Union of Teachers (34), and in an employers' organization like the Federation of British Industries (13). Names may differ—the B.M.A. has an Annual Representative Meeting and a Council, the N.U.T. a Conference and an Executive, the F.B.I. an Annual General Meeting and a Grand Council—but the substance is the same, in structural forms and in actual practices.

In nonpolitical adult organizations, from friendly societies and clubs to business organizations, smallness of scale and functional considerations generally lead to significant departures from these forms and practices, but in the vast majority of cases one finds in these organizations at least a great deal of imitation, if only as ritual, of the governmental pattern. Even small-scale neighborhood clubs, like the many lawn tennis and social clubs which dot the landscape of middle-class England, generally have their committees and secretaries, their relatively inconsequential elections and stable oligarchies, their formalities, petty constitutionalisms, and ritualistic annual meetings; and still more is this true of larger clubs and friendly societies, like the famous snob clubs of Pall Mall and that holiest of holies, the Marylebone Cricket Club. It may be easier in such small organizations for elites to maintain themselves in authority, and also for members to participate in decision making, if they wish, but the essential forms and actual patterns of authority do not differ very much from the great political associations.

In business organizations, greater departures from the typical pattern occur, but even in such organizations there is usually some acting out of the governmental forms (most conspicuously, much reliance on committees, both on the level of management and among workers). In business organizations, however, congruence with the authority patterns of the political organizations may be found mainly in seemingly inconsequential patterns of behavior, some of which have driven countless American efficiency teams, taking as their frame of reference behavior strictly "rational" in economic terms, to uncomprehending distraction—such as the tendency of British executives to keep civil service hours, and above all their tendency to carry on endless consultations instead of reaching quick and independent decisions. The general tone of relations among bosses and workers is also relevant here, although this is a matter difficult to deal with very explicitly. The typical British boss, like any other boss, is an authoritarian figure, but he is rarely an overbearing tyrant or a stern taskmaster. More often than not, he is a paternalistic authoritarian, in the general style of the British upper classes in relation to the British lower classes. It would not occur to him to be on intimate terms with his workers. Neither would it occur to him that his position might entitle him to treat his workers in an insulting manner, or to claim special privileges over them outside of the business organization, or that his functionally specific authority might extend to other aspects of his workers' lives.

Business organizations depart to a rather great extent from the governmental pattern, not only for obvious functional reasons, but also because of a fact just touched upon: they bring into close relation members of the upper and lower social classes. Wherever this occurs in British life, the authoritarian elements of the authority pattern tend to become enlarged and the democratic elements diminished. This is so not only in relations between economic bosses and their workers, but also between domestic servants and masters, enlisted men and officers, and members of the Administrative Class and other classes in the civil service. While all of these relations are governed by a high sense of propriety and functional limitation (by constitutionalist norms), those among members of the higher levels tend to be quite surprisingly democratic, or at least consultative and comradely; here again we might note the ubiquity of committees at every conceivable level in the higher civil service, the unusual use of staff committees in the military services, and the easy relations among officers of all ranks in military regiments, especially in elitist regiments like the Guards. But between members of the Administrative Class and their underlings, officers and their men, managers and their hired help, relations are highly non-consultative and certainly not comradely; the observance of propriety and functional limitations in these cases is complemented by a considerable separation of individuals from each other, a general lack of contact among them for purposes other than functional ones.

But all this is quite in keeping with a governmental pattern which is as markedly elitist as the British. In general, the governmental authority pattern is conformed to most in Britain in relations among members of the upper classes; it is conformed to less in relations among members of the lower classes and least in interclass relations. In other words, the more important the role in government that members of a social stratum are likely to play, the more their relations tend to be molded in the governmental pattern; and this is just what one would expect in a system like the British.

British schools and family life are at least partly responsible for this state of affairs. Family life in the lower strata is much more authoritarian than in the upper strata; there is less reasonableness, less consultation, less courtesy, less formality, more punishment, and more arbitrariness. Although even in the lower classes we can find no counterpart of the menacing *paterfamilias* of certain continental European families, the matriarchs whom Young and Willmott (35) found in Bethnal Green or the arbitrarily despotic fathers depicted in working-class novels, like those of Lawrence and Sillitoe, have no upper-class counterparts. The same thing applies to schools. A marked change of atmosphere occurs as one moves from the secondary modern and technical schools to the grammar schools and public schools, especially the latter. Of course, even on the upper levels, British schools, like British government itself, tend to be rather authoritarian—more so, certainly, than schools in the United States— but relations among masters and pupils involve also a great deal of rather formalized good fellowship (in school games, for example) and a strict adherence to well-defined codes of conduct, while behavior among pupils is modeled to a remarkable extent on the political system. A case in point is described in Duff Cooper's book of memoirs, *Old Men Forget* (6). In Cooper's days at Eton, and possibly still today, debates were conducted in a manner obviously a carbon copy of House of Commons procedure, even though political questions were never discussed. A motion would be introduced and any one of the students attending ("the House"!) might be called upon to captain the discussion; prior to "business," questions would be asked as in the Commons, and boys referred to one another as "honorable members" rather than by name. Not always do we find quite such faithful copies of governmental patterns in the higher educational institutions, but the governmental style is noticeable in almost every case; indeed, British politics has a readily recognizable style precisely because politicians are brought up to it practically from the time they wear rompers. Again, this is not to imply that relations among public school boys or grammar school boys are remarkably democratic or egalitarian; it would be absurd to call the prefect systems of British schools egalitarian. But then neither is British government remarkably egalitarian. And British schoolboys do enjoy an unusual degree of freedom from the direct supervision of their elders, a great amount of self-government, even though it is self-government modified by relatively well-defined authoritarian relations among themselves.

British life thus illustrates the congruence of social authority patterns in all its aspects and degrees. There is a great resemblance between the authority pattern of government and those most closely adjacent to it, parties and pressure groups. Between government and those authority patterns which least resemble it intervene authority structures which are to a fairly large extent like the governmental structure. At no point in the segmentation of British society is there any abrupt and large change in authority patterns, and throughout one finds at least some imitation of governmental forms. And resemblance to the governmental pattern is greater in elite structures than in those of the nonelite. This does not validate the present theory, but it does support it in the case of perhaps the most stable of all modern political systems.

For support from the opposite end of the spectrum, we might

look at one of the least stable of all modern governments, the Weimar Republic. How did the authority patterns of interwar Germany differ from modern Britain? Basically, in two ways. On one hand, the German governmental pattern was much more one-sidedly democratic, at any rate if we confine analysis to the level of parliamentary representation and decision making and do not take into account the instrumental adjuncts of government, bureaucracy, the military, and the judiciary. On the other hand, social life, including life in parties and political interest groups, was highly authoritarian and relatively little "constitutionalized" compared with Britain. Not only were society and polity to some degree incongruent; they existed in unprecedented contradiction with one another. And on the basis of the theory of congruence, in consequence, the Weimar Republic could only have been what indeed it was: nasty, brutish, and short-lived—unless, like the Third Republic, it had been more lucky than any political order can expect to be.

Democracy, in interwar Germany, was, for all practical purposes, isolated at the level of parliamentary government, but at that level it was organized in an almost absurdly pure and exaggerated manner. Weimar Germany was governed by a Reichstag chosen on the basis of universal suffrage and by means of one of the purest systems of proportional representation ever devised. The chief of state was a plebiscitary president, and an effort was made, through run-off provisions, to assure that he would have the support of an absolute, not merely a relative, majority. Ministers were easily removable both by the popularly elected Reichstag and popularly elected president, and government was conducted on the basis of a very lengthy and detailed bill of rights. The Weimar constitution was proclaimed in its day as the most perfect of all democratic constitutions, and for good reasons.

This unalleviated democracy was superimposed upon a society pervaded by authoritarian relationships and obsessed with authoritarianism. In his study of interwar German films, *From Caligari to Hitler* (21), Siegfried Kracauer has pointed out that a morbid concern with despotism, with raw power and arbitrary will, was a characteristic alike of reactionary and revolutionary German films, most obviously in films like *Caligari, Waxworks, Dr. Mabuse,* and *Mädchen in Uniform.* That the Germans should have been deeply preoccupied with naked power, large and petty, is hardly very surprising in a society democratized on its parliamentary surface, but shot through with large and petty tyrants in every other segment of life. Compared with their British counterparts, German family life, German schools, and German business firms were all exceedingly authoritarian. German families were dominated, more often than not, by tyrannical husbands and fathers, German schools by tyrannical teachers, German firms by tyrannical bosses. Insolence, gruffness, pettiness, arbitrariness, even violence were so widespread that one could certainly not consider them mere deviations from normal patterns. In a sense, throughout the whole of German interwar society one finds authority patterns which in Britain are confined to the nonelite strata, but even among the lower classes in Britain authority relations are not quite so arbitrary or so unrelenting as they were in Weimar Germany, nor afflicted by such omnipresent intimations of violence.

Families, schools, and occupational contexts are the most basic (that is, the most absorbing and demanding) segments of life, and the patterns existing in them are bound to affect all other social relations. But perhaps a high degree of authoritarianism in these patterns would not matter from the standpoint of democratic government if there were interposed between them and government certain institutions having mixed authority relations—institutions which might mediate between the pervasive despotism of the primary segments and the pure democracy of government, so that individuals would not be tossed abruptly from stark domination in one segment of life to stark liberty in another. But nothing remotely like this was the case in Weimar Germany. Political parties in imperial Germany had served as the principal model for Michels' iron law of oligarchy, and their internal political characteristics persisted in the Weimar period; at a later date, German political parties served as the chief illustration for Hermens' argument that proportional representation with the straight list system inevitably makes for a highly centralized and oligarchical party structure. Associational life in Weimar Germany presents, if anything, an even sharper contrast with Great Britain. Quite apart from the fact that the great interest groups were intimately involved in the party system—every major interest, economic, religious, or sectional, had a party of its own—the main "associations" offering men opportunities for escape from loneliness or from the primary social relations were extraordinarily authoritarian in structure. Germany was not a country of hushed snob clubs and demure whist drives, of jolly good fellowship and darts in the Public Bar, but a country of paramilitary organizations, trade union militants, beer hall conspirators, grimly serious *Turnvereine* and systematically joyful *Gesangvereine*. This, of course, is something of an exaggeration. Not all German associations were highly authoritarian in structure, and we have reason to think that there were important differences among the various regions of Germany in this regard—southern Germany, for example, being on the whole less monotonously authoritarian than northern Germany. But while any simple picture of any complex society will exaggerate and overemphasize to some extent, the essential picture of pervasive authoritarianism in German secondary associations given here probably does so relatively little. At the very least, we can say that life in German associations was much more authoritarian than it is in the great majority of democracies. Associations thus formed no bridge between government and the primary and occupational groups; if anything, they formed a barrier to their reconciliation. Certainly it is in organizations like the *Stahlhelm*, or the *Freikorps*, or the SA and SS, that we find the greatest contrast to the pattern of plebiscitary government (4, pp. 128-149, 165-169, 199-208).

The same argument applies to the instrumental appendages

of the parliamentary system, the civil and military service. Just as the imperial German parties had inspired Michels' theory of universal oligarchy, so the Prussian civil service, which persisted in form and to a large extent even in personnel under Weimar, had served as the chief model for Weber's ideal-type of bureaucracy, with its emphasis upon "hierarchical subordination" and "the distinct social esteem" of the official. To these characteristics, which are by no means found in anything like pure form in other modern countries (e.g., Britain), we might add another that innumerable works on German bureaucracy have remarked upon: its recruitment from the more authoritarian elements in German society and its open sympathy, throughout the Weimar period, for reactionary and authoritarian movements (4, pp. 174-198). As for the military, so frequently has the antagonism of its patterns and attitudes to the Weimar system been pointed out that nothing more need be said on this subject.

We have in the case of the Weimar Republic a government violently contradictory to all nongovernmental aspects of life. However, it would not be strictly accurate to say, as so many have said, that the Germans were simply thoroughgoing authoritarians who just had no use for political democracy, that in Germany governmental democracy was imposed upon a country which provided no basis at all for it, so that the first talented and lucky authoritarian to come along could easily demolish the whole structure. There is every reason to think that the great majority of Germans were convinced democrats during the Weimar period and even before—in their attitudes toward government. Imperial Germany was one of the first countries to have universal suffrage, and the fact that pro-democratic, liberal, center, and socialist parties consistently won somewhere between 80 and 90 per cent of the vote in elections before World War I is therefore a matter of some importance. This voting pattern, furthermore, continued under the Weimar Republic right up to the ill-starred elections of the early 1930's; the right-wing Nationalists (the DNVP), the party which best fits the stereotype of the unmitigatedly authoritarian German, rarely polled more than 10 per cent of the vote (32, pp. 400-401). Consequently, when one says that there was no basis for democracy in interwar Germany, one says something much more complicated than that Germans did not really want a governmental democracy. One says that Weimar Germany could provide no proper basis even for a governmental system which the great majority indeed wanted, while imperial Germany, ironically, did furnish a proper basis for a type of government which the great majority did not seem to want. Had the German taste for authoritarianism been absolute, the Germans would probably have constructed after World War I a much more stable, though not a purely democratic, government. The trouble was not that the Germans were so one-sidedly authoritarian; the trouble was rather that they were—and perhaps had always been (10, pp. 12-14)—so remarkably two-sided (i.e., incongruent) in their political beliefs and social practices. Profound ideological commitment to governmental democracy is not a sufficient basis for stable democracy; in fact, it can be worse, in the long run, than a more qualified commitment to democracy.

One more point regarding the incongruities in Weimar authority patterns may be worth mentioning. Although the constitution of the Weimar Republic was democratic to an unprecedented degree, it did contain some authoritarian elements. The executive, as in Britain, was given an unlimited power of dissolution; and under Article 48, the article which played such a villainous role in the legal destruction of German democracy, the president, with the cooperation of a chancellor appointed by himself, could wield enormous emergency powers, including the virtually absolute suspension of civil rights and a nearly unlimited power to govern by decrees. But these authoritarian elements of the constitution were reserved for particular periods when regular parliamentary processes no longer operated; contrary to the British case, they were not built into the everyday management of government. They were no part of the normal pattern of governmental authority. The constitution really left nothing to choose between absolute democracy in "normal" times—rare enough in the Weimar period—and an absolute lack of it in times of crisis. As a result, government was carried on not only in contradiction with society, but even in a sort of contradiction with itself; periods of pure parliamentary democracy alternated at a rapid rate with periods of practically unchecked executive dictatorship, much as in the last years of pre-Fascist Italian democracy and during the 1930's in France.

Motivational Basis of the Theory

In addition to the fact that it seems to fit the most unambiguous cases of stability and instability, the theory of congruence has, prior to any concerted testing, one other important point to recommend it: it leads one immediately to the motivational (or psychological) links between the variables it relates. This is important. Any generalization about human behavior obviously lacks an important element of plausibility if it makes no sense in terms of what we know about human motivations. Conceivably societies may involve certain purely mechanical relations which require no motivational explanation at all, but follow simply from the fact of interaction, whatever may underlie it; but even theories about competitive interdependence seem always to proceed from particular views of probable human conduct. In any event, to ask *why* certain relations exist in social life is always to ask what there is about one state of society that induces behavior leading to another.

Such motivational connections between different aspects of social life are by no means easy to see whenever one finds a positive correlation between social variables. Take the correlation between democracy and economic development. A positive relation of some sort seems to exist between the two, but why exactly should it? The only link which readily suggests itself is that a high degree of economic development leads to a high degree of economic satisfaction, and thus reconciles men to their condition of life, including their government. But this does not tell us why it should reconcile them particularly to democracy, and, what is more, militates against the obvious fact that economic satisfaction is always relative to economic expectations—expectations which might conceivably outstrip any rate of economic growth and any level of economic development. This is not to say that there is no link between democracy and economic development at all, but only that the motivational link between them is not readily apparent from the correlation itself and probably very indirect, if indeed it does exist.

The motivational basis of the theory of congruence, however, is quite readily apparent. This is due to the fact that the conditions described by the term "incongruity" are very similar to the conditions denoted by two other concepts of social science, two concepts, which, appropriately enough, denote both certain social conditions and certain psychological states, or propensities to act: the closely related concepts of anomie and strain.

Anomie exists, in its purest form, whenever there is a complete breakdown of a normative order governing action, when individuals lack clear and commanding guidelines to behavior, do not know what is expected of them, and are thus compelled to rely solely upon their egos, their "rational" calculations, to inform their conduct (16, pp. xi ff.; 30, p. 39). Anomie, in this sense, may be more or less acute and more or less widespread in a society; it may extend to few or many, important or unimportant, phases of life, and it may be found in society generally or only in certain of its members. It is always disturbing, but becomes, in its more acute form, unbearable; the actual responses to it depend, however, not only upon its acuteness but also upon the extent of its diffusion throughout a society. At its less acute levels, it manifests itself in merely annoying, possibly even constructive, anxieties, and the resort to perfectly innocuous means of relieving them. But in its more acute forms it has been linked, on the individual level, with serious functional disorders (even suicide), and, on the social level, with mass movements in general, particularly movements of religious fanaticism and political movements of a chiliastic and highly ideological character—in general, with movements which provide men with a sense of orientation, a sense of belonging to a bearable social order, or merely with the opportunity for escaping from the dilemmas of everyday life or submerging themselves in some comforting collectivity.

Anomie may result from many conditions. In individuals, it may be the result of inadequate socialization, or rapid mobility from one stratum of society to another, or transplantation from one culture to another, or indeed any important change in one's condition in life. In societies it may result from any social change (especially rapid change) requiring important adjustments in conduct, or from a widely successful attack upon traditional norms, or from large-scale mobility.

Among these many conditions which can give rise to anomie, the condition of "strain" is perhaps the most common in any complex society. "Strain" is used here in a technical sense; it refers, not to the utter lack of settled guides to behavior, or to ambiguous norms, but to *ambivalent* expectations—that is, the coexistence of different, perhaps even contradictory, norms of conduct in regard to a particular set of actions or an individual's actions in general (30, p. 253). We may speak of strain whenever men are expected to conform to different, but equally legitimized, norms of conduct—as, for example, when a man simultaneously performs some roles involving universalistic norms and others involving particularistic norms, or some roles permitting affective responses and others demanding affective neutrality; and strains are of course particularly acute if a single role makes contradictory normative demands. Strain exists between the role of a man who is given access to the female body as a doctor and who seeks access to the female body as a lover, and strain will be particularly great in that case if patient and lover are one and the same person.

Incongruity between the authority patterns of a society, like any other incongruity among social patterns, is an obvious source of strain, and through strain of anomie, and through anomie of behavior potentially destructive to the stability of any pattern of government. This seems obvious; yet one cannot let the argument go at that. Conflicting expectations inevitably exist in any highly differentiated society, and are perhaps given in the very nature of the human condition, for human beings are inherently multifaceted. One can no more imagine a bearable existence which is utterly devoid of affect than one which consists only of emotional responses; pure and complete universalism is unattainable, men being what they are, and pure and complete particularism leads to chaos and gross inefficiency in any kind of social life. It is not, therefore, the simple absence of strains which distinguishes an integrated and stable society from one which is unintegrated and unstable, but rather the successful reduction and management of strains which can never be eliminated. How then can strains be "managed," in order to prevent them from leading to acute anomie?

Perhaps the only reliable way is through the institutionalized segregation of roles—through preventing one role as much as possible from impinging upon, or even being mentally associated with, another, if the other makes conflicting normative demands. Such segregation of roles is in fact a feature of any society which is functionally differentiated to a high degree; it may be physical (note, for example, the fact that the doctor's office is generally separated from his domicile) or "psychological"—that is, achieved only through the widespread mental disjunction of particular roles. Why then should not incongruities in authority patterns be similarly "manageable" through segregation? Why should it matter, for example, that authority is strong in one context and weak in another?

A number of things need to be said about this issue. First of all, the theory here sketched does not assert that *any* disparity among authority patterns is disastrous; it only asserts that disparities of a particular kind and degree have fatal consequences. After all, I have already argued that the very notion of congruence encompasses certain kinds of disparities. Some disparate authority patterns can be tolerated well enough— anyway, without serious anomic consequences; the argument here is merely that *incongruent* patterns cannot be tolerated, partly because they are, by definition, patterns in which disparities are particularly stark and great, and partly because strains arising from incongruent authority patterns are not alleviated by "intermediate" patterns which help to reconcile the starkly disparate patterns in relatively distant segments of society. In any case, no one would argue that all strains can be "managed" equally well; and, obviously, the greater the strain, the more unlikely it is to be successfully managed.

Another point to bear in mind is that "managing" a strain is not the same thing as abolishing it; when we manage strains, we merely reduce them to a tolerable level, or, without reducing them, in some way accommodate ourselves to their existence. The strains, however, persist, and may at any time lead to behavior modifying the social relations which give rise to them. What is more, certain kinds of strains are hard to reduce or tolerate and strains among authority patterns, in my view, are of this type. The reason is precisely that authority relations are nearly universal in social relations, aspects of almost every social role, a fact which makes it inherently difficult to "segregate" authority patterns from one another. Whether a man is acting the role of father, teacher, boss, or politician, he is almost always in some context involving authority; the operation of authority is one of the more inescapable facets of life. Not so for a man playing both the affective husband and affectively neutral professional, or both the particularistic father and universalistic boss. In these cases, not only the structures but the functions also are different. There is, in other words, a crucial difference between performing different functions in different ways and performing the same function in different ways; conflicts of the latter sort obviously impose uncomparably the greater psychological burden. Imagine, on one hand, a doctor who is expected to take a coldly scientific attitude toward his female patients and a warmly unscientific attitude toward his wife; imagine, on the other, a doctor who is expected to administer only to his wealthy patients but wash his hands of others, or who is supposed to help friends and kin but let strangers suffer, or to alleviate the pains of adults but not those of children. In the latter cases strain is bound to be the more severe, whatever grotesque value system might be used to legitimize such behavior—and functioning in incongruent authority relations is like the latter cases rather than the former.

This is not to say that a single man cannot rule in one context and be ruled in another. Although such a duality of positions does create strains which, apparently, are unmanageable by some people, most of us do just that most of the time. The question here is one of operating in conflicting authority patterns, not of occupying different positions in similar authority patterns. When one is subordinated in one pattern of authority, one may in fact learn very well how properly to be dominant in a similar pattern of authority, but being tossed back and forth among radically different authority patterns is another matter.[4]

To some extent, however, it may be possible to "segregate" even very disparate patterns in the performance of the same or similar roles through highly rigid institutionalization. The likelihood of this is small, but not absolutely zero. Human ingenuity in ridding life of strains, or in creating the delusion that strains do not really exist, is very great. Political science itself furnishes a striking example of how far such delusions may go, in the long-held, and still carefully nurtured, belief that authority is characteristic only of the state, not of anything outside the state. This belief is quite modern in origin, and has

[4] Actually, Kornhauser's theory does not deal directly with the problem of stable democracy. It tries rather to account for large-scale illegitimate movements subversive of "libertarian" governments. But the existence of such movements is one of the "obvious" conditions which lead to instability in democracies. For our purposes, therefore, we can consider his a theory of stable democracy.

been dominant mainly in the liberal West. Why has it been dominant there? Has it become established only because of the development of political science departments in search of some subject matter entirely their own? Or because of the effects of the theory of sovereignty? Or because of the gradual development of functionally differentiated, specialized structures of government? Or is it really a delusion which keeps liberal democrats from having to face up to the inevitable lack of real democracy in nongovernmental phases of social life? On the face of it, the notion that authority is a property solely of the state is so absurdly untenable that the compulsions making for it among eminently sensible people must be very great indeed. And that lends credence to the view that the notion performs neither an academic, nor a legal, but a psychological function: that it helps preserve the myth of democracy by keeping men from having to face up to, and incorporate in their political theories, uncomfortable disparities between governmental and nongovernmental life. In this connection, note that it has been mainly men out of sympathy with classical democratic ideas who have maintained a different position: pluralists, like Laski and Cole; Marxists, most obviously; and power theorists, like Lasswell and Michels.

Undoubtedly, men are able—and must be able—to make bearable, by all sorts of devices, even the most crushing strains. Under one condition, however, we can be sure that the chances of successful role segregation are not merely small, but practically zero: if nongovernmental social relations are themselves highly politicized—that is to say, if they are greatly concerned with governmental politics. One of the characteristics of life under the Weimar Republic was that social formations, in addition to being extraordinarily authoritarian, were concerned, to an extraordinary extent and with extraordinary fervor, with matters of government; many voluntary societies— even some of the least of gymnastic or choral groups—seemed to have some sort of governmental ideology, or even some affiliation with political parties or movements. Where this is the case, it is obviously much more difficult, indeed impossible, to segregate discrepancies in expected behavior, for the simple reason that government itself cannot then appear as a segregated social context. And in a democracy some politicalization of nongovernmental life is always unavoidable, even necessary; how otherwise could there be any political competition? Democracy presupposes, at the very least, some organized party life, and party life tends to draw into politics all sorts of other social units; it diffuses governmental politics throughout society, now more, now less, but always to some extent, and thus makes the management of strains by role segregation particularly unlikely.

But my purpose here is not to show that strains arising from incongruent authority patterns cannot be managed or tolerated under any circumstances. Rather it is to show that, among the manifold strains of life in a complex society, such strains are unusually, perhaps incomparably, difficult to manage, so that it seems logical for men to try and cope with them by reducing them at the source, that is, ordinarily, by changing the governmental patterns under which they live. Even if this is not granted, however, one fact is surely beyond doubt: societies possessing congruent authority patterns possess an enormous "economic" advantage over those that do not. In the more extreme cases, like Great Britain, individuals are in effect socialized into almost all authority patterns simultaneously (even if they belong to the nonelite strata), while in highly incongruent societies men must repeatedly be resocialized for participation in various parts of social life. For society, then, congruence in regard to authority patterns, at the very least, saves much effort; for individuals, it saves much psychological wear and tear resulting from uncertainty and ambivalence. In that basic and indisputable sense, the congruent society starts with a great advantage over the incongruent society; and we have many reasons to think that it enjoys greater advantages still.

If it is true that incongruities among authority patterns can be reduced only at the source (in democracies, and perhaps other systems of government as well), and if it is true that such incongruities are particularly hard to bear, then all sorts of things which are otherwise mysterious become more comprehensible. To cite only one example: perhaps these points explain why in totalitarian systems such massive efforts are made to accomplish seemingly trivial, even self-destructive, ends, particularly efforts to reshape all social relations, from the family up, in the totalitarian image—or else to destroy them. "What rational balance sheet," asks Inkeles, speaking of early Soviet attacks on family and church, "would have led a group of leaders who were concerned first and foremost with preserving their power to attempt that particular diversion of energy with its obvious consequences of social resentment and popular hostility" (17, p. 19)? His own solution is that the Soviet leaders' actions can be explained only by their messianic visions of an utterly transformed society; the theory of congruence, however, provides a still more "rational" explanation, even if it was only felt in some intuitive way, not grasped in the sense in which it is stated here, by Soviet leaders.

But the subject here is democracy, not totalitarianism; and for the analysis of democratic government another important deduction can be made from the proposition that strains due to ambivalences in authority patterns can be relieved only by reducing the ambivalences themselves: there must always be *some* strains among authority patterns in a democracy. Such strains will be nonexistent only if a society's authority patterns are identical, a condition quite unrealizable in a democracy, as we have seen. Obviously, however, they can be kept at a relatively low level if the society provides sufficient opportunities for learning patterns of action appropriate to democracy (if, that is, a good many of the authority patterns in a democracy are significantly democratized); and this will be all the more the case if the more congruent patterns are directly associated with government or involve mainly interactions among the political elite. And there is also a second possibility: strains might be kept within tolerable limits in democratic governments

which have certain characteristics rather than others—there
are, after all, many varieties of democracy.

This is a subject better dealt with under the second theory
we require, a theory which specifies the particular conditions
which must exist if democracy, rather than government in
general, is to be stable.

IV. BALANCED DISPARITIES IN THE GOVERNMENTAL PATTERN

What then are the special conditions that democracies must
fulfill if they are to be stable? Undoubtedly one could list here
a massive catalog of social characteristics which favor stable
democracy, but if we confine ourselves to conditions not merely
favorable but indispensable, to necessary conditions, we can
deal with this question rather briefly. The most essential special
requirement of stable democracy can in fact be deduced from
the theory of the congruence of authority patterns—as indeed
ought to be the case, since special theories should always be
derivable from general theories. If governments tend to be
stable when social authority patterns are congruent; if a great
many social relations cannot be organized on a purely democratic basis without seriously dysfunctional consequences; and
if some of these relations resistant to democratic structure exist
in social segments adjacent or close to government; then it follows that *governmental democracy will tend to be stable only if
it is to a significant extent impure—if, in short, the governmental authority pattern contains a balance of disparate elements, of which democracy is an important part (but only a
part).*

To forestall a tempting, but unjustified, retort to this proposition, it should perhaps be pointed out immediately that I am
not now asserting, after arguing that governmental stability
requires congruent authority patterns, that stable democracy
requires an *incongruent* authority pattern after all. The notion
of congruence applies to the relations between governmental

and nongovernmental authority patterns, while the present point relates only to governmental patterns. It asserts merely that intolerable strains between governmental and nongovernmental patterns are likely to be avoided if the governmental pattern is not extremely, i.e. purely, democratic.

One could even argue that the very minimum definition of congruence cannot be satisfied in a pure governmental democracy. Not only are the primary and occupational relationships of social life inhospitable to democratic organization, but we have every reason to think that associations, parties, and pressure groups also resist democratization after a point—not to mention the still more obvious cases of the civil and military service. Parties, for example, are competitive organizations— Michels called them fighting organizations (29, pp. 46-49)— which can hardly afford the luxuries of plebiscitary democracy; so are pressure groups. Associations in general are rarely very democratic, if only because of the relatively low rate of participation by members in their affairs, in the great majority of cases (26)—not to mention functional requirements which act as barriers against democratization. The iron law of oligarchy seems to hold pretty well, which is not to say that democracy must always be a chimera in any form. It follows that between a governmental pattern as purely democratic as that of Weimar Germany and *any* kind of social life, even in the least authoritarian of political cultures, there are bound to be glaring, perhaps insurmountable, disjunctions. Governmental democracy, of course, is never really pure in practice; but, as the case of Weimar shows, it can come very close, certainly in the forms and myths of authority, if not quite so readily in actual practices.

It is certainly curious how often one finds mixtures of heterogeneous characteristics, sometimes even contradictory characteristics, in stable democracies. Take Great Britain once more as the obvious and most essential case in point. British government and British authority beliefs, as already pointed out, are a mixture of all the elements out of which governmental authority can be concocted: popular government, the government of an autonomous elite, and government under an impersonal law; and none of these elements is clearly dominant over the others. British government combines (in a surprisingly easy fit) authority, responsibility, and responsiveness—the dominion of rulers, rules, and the ruled; for this reason there is something in British government to which every aspect of British social life, whether permissive or compulsive, traditional or modern, can have an affinity. Nor is this mixture of basic authority patterns the only balance of disparities which British government contains. We find in it a similar mixture of ceremonial and "efficient" institutions, of sober business and gaudy show. We find in it also a mixture of integration and pluralistic competition. Authority is concentrated in the cabinet, but the cabinet, being a collective entity, is itself a pluralistic structure and, under modern conditions, functions less as a single, cohesive unit than through a large number of committees and subcommittees, formal and informal, permanent and ad hoc; normally this structure works slowly, by patient bargaining and consultation, like all polycentric structures, but the myth of the fusion of authority can accommodate on occasion swift and autonomous action, by a prime minister or an inner cabinet. So also the monolithic character of the disciplined mass parties is balanced by a highly pluralistic universe of active and influential pressure groups, acting, by and large, directly upon government, rather than through the instrumentalities of the parties.

Not least, British politicians strike a most remarkable balance between dogmatism and pragmatism in their behavior. They tend to be neither absolute ideologists (in the manner of most Weimar politicians) nor utterly unprincipled opportunists (in the manner of the "trasformists" of pre-Fascist Italy); parliamentary behavior in Britain is characterized neither by unstable maneuvering for power nor by intransigent insistence upon ideals. K. B. Smellie has said that British politicians, while not unprincipled opportunists, are nevertheless "hard to work up to the dogmatic level"—suggesting that they are, on the average, men of principle, but lukewarm, phlegmatic, and tentative in the principles they hold. This, however, is not what I want to suggest at all. What is involved here is not a matter of temperament. The crucial point is rather that dogma and principle are concentrated upon some aspects of government and kept almost entirely out of others. In essence, the British invest with very high affect the procedural aspects of their government and with very low affect its substantive aspects; they behave like ideologists in regard to rules and like pragmatists in regard to policies. Procedures, to them, are not merely procedures, but sacred ritual. Neither the Tories nor the Whigs appear to have the slightest difficulty in stealing one another's clothes; yet in Britain any procedural reform, even the slightest and most sensible, seems to run into the most intractable and irrational obstacles. Massive evidence for this point is provided by the heaps of fruitless proposals on parliamentary reform, piled up both by private individuals (from Jennings to Crick) (18; 7) and by Select Committees. Herbert Morrison's *Government and Parliament* contains some particularly arresting examples, especially in regard to the complex, time-devouring, and needlessly repetitious financial procedures in the House of Commons. This explains not only why the British fit neither the extreme model of the Weimar ideologists nor that of the Italian "trasformists," but also why they do indeed sometimes behave as if they were ideologists in regard to policy. They do so when policy problems appear in procedural guise, as in the case of the House of Lords crisis of 1909-1911, and more recently (and not on the governmental level) in the Labour Party disputes over nuclear weapons.

The theory of congruence gives us one reason, but only one of several, for the assertion that such balanced disparities are necessary if democracy is to be stable. Others are perhaps even more obvious. Democratic governments require a healthy element of authoritarianism not only for the sake of congruence between government and other aspects of society, but for the even simpler reason that a representative government must govern as well as represent—must satisfy two values which, on the evidence, are not easily reconcilable. This point can in fact be stated in a much less truistic form, and tied in with the motivational basis of the theory of congruence sketched above. That strains in the definition of political roles can produce governmental instability seems manifest; but can governmental stability also be affected by nonpolitical strains? There is at least a possibility that acute anomie, in whatever segment of life it may appear, will have destructive consequences upon government, and not only because it may alienate men from their general condition of life. If intolerable strains exist in some social relations, but not in authority patterns, it is particularly likely that attempts will be made to manage the existing strains through governmental means; it seems natural that men should attempt to modify unacceptable relations through whatever relations they accept. But if government, under these conditions, is incapable of realizing important special changes through political direction, it will itself become identified with the unbearable aspects of social life. Hence, a particular need for some measure of authoritarianism in the governmental pattern, or, to put the same point slightly differently, a high capacity to control social relations toward desired ends. This capacity is always necessary—it is inherent in the governmental function; but it is particularly necessary if society needs a solvent for nonpolitical tensions.

We could rest this point, and others, on an even simpler psychological basis: human beings just are not one-sided. They have superegos and libidos as well as egos. For that reason, as Bagehot so clearly saw, a government which provides no food for the sentiments, a purely businesslike, perfectly rationalized government, is unlikely to get very much support and likely to engender a rash of hysterical social movements to satisfy the instincts it neglects. And as Bagehot also clearly saw, a government which provides no clear and focussed leadership, no easily recognized source of directives for conduct, is equally unlikely to succeed. The superego requires such a definite source of directives, even if only an imaginary one, just as the libido requires that it be invested with high affect; and a political system also requires it for operational purposes, above all in times of crisis. These two points may explain why constitutional monarchies seem to work better than parliamentary republics, and why presidential government seems preferable wherever monarchy no longer exists—two very old theories of political science.

We might speak in this connection of a second kind of "strain" which can afflict human behavior—strain which results from overconcentration on any pattern of behavior satisfying to only one aspect of the human psyche. Certainly we can regard the compulsive ritualism of political movements in the Weimar Republic as attempts to satisfy needs frustrated by the insipid matter-of-factness of the Weimar government; and we can regard the American penchant for giving officers of private associations stately titles (High Potentate, Grand Marshal, Sultan, and the like) in the same light. Indeed, one could argue that strain, in one sense or the other, is a condition inherent in human life, for anything which decreases strain in the first sense tends to increase it in the second. And if this is true, then it is clear that a stable government is never one lacking in strains, but one which strikes a tolerable balance between disparate strains; between strains resulting from the existence of inconsistent norms and strains resulting from over-consistent norms. This lends support to the still older theory of political science that mixed government is the most stable form of government—and puts it also in a new light.

As for the need to balance pragmatism and ideologism in politics, an explanation not quite so manifestly relevant to the present theory is required. A high degree of pragmatic behavior in politics is obviously desirable because it makes possible political integration, either on the party or the parliamentary level. Because of the great multiplicity of interests existing in any modern society, both a two-party system and stable coalition government presuppose a great deal of compromise, and compromise in turn presupposes a relatively low degree of affect and dogma in political competition. Pragmatic attitudes in politics also help to keep political problems in proper focus and on a proper level of significance, and thus facilitate rational and relevant decision making. Political ideologies tend to elevate even the most minor matters to major importance, so that energies tend to be dissipated upon insignificant questions while great problems go begging for solution; they invest everything with "world significance," to translate literally an untranslatable German word. But if too much principle can kill a government, so can the lack of any principle at all. Spiro (33, p. 189) has pointed out, quite rightly, that too unprincipled an approach to politics will lead to a lack of consistent and long-range policies, to an eclectic flitting to and fro from policy to policy which may prove destructive to a government by setting it internally at cross-purposes; what is wanted is "programmatic" government, and this must of necessity blend principle with pragmatic adjustment. One can add to this another, perhaps still more serious point. Pragmatic politics, absolutely unburdened by affect and principle, can lead to only one kind of political behavior: sheer opportunism—mere maneuvering lacking any higher purpose. That is what Italian politics was like before Giolitti's grant of universal suffrage, and, judging from the works of Mosca and Pareto, opportunism did more than anything else to discredit democratic institutions in Italian minds. Nor should one overlook that the most unprincipled and adaptable politican is likely also to be the most cynical (and effective) manipulator of symbols for unscrupulous ends; Richard Rovere's fascinating analysis of McCarthy provides a perfect case in point. And just as ceremony feeds the emotions, so principle feeds the superego—narrows the range of decisions requiring "rational" adjustment, and thus makes pragmatic reasoning a more tolerable burden. In this last sense, a proper balance between commitment and moderation is part and parcel of those manifold counterweights which preserve a tolerable balance of strains in social life.

V. RELIGION, ECONOMIC DEVELOPMENT, AND MASS SOCIETY: AN APPRAISAL OF OTHER THEORIES

No attempt will be made here to test the theory I have sketched directly, that is, by broad-scale, comparative analysis; but, as pointed out at the beginning, one can to some extent test a theory indirectly by viewing it in light of other, well-substantiated theories. If the latter can be subsumed to the theory proposed, that is certainly a powerful argument for it. If one can show on the basis of a proposed theory *why* certain other correlations between variables hold, that is a still more powerful argument for it. And if one can show that the theory not only explains such correlations but also explains why they are not better correlations, then one has as cogent a case as can be made for it short of direct testing.

The propositions I should like to consider in light of the present theory are the following: (1) that countries with large, or predominant, Catholic populations do not produce stable democracy; (2) that a high degree of economic development correlates positively with stable democracy; and (3) that stable democracy correlates positively with vigorous associational life in a society and negatively with "mass societies," societies in which men are highly individuated or in which very strong primary group attachments exist. The first proposition has been stated in a great many sources, but perhaps most strongly and unequivocally by certain French writers, e.g., André Gide (15, p. 122) and Raymond Aron. The second has been argued most strongly by Lipset (25, ch. 2). The third comes from Kornhauser's *The Politics of Mass Society* (20).

These three propositions hold up very well; certainly they are the best propositions about the basic conditions of stable democracy available at present. Other propositions—e.g., those relating stable democracy to integrated party systems or to a high degree of political consensus—may hold up even better, but deal with the subject on a much more superficial (or at any rate, a different) level. But however cogent, each of the three propositions leaves something to be desired when properly tested. For this, there may be several possible explanations. One possibility is that the phenomenon which the theories are meant to explain may be "multicausal," and that certain additional factors must be invoked in each case to make the theories entirely satisfactory. Another is that imperfections in the correlations arise because of the operation, in some cases, of accidental circumstances, the sort of circumstances which, I have argued, led to the longevity of the French Third Republic. Here is also a third possibility, namely, that the conditions singled out in the propositions are not directly responsible for the stability or instability of democracies, but are linked to these only through some other condition—a condition which they either help to bring about or of which they are frequently a manifestation. My argument is that the last is indeed the case: that religion, economic development, and a society's structure of participation affect the stability of democracy only in so far as they affect or reflect the relations among its patterns of authority. This is the preferable explanation of the imperfections of the three theories for several reasons: first, because in each case it can in fact be shown that the theories hold to the extent that they are special cases of the present theory and fail to hold to the extent that they are not; second, because we can never tell when our subject matter intrinsically requires complex explanations (as distinguished from complex explanations which are required merely because we cling to highly imperfect hypotheses); and third, because it is very unlikely that fortuitous circumstances could account for the whole combination of conditions here identified as stable democracy, even if they can account for the mere survival of a political order.

Democracy and Catholicism

The proposition that countries with large, or predominant, Catholic populations tend not to be stable democracies certainly contains some truth, but the correlation between stable democracy and Catholicism is highly imperfect. For one thing, it is by no means established that predominantly non-Catholic countries tend to be markedly more stable democracies; it may be that stable democracy is simply very rare, no matter what a society's religious composition, in which case the failure of most predominantly Catholic countries to produce it indicates a condition pertaining to mankind, not just to such countries. Even granted that the most conspicuously stable democracies have existed in largely Protestant countries, some uncomfortable facts remain. Among the more stable democracies are several with very sizable Catholic populations, for example, Australia, Canada, Switzerland, and the United States. At least one almost exclusively Catholic country, Ireland, is a highly stable democracy. Present-day West Germany, with a government verging upon hyperstability, is much more highly Catholic than was the unified Germany of the Weimar Republic. And there are even some reasonably stable Latin American democracies, like Costa Rica and (until very recently, and perhaps still today) Uruguay.

Furthermore, most of the familiar arguments used to link Catholicism with unstable democracy (arguments used to *explain* the supposed correlation) simply do not stand up to close examination. Catholicism, being a highly dogmatic religion, is supposed to make for ideological intransigence in politics, yet nothing more pragmatic or accommodating can be imagined than political behavior in Italy before World War I, or the attitudes of the French Center of the Fourth Republic described by Leites. Catholicism, being authoritarian in structure, is supposed to engender a preference for highly authoritarian government, yet in France it appeared rather to engender a preference for near anarchy. Catholicism, by intruding clerical issues into political life, is supposed to prevent the consensus required in a highly integrated political system, yet nothing more consensual could be imagined than Italian politics in the post-unification era.

It is reasonable to suspect, therefore, that if the imperfect correlation between Catholicism and unstable democracy does indeed represent some sort of causal relation—if it is not just a spurious correlation—then Catholicism must frequently be associated with some other factor, which can also exist in non-Catholic countries, which need not invariably exist in Catholic countries, and which leads more invariably to unstable democracy than Catholicism itself. The moment the question is viewed in this way, it becomes apparent that the theories proposed here can make very good sense both of the correlation and of its imperfections.

Catholicism, by subjecting its adherents to a highly authoritarian relationship, and one which involves extremely powerful psychological sanctions, certainly does nothing itself to reinforce democracy. Potentially it always threatens to introduce an incongruity into a democratic society, so that in any democracy there exists a fair probability that Catholicism will have dysfunctional consequences. But no more than a fair probability. If a democracy is sufficiently hedged about with authoritarian elements, the incongruity between government and church need not be very great. Moreover, if the church does not play a very important role in the associational life of a society, or if between church and government there exists a multiplicity of less authoritarian associations, even associations with a religious tinge, the incongruities will be diminished, in the sense of being mediated and reconciled. Whether or not Catholicism will inhibit or undermine stable democracy depends, therefore, not only on the inherent characteristics of Catholicism, but also on the nature of the governmental pattern and the vigor (and particular characteristics) of associational life in a society. This is why there neither is nor could be a very close correspondence between stability of democracy and size of Catholic population, and yet why there is some such correspondence.

Catholics certainly have no difficulty in acting as constructive democratic citizens in countries offering the chance to participate in a large variety of nonecclesiastical associations, particularly in countries like the United States and Switzerland, perhaps even Britain, where they account for a large but not predominant part of the population. It has been argued, of course, that in these countries Catholics are a minority (although a very large minority) and that this makes all the difference in the effect they can have on politics. Perhaps so, though obviously a group comprising from 20 to 40 per cent of the population can affect the political life of a nation a great deal; but this hardly explains why Catholics themselves should be relatively unaffected by Catholicism in these countries—why, for example, they should not themselves be markedly more authoritarian or ideological in political behavior, but fit instead so easily into the overall political culture of their society. Nor are Catholics a crashingly discordant element in what we might call "authoritarian democracies," like the *Kanzlerdemokratie* of the Bonn Federal Republic and the cabinet system of Britain. The real trouble lies in societies which combine a large Catholic population with a very pure democracy and in which nonsectarian associational life is poorly articulated. France of the Third and Fourth republics, for example, had not only a predominantly Catholic population but also one of the world's most unmitigated democracies and, relatively speaking, an unintensive associational life; such as it was, moreover, a good deal of its associational life was directly centered upon the Church. From this standpoint, the Fifth Republic ought to be a good deal more stable than the Third and Fourth, just as Germany under Adenauer (but not solely because of Adenauer) has been more stable than Weimar Germany. Certainly Gaullist France ought to be more stable than postwar Italy, a system which, under the understandable impression that pre-Fascist Italy was destroyed by Mussolini and not by its own weaknesses, has hedged against the possibility of excessive executive authority much more than it has provided against an insufficient amount of it. It is, of course, too early to assess the stability of the Fifth Republic, but just because of that—and because of

to be well established. But is there really a close connection between democracy and economic development?

The evidence suggests strongly that there is. Lipset, for example, found a positive correlation of sorts between stable democracy (in *his* sense of the term) and almost every conceivable index of economic development. Average per capita income in European and English-speaking stable democracies he found to be (in 1949 and 1950) $695, in unstable democracies only $308. Stable democracies had one doctor for every 860 persons, unstable democracies one for every 1,400 persons. There were 17 persons per motor vehicle in one case, 143 in the other; on one side, there were 205 telephones, 350 radios, and 341 newspapers per 1,000 persons, on the other only 58 telephones, 160 radios, and 167 newspapers. Stable European democracies had a male agricultural population of 21 per cent, European dictatorships one of 41 per cent. No less than 43 per cent of the population in stable European democracies lived in urban areas (cities over 20,000), but only 24 per cent did so in European dictatorships. And so on. These findings are supported by Coleman (in the Conclusion of *The Politics of the Developing Areas*), countries with "competitive" political systems in the "developing areas" coming out much better, on the indices used also by Lipset, than "semi-competitive" and "authoritarian" countries (1, pp. 579-581). And Deutsch's work (9) also lends credence to the thesis, since the great majority of the countries located at the highest extreme of economic development in his "country profiles" are also stable democracies—e.g., Switzerland, Australia, New Zealand, Sweden, Norway, Denmark, the United Kingdom, and the United States.

This is a lot of evidence—but far from conclusive. If we look, not at overall averages, but at specific cases and at ranges of economic differences among countries in the same governmental categories, it becomes apparent that we have here a rather weak correlation, not a strong one. A few countries which have been anything but paragons of democratic stability rank quite high in economic development. France, Venezuela, and the USSR (not to mention Kuwait) rank high now, and Weimar Germany did in its own day. It is true that the half-dozen countries which are most highly developed are also stable democracies, but difficulties seem to arise only a very little below their level. And the ranges between the most and the least developed stable democracies, as well as the most and the least developed unstable democracies (and nondemocracies), are enormous. The least developed stable European democracy had, according to Lipset, an average per capita income of $420, the most developed European dictatorship one of $482. Stable democracies have as many as 62 persons per motor vehicle, dictatorships as few as 10; one has as many as 46 per cent of males employed in agriculture, the other as few as 16; in one case as few as 28 per cent of the population live in cities, in the other as many as 44 per cent. Such overlaps, varying in size, but all large, are found for every index.

It follows that between the great extremes of economic development and economic underdevelopment is a large no-man's-land where apparently any governmental order, from stable democracy to totalitarianism, can exist—and at the great extremes there are not many cases. That stable democracy is not found at the very lowest levels is, of course, not surprising. At that level of underdevelopment the more obvious requisites for any democracy at all, stable or unstable—a certain minimum level of literacy, information, and communications—are not satisfied. But beyond that extreme, in the higher and intermediate ranges of economic development, everything is puzzling and indeterminate, if one assumes a simple correlation between democracy and economic level.

Lipset himself seems well aware of this, for his theory does not stop with economic development, but uses also a large number of other factors to explain the stability or instability of democracies: rapidity (rather than level) of economic development; "legitimacy" (that is, acceptance of a regime as right for a society), with special emphasis on the support of conservative groups; religion; historical development; and governmental structure. By adding all of these conditions to qualify the correlation with economic development, the theory can be made to come out right in every case, but so could any theory whatever; the whole procedure smacks of the familiar methodological fallacy of "saving the hypothesis." Moreover, the theory which finally emerges from all these modifications is extremely complicated, to say the least. It does not blatantly violate the rule of parsimony, for it is not established that a simpler theory with equal explanatory power is available; but it is very cumbersome to use and the significance of any of its variables almost impossible to establish, owing to the number of variables alleged to be independently capable of producing unstable democracy.

For these reasons alone one ought to look for another way to deal with the imperfections of the correlation, and such a way is provided by the present theory. Like religion, we can regard economic development as an aspect of society which correlates with stable (or unstable) democracy only in so far as it has an impact upon the congruence of authority patterns in society and the balancing of disparate patterns in government—as it does frequently (hence the positive correlation) but certainly not always (hence its imperfections).

That this is probably the right way to proceed is suggested by the most important modification Lipset himself makes in his theory. Not only the *level* of economic development seems to him to be associated with the performance of democracies, but also the *rate* of economic development; very rapid economic development, he argues, has consequences inimical to democracy, more gradual economic development supports it. On the evidence, this is a very strong argument—and exactly what one would expect on the basis of the present theory. Rapid industrialization from a traditional base, whatever its long-run effects, obviously introduces into society profound incongruities, particularly if it is imposed by direction, in one form or another. If economic development is relatively slow, strains between the economic and other sectors of life can be kept at tolerable levels by the gradual adaptation of other social institutions to the slowly evolving industrial economy. Nor is this the only reason why rapid economic development has political consequences different from gradual economic development. In the course of rapid economic development, the social order (appearing, as it must, as a barrier to development) is usually attacked in all its aspects, and in that process even aspects of social life which are, if not perfectly, then at least sufficiently, compatible with a modernized economy may be uprooted. Even if social life is not coercively uprooted by those who want to industrialize rapidly, it may nevertheless be uprooted by revolutionary violence resulting from the great strains attendant upon rapid industrialization. In either event, the outcome is the same: society and government will not consist of that mixture of modern and premodern patterns, that blending of disparities, which is characteristic of the more stable democracies. Furthermore, rapid industrialization usually occurs, for obvious reasons, at a relatively late stage in the history of industrialism; because of this, the desire for rapid economic modernization is likely for manifest historical reasons to be accompanied by expectations of relatively advanced democracy. Rapid industrialization in nontotalitarian countries will therefore tend to be accompanied by the creation of especially pure democracies, and these are always more tenuous than impure democracies; and if democracy is achieved by revolution, the result is, of course, the same. Worst of all, the sudden creation of an advanced democracy will abruptly liberate men politically, while the exigencies of rapid industrialization will subject them, in the short run, to unprecedented disciplines and compulsions. In this way, rapid industrialization not only unsettles the social order in general, but tends to create particularly great strains between government and other aspects of social life.

The theories of congruence and balanced disparities can thus account comprehensively for the deleterious impact upon democracy of rapid industrialization. But what of the positive correlation between economic development and stable democracy in general? If rapid industrialization is indeed inimical to democracy, and if it leads, as it must, to the attainment of relatively high levels of development in relatively little time, then surely this correlation is rather puzzling—until one remembers that the most advanced industrial societies (at present, or at any rate when Lipset collected his data) are precisely those which developed industry most gradually, but still lead the field because of their early start. In these countries—Great Britain, the United States, Switzerland, Sweden, and Canada—industrialization was associated with the relatively slow growth of populistic democracy and the gradual adaptation, never complete displacement, of preindustrial patterns, or else the forming of society itself simultaneously with the growth of industry and democracy. When this is realized, it becomes apparent that level of economic development, the moment one goes beyond extreme underdevelopment, matters only because speed of economic development matters; and from this it also follows that the present theory can account for Lipset's general proposition, no less than for the supposed modification of it which he introduces. This is because the modification is, in fact, the really crucial theory.

Economic development thus correlates very imperfectly with stable democracy because certain forms of development produce precisely those incongruities and imbalances which endanger democracy. That is why some very highly developed countries are unstable democracies, or not democracies at all. But economic development need not produce these deleterious consequences, and has not produced them in the (presently) most highly developed countries—that is why there is, nevertheless, a positive correlation between level of economic development and stable democracy. Indirectly, in the ways Lipset mentions, industrialization may even create conditions favorable to democracy, provided it is achieved in the right way. It is even more likely, however, that the two are associated simply because their roots lie in the same historical conditions —that is to say, because the processes of industrialization and democratization coincided, and did not, while both were being achieved gradually, frustrate one another.

If this is so, then it would clearly be unwise to base on the correlation any optimistic predictions about the future impact of industrialization upon the stability of democracies. The only predictions which seem to follow from this analysis are that late industrialization is, in the typical case, likely to have political consequences directly opposite to those of early industrialization, and that rapid industrialization is particularly dangerous to democracy if, paradoxical though it may seem, it is accompanied by rapid democratization.

Democracy and Mass Society

The third theory I wish to consider has now become associated mainly with William Kornhauser—although Kornhauser himself acknowledges the great role played in its formulation by such diverse people as Jacob Burckhardt, Gustave Le Bon, Ortega y Gasset, Karl Mannheim, and, above all perhaps, Emile Durkheim, Emil Lederer, and Hannah Arendt. This theory attributes unstable democracy primarily to "mass society," a technical term denoting societies without a vigorous corporate life, societies in which elites have "direct access" to nonelites, and nonelites to elites, owing to the weakness of organizations mediating between government and primary social relations. Such societies leave men, so to speak, "naked" before the state, and the state naked before men, unlike "pluralistic" societies, in which sovereign and subject are separated by many autonomous social formations, through which each must act upon the other.

With this theory we can deal rather more briefly than with the others, not because it is transparently bad, but, on the contrary, because it is so very well established. The theory of mass society is by all odds the best substantiated of the theories we have considered, and just because of that requires the least reinterpretation. Kornhauser supports it with truly massive evidence—evidence which shows not only that the more unstable democracies fit the model of mass society but also that the most apathetic and extremist antidemocrats, even in stable democracies, are found among the most "socially isolated" members of all classes and walks of life, among the "nonparticipants" who exist, in greater or smaller numbers, in any society. Kornhauser, in other words, not only links variables on the social level, but also, by looking at individual behavior in a great variety of contexts, shows that these relations have a clear and definite motivational basis. All that is necessary here, therefore, is to show that the theory of mass society is intimately related to the theory I have sketched—indeed, it is almost the same—and that the very slight imperfections which exist in it are attributable to the very slight ways in which it departs from the present theory.[5]

That the two theories are closely related should be manifest without long explication. If it is true that democratic government is inherently and profoundly in tension with the primary and occupational relations of social life, then it follows from the present theory that vigorous interactions upon the "intermediate" (or secondary) levels are required to produce congruity of authority patterns in democracies. Only a wide variety of intermediate associations can keep the inherent contradictions between democracy and life at the primary social levels from directly leading to insupportable strains; only intermediate associations can provide opportunities for learning democratic behavior patterns. This is even more important than the fact, of which Kornhauser makes a great deal, that such associations act as buffers against overbearing rulers, for while this fact may explain why vigorous associational life can

[5] Authority is not, of course, the only kind of social relation which is found in many different social contexts, but not all types of social relations are universal or near-universal in societies. One might suggest the hypothesis that the degree of success with which strains can be managed through role segregation is inversely proportional to the diffusion of a social relationship among various social contexts.

be a barrier to totalitarianism, it does not explain why it should be particularly compatible with stable democracy; after all, impeding totalitarianism is not at all the same thing as facilitating stable democracy—there are unstable democracies and nontotalitarian autocracies as well. Kornhauser's emphasis upon the protective effect of secondary associations seems therefore to miss the really crucial relation between associational life and stable democracy—except in one sense. Kornhauser argues that associations not only act as buffers shielding the ruled from their rulers, but that they also work in the opposite direction: that they provide the rulers with a certain autonomy from the ruled, while still subjecting them to exigent social pressures. If this is so, and it seems cogent, then it is apparent that a vigorous associational life not only permits authority patterns to be congruent, but leads also to one of the balanced disparities that democracy seems to require—a balance between governmental autonomy and dependence, "democracy" and "authoritarianism."

The two theories thus closely fit one another. Do they in any way differ? The answer is that in one way they clearly do: if a society has a vigorous associational life, but if the associations themselves are highly undemocratic, then, upon my theory, democracy should not be stable, and upon Kornhauser's, it should (at any rate, one condition making for unstable democracy—large-scale, illegitimate, antilibertarian movements—should not exist). It is, of course, perfectly possible for intermediate associations to be as undemocratic as primary groups, or even more so. It is improbable, but not impossible—and it has happened. Weimar Germany is itself a case in point, though admittedly there are not many others, for intermediate associations resist absolute authoritarianism nearly as much as they resist utter democracy. But the Weimar example suggests that, in so far as the two theories differ, the present one is the more powerful—for it is just in improbable cases like Weimar Germany that the theory of mass society fails to hold.

In this connection it is worth noting that, in a book which

teems with apposite evidence, data relating to Germany are conspicuously sparse and unapropos. Some of the evidence intended to show unintensive associational life in Germany actually relates to the Bonn period (cf. pp. 170-171); some of it shows that German associations tend to be engaged in politics to an unusual extent, not that there is a scarcity of associations or of participation in them (cf. p. 88); and the rest either shows what is true of all societies, that participants are disposed more favorably to democracy than nonparticipants, or that certain other conditions unfavorable to democracy existed in Weimar days. In actual fact, life upon the secondary levels was very vigorous in the Weimar period—and very incongruent with democracy. One might perhaps argue that large-scale participation in illiberal organizations was itself a response to social atomization, but this would be transparent sophistry, for it implies that illiberal associations simply do not count when one evaluates the extent to which a society is atomized, a position for which there can be no possible justification. If only mass movements like the Nazi and Communist parties had existed at the intermediate levels in Weimar Germany, such an argument would be sensible enough, but in fact one finds at those levels a great many organizations—most of them of a piece, from the standpoint of authority relations.

VI. Conclusion

However easily other theories can be subsumed to, and even improved by, the theory I have proposed here, it should be admitted that at this stage the theory is still little more than plausible. It is deficient, most obviously, in that no rigorous validation of it has been undertaken; the data used here illustrate the propositions, but do not validate them. Moreover, before the theory can be adequately tested, much more theoretical work is required. Testing the theory will not be just a matter of looking at the relevant data. For one thing, to test the theory we need a much better set of categories for classifying authority patterns than we now possess. Terms like democratic, authoritarian, and constitutionalist may do in the initial formulation of the idea, but for any large-scale comparative analysis a more discriminating and less ambiguous set of categories seems required. Such categories ought to be applicable to any kind of authority pattern, not just to government, a point which rules out many of the typologies now in use in political science. It is also necessary to find ways to measure with some exactness the extent to which different kinds of authority are present in actual cases, so that degrees of correspondence and disparity between authority patterns can be precisely established and, even more important, so that the very idea of congruence can be given a more precise formulation. In addition to measurable categories of authority, we need such categories for different types and degrees of instability; we need to relate types and degrees of instability to types and degrees of incongruence and imbalance; and, not least, we should be able to establish direct connections between incongruence and imbalance of authority patterns and the obvious conditions and system failures associated with unstable democracy.

Apart from these tasks, a staggering amount of empirical work still seems required before validity can be claimed for the theory. Because of the traditional emphasis on the state in political science, and on nonpolitical matters in other social sciences, studies of authority in general social life are pitifully meager and, for the most part, inadequate. Political scientists have charted little more than the visible part of their world; the massive infrastructure of political life is still largely *terra incognita*. This applies even to the data given here about authority in British and German life. By and large, these data are derived from my own and other people's personal impressions, and from allusions to the subject in works not directly concerned with the rigorous and intensive investigation of authority relations.

In short, almost everything needed to establish the theory

still needs doing, and an enormous amount of work is required if these things are to be done. Hence the claims made for the theory here are very modest. Nevertheless I do make some claims for it. I claim that it is at least plausible; I claim that it fits what is known about the more obvious cases of stable and unstable democracy; I claim that it can make still more convincing propositions about stable democracy which are already convincing to a degree; and I claim that it not only relates variables but gives immediate insight into the motivational forces which link them. Not least, I claim that the theory can account for a crucial fact not yet touched upon—perhaps the most important fact with which the study of democracy confronts us. This is that stable democracy is immensely difficult to achieve, and has in fact been achieved only in very few cases —that it is unstable democracy, not stable democracy, which is, by any reasonable measurement, the "normal" case.

Every aspect of the paper suggests how very tenuous and improbable are the foundations of stable democratic government. Stable democracy requires congruence of authority patterns between government and segments of social life which resist democratization; it requires balances of contradictory behavior patterns, in such a way that the balances do not lead to undue strain and intolerable anomie; it requires a certain similarity among authority patterns, but not to the extent that basic human needs are thwarted. Surely, if these conditions are indeed required, then the existence of a stable democracy requires much explaining, while unstable democracies practically explain themselves. Perhaps this is why writers like Lipset find so many factors that can of themselves prevent stable democracy, and none that can of themselves assure it. What, after all, is a complex multicausal explanation if not an assertion that a great many factors must coincide if a phenomenon is to exist—and that its existence is, for that reason alone, improbable?

Given the evidence of our times, this seems a most appropriate conclusion. The age when men had some reason confidently to expect the universal reign of democracy (and, more than that, the end of fundamental political change, because of a supposedly inherent affinity of human nature to democracy) ended with Bryce—and the trials of Weimar. For our own world we need a more pessimistic approach to democratic government, one not based upon the bland assumption that men are natural democrats, but one which directs attention to those calamitously improbable combinations of circumstances which actually make democracy work.

For the present purpose this is certainly the most important deduction which can be drawn from the theory. But still larger implications, which might be briefly indicated, follow from it. One could argue, for example, that the conditions which make stable democracy improbable also make stable totalitarianism improbable: not only is totalitarianism a very "pure" governmental system but also one fundamentally incongruent with certain functionally indispensable social relations. By the same token, semiauthoritarian government—government in which strong, preferably ascriptive, authority is mitigated by adherence to impersonal rules, paternalistic benevolence, institutionalized channels of representation, and a vigorous corporate life—is bound to be the most stable of all possible governments, owing precisely to its impurity and easy congruence with primary group patterns. This corresponds to Weber's view that "traditional" authority is the most stable of his three ideal types.

But still more convincing would be the deduction that, while degrees of stability, or rates of change, may vary, no form of government can be inherently stable—if only because no form of government can escape the dilemma of managing some strains by increasing the probability of others. The present theory leads logically to an inherently dynamic conception of government, in which strains, and, through strains, change, are the rule rather than the exception; stable governments, upon this view, are the product of "accidental" (extremely improbable) conjunctions of conditions which do sometimes, but rarely, occur in actual societies. Such a dynamic view of governmental change—a view positing change as normal and constant, but, unlike Marxism and other historicist theories, specifying no concrete content or goal for the process of change —seems, on the face of it, more in tune with the manifest testimony of history than theories which take stability for granted and attribute change to external, rather than immanent, conditions. But this takes us far beyond the subject of stable democracy, and obviously requires a more thorough treatment than can be given here.

REFERENCES TO
APPENDIX B

1. Almond, G. A., and J. S. Coleman, *The Politics of the Developing Areas*, Princeton, 1960.
2. Apter, David E., "A Comparative Method for the Study of Politics," *American Journal of Sociology*, LXIV (Nov. 1958), 221-237.
3. Beer, S. H., "Great Britain: From Governing Elite to Organized Mass Parties," in *Modern Political Parties* (S. Neumann, ed.), Chicago, 1956, pp. 9-57.
4. Bracher, Karl Dietrich, *Die Auflösung der Weimarer Republik*, Stuttgart and Düsseldorf, 1957.
5. Catlin, G. E. G., *Principles of Politics*, London, 1930.
6. Cooper, Duff, *Old Men Forget*, London, 1953.
7. Crick, Bernard, *Reform of the Commons*, London, 1959.
8. Dahl, Robert A., "Business and Politics: An Appraisal of Political Science," *American Political Science Review*, LIII (March 1959), 1-34.
9. Deutsch, K. W., "Toward an Inventory of Basic Trends and Patterns in Comparative and International Politics," *American Political Science Review*, LIV (March 1960), 34-57.
10. Deutsch, K. W., and L. J. Edinger, *Germany Rejoins the Powers*, Stanford, 1959.
11. Deutsch, M., "A Theory of Cooperation and Competition," *Human Relations*, II (1949), 129-152.
12. Eckstein, Harry, *Pressure Group Politics: The Case of the B. M. A.*, London, 1960.
13. Finer, S. E., "The Federation of British Industries," *Political Studies*, IV (Feb. 1956), 61-82.
14. Friedrich, C. J., *Constitutional Government and Democracy*, 2nd ed., Boston, 1941.
15. Gide, André, *Journals*, IV, New York, 1951.

16. de Grazia, Sebastian, *The Political Community: A Study of Anomie,* Chicago, 1948.
17. Inkeles, Alex, "The Totalitarian Mystique: Some Impressions of the Dynamics of Totalitarian Society," in *Totalitarianism* (C. J. Friedrich, ed.), Cambridge, Mass., 1954.
18. Jennings, Sir Ivor, *Parliamentary Reform,* London, 1934.
19. de Jouvenel, Bertrand, *Sovereignty, An Inquiry into the Political Good,* Chicago, 1957.
20. Kornhauser, William, *The Politics of Mass Society,* Glencoe, Ill., 1959.
21. Kracauer, Siegfried, *From Caligari to Hitler,* Princeton, 1947.
22. Lasswell, Harold, *Politics: Who Gets What, When, How,* New York, 1936.
23. Lasswell, Harold, and Abraham Kaplan, *Power and Society,* New Haven, 1950.
24. Levy, Marion J., Jr., *The Structure of Society,* Princeton, 1952.
25. Lipset, S. M., *Political Man,* New York, 1960.
26. Lipset, S. M., M. A. Trow, and J. S. Coleman, *Union Democracy,* Glencoe, Ill., 1956.
27. McKenzie, R. T., *British Political Parties,* London, 1955.
28. Merriam, Charles, *Public and Private Government,* New Haven, 1944.
29. Michels, Robert, *Political Parties,* Glencoe, Ill., 1958.
30. Parsons, Talcott, *The Social System,* Glencoe, Ill., 1951.
31. Potter, Allen, "Attitude Groups," *Political Quarterly,* XXIX (Jan.-March 1958), 72-82.
32. Spiro, Herbert J., "The German Political System," in *Patterns of Government* (S. H. Beer and A. B. Ulam, eds.), New York, 1958.
33. Spiro, Herbert J., *Government by Constitution: The Political Systems of Democracy,* New York, 1959.
34. Tropp, Asher, *The School Teachers,* London, 1957.
35. Young, Michael, and Peter Willmott, *Family and Kinship in East London,* Glencoe, Ill., 1957.

Index

BOOKS WRITTEN
UNDER THE AUSPICES OF THE
CENTER OF INTERNATIONAL STUDIES
PRINCETON UNIVERSITY

Gabriel A. Almond, *The Appeals of Communism* (Princeton University Press 1954)

William W. Kaufmann, ed., *Military Policy and National Security* (Princeton University Press 1956)

Klaus Knorr, *The War Potential of Nations* (Princeton University Press 1956)

Lucian W. Pye, *Guerrilla Communism in Malaya* (Princeton University Press 1956)

Charles De Visscher, *Theory and Reality in Public International Law*, trans. by P. E. Corbett (Princeton University Press 1957; rev. ed. 1968)

Bernard C. Cohen, *The Political Process and Foreign Policy: The Making of the Japanese Peace Settlement* (Princeton University Press 1959)

Myron Weiner, *Party Politics in India: The Development of a Multi-Party System* (Princeton University Press 1957)

Percy E. Corbett, *Law in Diplomacy* (Princeton University Press 1959)

Rolf Sannwald and Jacques Stohler, *Economic Integration: Theoretical Assumptions and Consequences of European Unification*, trans. by Herman Karreman (Princeton University Press 1959)

Klaus Knorr, ed., *NATO and American Security* (Princeton University Press 1959)

Gabriel A. Almond and James S. Coleman, eds., *The Politics of the Developing Areas* (Princeton University Press 1960)

Herman Kahn, *On Thermonuclear War* (Princeton University Press 1960)

Sidney Verba, *Small Groups and Political Behavior: A Study of Leadership* (Princeton University Press 1961)

Robert J. C. Butow, *Tojo and the Coming of the War* (Princeton University Press 1961)

Glenn H. Snyder, *Deterrence and Defense: Toward a Theory of National Security* (Princeton University Press 1961)

Klaus Knorr and Sidney Verba, eds., *The International System: Theoretical Essays* (Princeton University Press 1961)

Peter Paret and John W. Shy, *Guerrillas in the 1960's* (Praeger 1962)

George Modelski, *A Theory of Foreign Policy* (Praeger 1962)

Klaus Knorr and Thornton Read, eds., *Limited Strategic War* (Praeger 1963)

Frederick S. Dunn, *Peace-Making and the Settlement with Japan* (Princeton University Press 1963)

Arthur L. Burns and Nina Heathcote, *Peace-Keeping by United Nations Forces* (Praeger 1963)

Richard A. Falk, *Law, Morality, and War in the Contemporary World* (Praeger 1963)

James N. Rosenau, *National Leadership and Foreign Policy: A Case Study in the Mobilization of Public Support* (Princeton University Press 1963)

Gabriel A. Almond and Sidney Verba, *The Civic Culture: Political Attitudes and Democracy in Five Nations* (Princeton University Press 1963)

Bernard C. Cohen, *The Press and Foreign Policy* (Princeton University Press 1963)

Richard L. Sklar, *Nigerian Political Parties: Power in an Emergent African Nation* (Princeton University Press 1963)

Peter Paret, *French Revolutionary Warfare from Indochina to Algeria: The Analysis of a Political and Military Doctrine* (Praeger 1964)

Harry Eckstein, ed., *Internal War: Problems and Approaches* (Free Press 1964)

Cyril E. Black and Thomas P. Thornton, eds., *Communism and Revolution: The Strategic Uses of Political Violence* (Princeton University Press 1964)

Miriam Camps, *Britain and the European Community 1955-1963* (Princeton University Press 1964)

Thomas P. Thornton, ed., *The Third World in Soviet Perspective: Studies by Soviet Writers on the Developing Areas* (Princeton University Press 1964)

James N. Rosenau, ed., *International Aspects of Civil Strife* (Princeton University Press 1964)

Sidney I. Ploss, *Conflict and Decision-Making in Soviet Russia: A Case Study of Agricultural Policy, 1953-1963* (Princeton University Press 1965)

Richard A. Falk and Richard J. Barnet, eds., *Security in Disarmament* (Princeton University Press 1965)

Karl von Vorys, *Political Development in Pakistan* (Princeton University Press 1965)

Harold and Margaret Sprout, *The Ecological Perspective on Human Affairs, With Special Reference to International Politics* (Princeton University Press 1965)

Klaus Knorr, *On the Uses of Military Power in the Nuclear Age* (Princeton University Press 1966)

Harry Eckstein, *Division and Cohesion in Democracy: A Study of Norway* (Princeton University Press 1966)

Cyril E. Black, *The Dynamics of Modernization: A Study in Comparative History* (Harper and Row 1966)

Peter Kunstadter, ed., *Southeast Asian Tribes, Minorities, and Nations* (Princeton University Press 1967)

E. Victor Wolfenstein, *The Revolutionary Personality: Lenin, Trotsky, Gandhi* (Princeton University Press 1967)

Leon Gordenker, *The UN Secretary-General and the Maintenance of Peace* (Columbia University Press 1967)

Oran R. Young, *The Intermediaries: Third Parties in International Crises* (Princeton University Press 1967)

James N. Rosenau, ed., *Domestic Sources of Foreign Policy* (Free Press 1967)

Richard F. Hamilton, *Affluence and the French Worker in the Fourth Republic* (Princeton University Press 1967)

Linda B. Miller, *World Order and Local Disorder: The United Nations and Internal Conflicts* (Princeton University Press 1967)

Henry Bienen, *Tanzania: Party Transformation and Economic Development* (Princeton University Press 1967)

Wolfram F. Hanrieder, *West German Foreign Policy, 1949-1963: International Pressures and Domestic Response* (Stanford University Press 1967)

Richard H. Ullman, *Britain and the Russian Civil War: November 1918-February 1920* (Princeton University Press 1968)

Robert Gilpin, *France in the Age of the Scientific State* (Princeton University Press 1968)

William B. Bader, *The United States and the Spread of Nuclear Weapons* (Pegasus 1968)

Richard A. Falk, *Legal Order in a Violent World* (Princeton University Press 1968)

Cyril E. Black, Richard A. Falk, Klaus Knorr, and Oran R. Young, *Neutralization and World Politics* (Princeton University Press 1968)

Oran R. Young, *The Politics of Force: Bargaining During International Crises* (Princeton University Press 1969)

Klaus Knorr and James N. Rosenau, eds., *Contending Approaches to International Politics* (Princeton University Press 1969)

James N. Rosenau, ed., *Linkage Politics: Essays on the Convergence of National and International Systems* (Free Press 1969)

John T. McAlister, Jr., *Viet Nam: The Origins of Revolution* (Knopf 1969)

Jean Edward Smith, *Germany Beyond the Wall: People, Politics and Prosperity* (Little, Brown 1969)

James Barros, *Betrayal from Within: Joseph Avenol Secretary-General of the League of Nations, 1933-1940* (Yale University Press 1969)

Charles Hermann, *Crises in Foreign Policy: A Simulation Analysis* (Bobbs-Merrill 1969)

Robert C. Tucker, *The Marxian Revolutionary Idea: Essays on Marxist Thought and Its Impact on Radical Movements* (W. W. Norton 1969)

Harvey Waterman, *Political Change in Contemporary France: The Politics of an Industrial Democracy* (Charles E. Merrill 1969)